The Last Temptation™

writer
NEIL GAIMAN

illustrator
MICHAEL ZULLI

letterer
TODD KLEIN

BASED ON A STORY BY
NEIL GAIMAN AND ALICE COOPER

NEIL'S DEDICATION:
This book is for the remarkable Cindy Wall,
who worked hard and long, and over and above,
on the project, all those years ago, and for Jack Wall,
and for Grace, when she's old enough.

———————————

MICHAEL'S DEDICATION:
To Big Steve K. and to Alice,
who have walked the walk. And to all the little
Stevens out there … there is no Mercy.

INTRODUCTION
by Neil Gaiman

It seems only natural that the House of Wax is next to the graveyard. It's cold and dark, and a low mist smudges the light of the gas lamps that flicker unreliably outside the House of Wax. You walk through the graveyard, thick clay sticking to your boots, weighing you down.

The House of Wax is a huge tent, made of thin brown leather which hangs lifelessly in the windless mist. You walk through the entrance, muddy boots rustling through dead leaves.

The mist curls and writhes in the corner of the tent. You step back, nervously.

"You've come to see the sideshow," says a voice from behind you.

"I have?"

"Of course you have."

You turn and look at the man. His clothes were once elegant, but are now shiny and frayed at the edges. His hair is long and black, his face thin, his eyes set deep in his head. He raises his top hat to you, and grins like a wolf.

He gestures with his stick. A hundred candles burst into flame, illuminating a bad place.

Wax statues stand in the tent, each on its own raised pedestal.

The Showman walks you over to a statue. He runs a finger down its spangled side.

The life-sized wax figure is clasping a microphone. It is a rock-and-roll star, black make-up outlining its eyes and mouth. The sign next to it reads ALICE COOPER.

"He looks like you," you tell the Showman.

"There's a certain family resemblance," he admits.

You walk past a wax statue of an artist, a tall man with mustachios and beard that Dali might have envied, painting at an easel. The word ZULLI is painted, carefully, on his back.

Next to him is a wax statue of a man wearing a leather jacket and dark glasses. He has dark hair, and black jeans. He is holding a placard with the word WRITER on it.

"Do you want to hear what he has to say?" asks the Showman.

You shrug. There's a rustling at the edge of the tent; you dart a glance, but see nothing other than wax statues frozen in awkward poses.

The Showman takes a tarnished silver coin from his pocket, and forces it between the lips of the statue. "That's the motto of the lot," he tells you, his voice little more than a whisper. "Put a penny in the slot."

The statue of the writer moves, mechanically. A hand raises, in slow, jerking movements. A head tilts. The lips part, revealing no sign of the coin the Showman placed between them.

It begins to talk to us.

I was sitting in my study in England, almost a decade of years ago, when the phone rang. I answered it. I like answering the phone.

"This is Bob Pfeifer. That's P-f-e-i-one-f-e-r. I'm from Epic Records in Los Angeles," he said.

"Hello," I said. I couldn't think why someone from a record company would be calling me. It was, I supposed, vaguely conceivable that someone had taped me singing in the shower; that a bootleg — The Gaiman Shower Tapes — had been released without my knowledge; it was even conceivable such tapes had made it across the Atlantic all the way to L.A. It was slightly more likely that I'd been elected Prime Minister of Lichtenstein and no one had told me.

"Yeah. Anyway. One of my artists is a big fan of yours. Well, we're all big fans of yours. *Sandman*, all that. My assistant, Jason, he's a huge fan of yours."

"That's nice."

"Yeah. So, like I say. This artist I was talking about. He's going to make a concept album."

"And?"

"Well, we were wondering if you could work with the artist on the concept. Are you interested?"

"Who are we talking about here?"

"Well, that's kind of confidential. But it's Alice Cooper."

Alice Cooper?

I *liked* Alice Cooper. I liked *School's Out* and *Billion Dollar Babies* and *Teenage Lament '74*. I thought *Welcome to My Nightmare* was one of the great rock-and-roll records. I thought *Trash* was a remarkable comeback album.

My head swam with snakes and swords, top hats and black-rimmed eyes.

"Maybe," I said. "I'd like to meet him first."

Wayne's World had been out a week when I met Alice Cooper, although I hadn't seen it, and knew nothing about it.

I sat in the hotel restaurant with Bob Pfeifer, who is younger and funnier and lankier than he sounds on the phone, and is always magnificently stressed-out. We were in Phoenix, Arizona.

"There he is," said Bob, pointing out of the restaurant window at a tall man climbing out of a sports car. White T-shirt, blue jeans, long black hair.

Heads turned as he came into the restaurant.

Alice Cooper in person is tall, shaggy, suntanned. His eyes are sharp and good-humoured and alive. He knows more about bad Italian horror movies than anyone who doesn't write books about them for a living.

We ate sandwiches then went up to my hotel room to talk. On the way out of the restaurant a couple ran over to Alice and threw themselves onto their knees.

"We're not worthy," they wailed.

He took it pleasantly. When I asked him about it, he explained that this was but a small token of the respect he was shown in Phoenix; later he admitted that it was from a new movie called *Wayne's World*.

Every time I've seen Alice in public since then, someone has come over to him, bowed low, said, "We're not worthy." Every time he has treated them with good humour, nodded, smiled, and bowed back.

In the hotel room we talked about horror fiction, about stories, about what we'd like to do with the story of the album. We talked about the *Grand Guignol*, the French theatre of blood and horror, popular in the early years of this century. We talked about bad Italian horror movies. We talked about the story of Faust.

Alice Cooper sometimes talked about Alice Cooper in the third person. "Alice wouldn't do that," he explained.

I learned there were two Alice Coopers, the person and the icon.

I found this very comfortable: Alice Cooper the person was his own affair; Alice Cooper the character was something else again. He's larger than life. He's theatre.

Alice Cooper is a horror icon. He's up there with Larry Talbot, and Count Dracula, with Jason and Freddie. Alice Cooper is hung and guillotined; Alice writhes with snakes and flees the madhouse. He was even the star of his own Marvel comic.

I liked Alice the person enormously. And I liked the idea of creating a story with Alice the character — something that could be used to build an album or a stage show.

Somewhere in there things changed. We were no longer feeling each other out, deciding whether or not we wanted to work together. We *were* working together.

I suggested a few ideas to him. He liked some of them, wasn't as keen on others. We talked about the feel we wanted, the shape, the characters.

I went home to England, talked with Alice some more on the phone, and began to write the story we seemed to be evolving. It was the tale of a boy named Steven, and a strange theatre, and a Showman with a strange resemblance to Alice Cooper — part Machiavellian ghost, part commentator, part demon. It was the story of a deal Steven is offered; of a theatrical performance he attends; of his parents, his school friends, his teachers, and, ultimately, his temptation.

The story wasn't a story I would have come up with alone: it was too clear-cut. God was looking out for the innocent, and the serpent was always looking for a way into your heart. But it was a good story, and it worked.

The next time I saw Alice six months

had passed, and we were back in the same hotel in Phoenix. We sat in Bob Pfeifer's hotel room and I listened to tapes of the first few songs they'd written, and I watched Alice and his collaborators write another three songs — while I sat on a bed, occasionally making suggestions for lyrics and song titles.

A lightning storm came in from the desert, and we sat outside on the hotel balcony and watched the storm buffet the eucalyptus trees, while Alice told us about The Time He Met Elvis. Linda Lovelace was in the story, and karate, and guns.

Another few months went by, and now I was in a recording studio in Los Angeles, listening to them record *Lost in America*.

It's odd: one minute it was just a plot in my head, the next it's an honest-to-goodness rock-and-roll concept album. Real musicians. Real Alice Cooper. Dave McKean even agreed to do the album cover.

I'm not sure when it was suggested, or by whom, that we should do a comic.

It wasn't a hard decision to make, though. I found the idea challenging. Rock stars have been cropping up in comics for decades — Kiss emptied their veins into the first printing of their comic, or so we were told, and Jimmy Olsen, if I remember correctly, was the Stone-Age Beatle of 30,000 B.C. But the comics on the whole (we might as well be honest here, just between ourselves) weren't terribly good. And I didn't see why there *couldn't* be a good rock comic.

There were chunks of plot that hadn't made it onto the album, after all. It would be good to get it all down.

Michael Zulli, Salvador Dali look-alike, artist and co-creator of the ecological SF series *Puma Blues*, author of by far the strangest and darkest interpretation of the

Teenage Mutant Ninja Turtles; occasional interpreter, with me, of *The Sandman*, and my partner in crime in the mysteriously lost *Sweeney Todd, The Demon Barber of Fleet Street*, is one of the most fascinating, grim, and delightful artists in the business, and would be the perfect artist for the project — if he was interested.

I called him, and he was.

The award-winning Todd Klein was willing to letter the comic.

And the album came out, and the comic came out, and Alice and I stumbled around Europe promoting it. I fulfilled a childhood dream and found myself backstage on BBC TV's *Top of the Pops*, as Alice and the band performed *Lost in America* in front of a twenty-foot-high reproduction of Michael's double-page splash from part one. We were treated a little like kings in Germany, and a little like gods in Scandinavia.

The reviews were good — people as diverse as the rock critics of *Rolling Stone* and of the *Times* of London proclaimed it Alice's finest album in fifteen years. And it sold pretty well too — it charted all over the world, and continues to sell in respectable numbers to this day.

As for the comic, I wanted to create something that was, essentially, the comics equivalent of several pop singles: nothing too deep, nothing too ambiguous. A campfire tale, that was what I wanted it to be. A comic to read with the album playing in the background. A comic for when the leaves begin to crisp and fall. Light reading for what Ray Bradbury called the October Country.

It had been out of print for several years, and I was delighted that Dark Horse were willing to make it available again, and to present it in a format that allows the artwork to shine.

The wax statue of the writer smiles, nods, closes its mouth, and, mechanically, returns to the position it was in to begin with. Its skin has the sheen of old wax, or of a fresh corpse.

The Showman turns to you.

There's something feral in his smile, something wolf-like in his eyes.

"Is there anything else you need to know?" he asks.

You shake your head, nervously, and begin to back away through the tent and the wax people. You would feel far more comfortable back in the graveyard, of that you have no doubt at all.

The Showman gestures.

One by one the candles that illuminate the tent flicker and go out, casting strange shadows across the inside of the tent as they die, shadows that make the wax figures seem to move, to clamber down from their pedestals, to walk towards you.

You aren't moving. You are frozen in place. You can't look away.

"Don't go," says the Showman. "We've got other things to show you." He is fumbling with one gloved hand at the side of his face. "Look."

His face comes away, as if it's hinged, revealing a skull the yellow of old ivory. A tiny snake, the green of a fresh-cut emerald, writhes in an empty eye socket.

It hisses at you, and bares its fangs.

The spell is broken. You can move once more: you take a step back, then begin to run, looking around frantically for the way out. Somewhere there must be a way out …

You're all alone.

The rustling gets louder now. It seems to come from all around you.

And then the last candle goes out.

Act One: Bad Place Alone

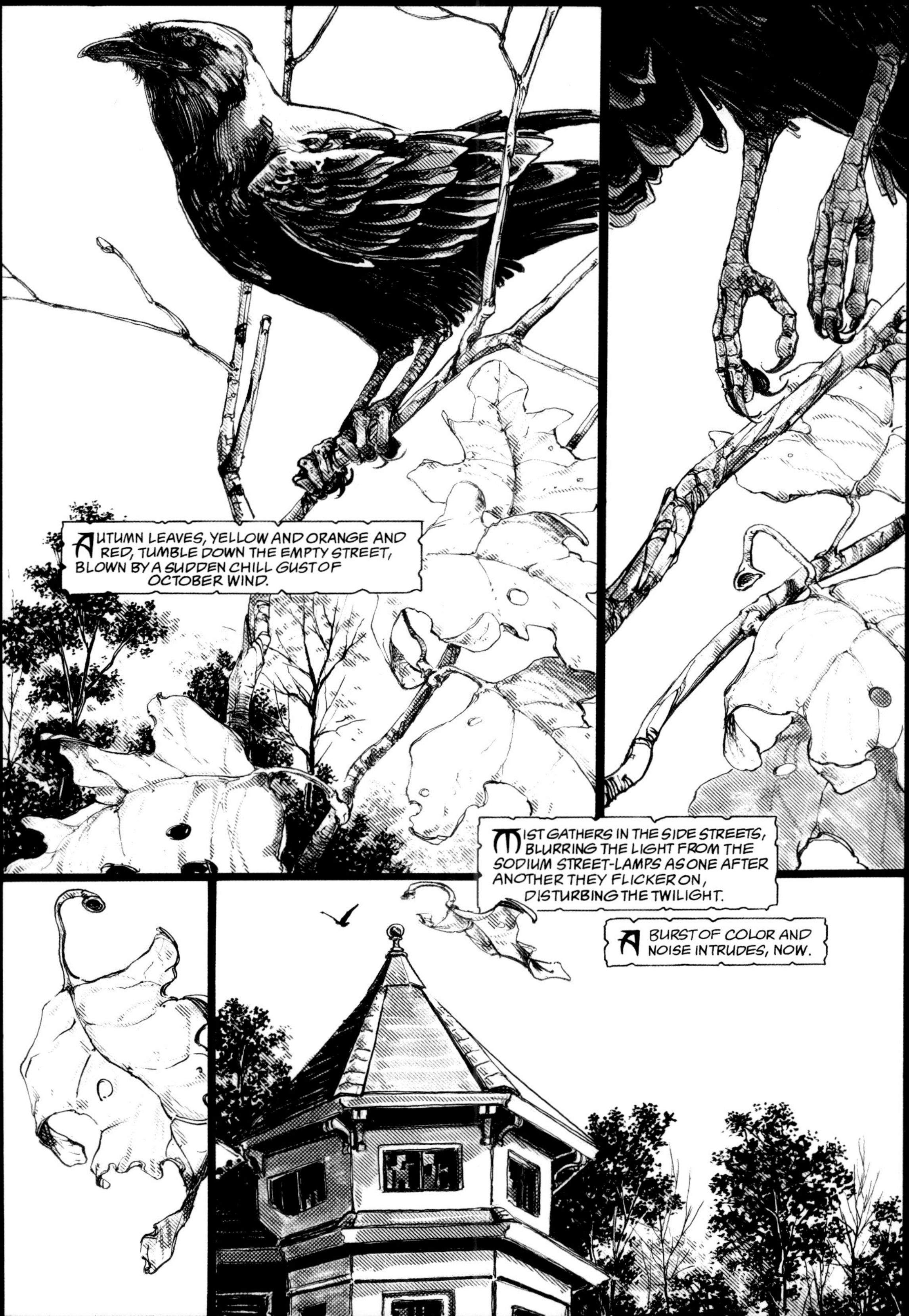
AUTUMN LEAVES, YELLOW AND ORANGE AND RED, TUMBLE DOWN THE EMPTY STREET, BLOWN BY A SUDDEN CHILL GUST OF OCTOBER WIND.
MIST GATHERS IN THE SIDE STREETS, BLURRING THE LIGHT FROM THE SODIUM STREET-LAMPS AS ONE AFTER ANOTHER THEY FLICKER ON, DISTURBING THE TWILIGHT.
A BURST OF COLOR AND NOISE INTRUDES, NOW.

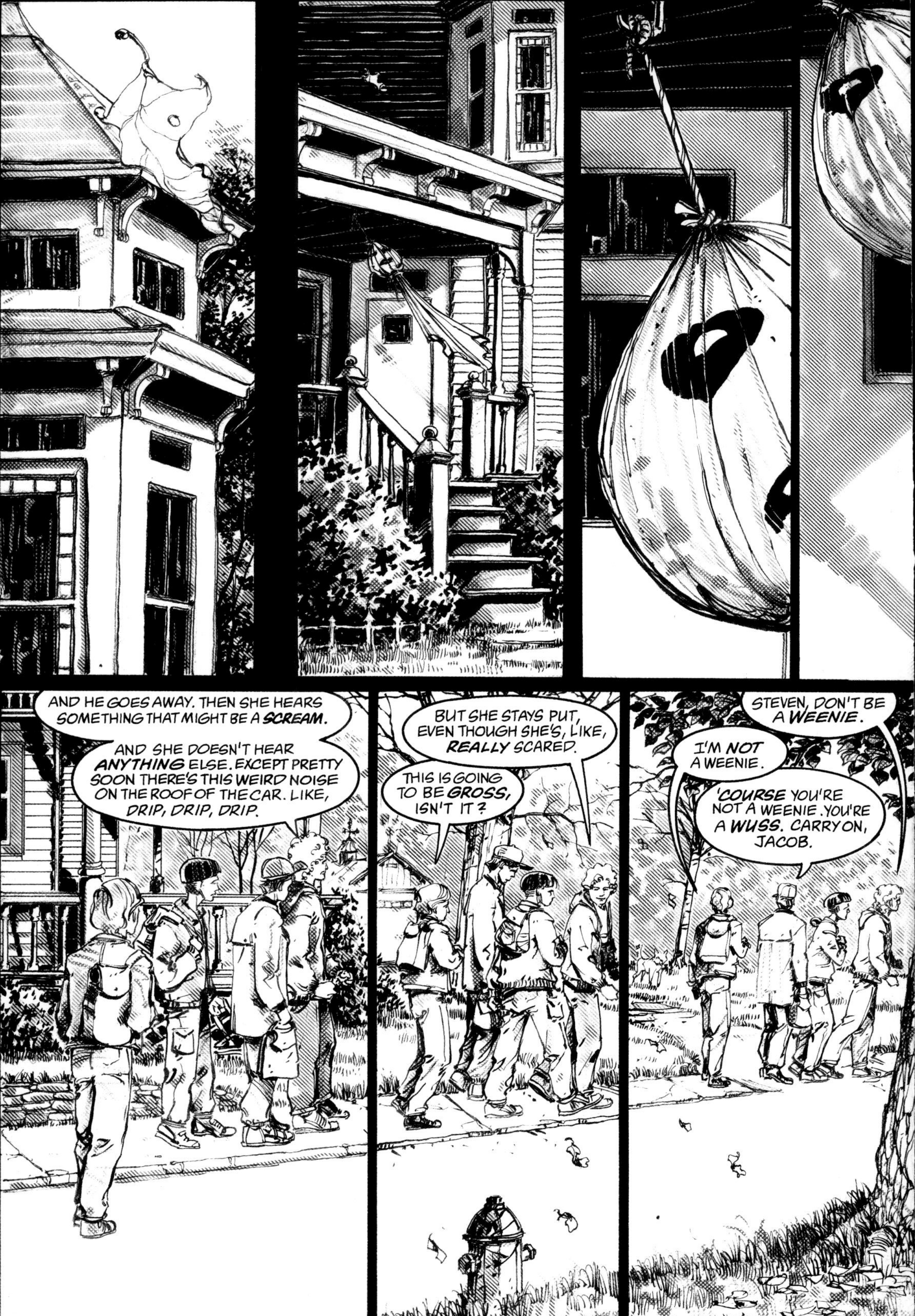
AND HE GOES AWAY. THEN SHE HEARS SOMETHING THAT MIGHT BE A SCREAM.
AND SHE DOESN'T HEAR ANYTHING ELSE. EXCEPT PRETTY SOON THERE'S THIS WEIRD NOISE ON THE ROOF OF THE CAR. LIKE, DRIP, DRIP, DRIP.
BUT SHE STAYS PUT, EVEN THOUGH SHE'S, LIKE, REALLY SCARED.
THIS IS GOING TO BE GROSS, ISN'T IT?
STEVEN, DON'T BE A WEENIE.
I'M NOT A WEENIE.
'COURSE YOU'RE NOT A WEENIE. YOU'RE A WUSS. CARRY ON, JACOB.

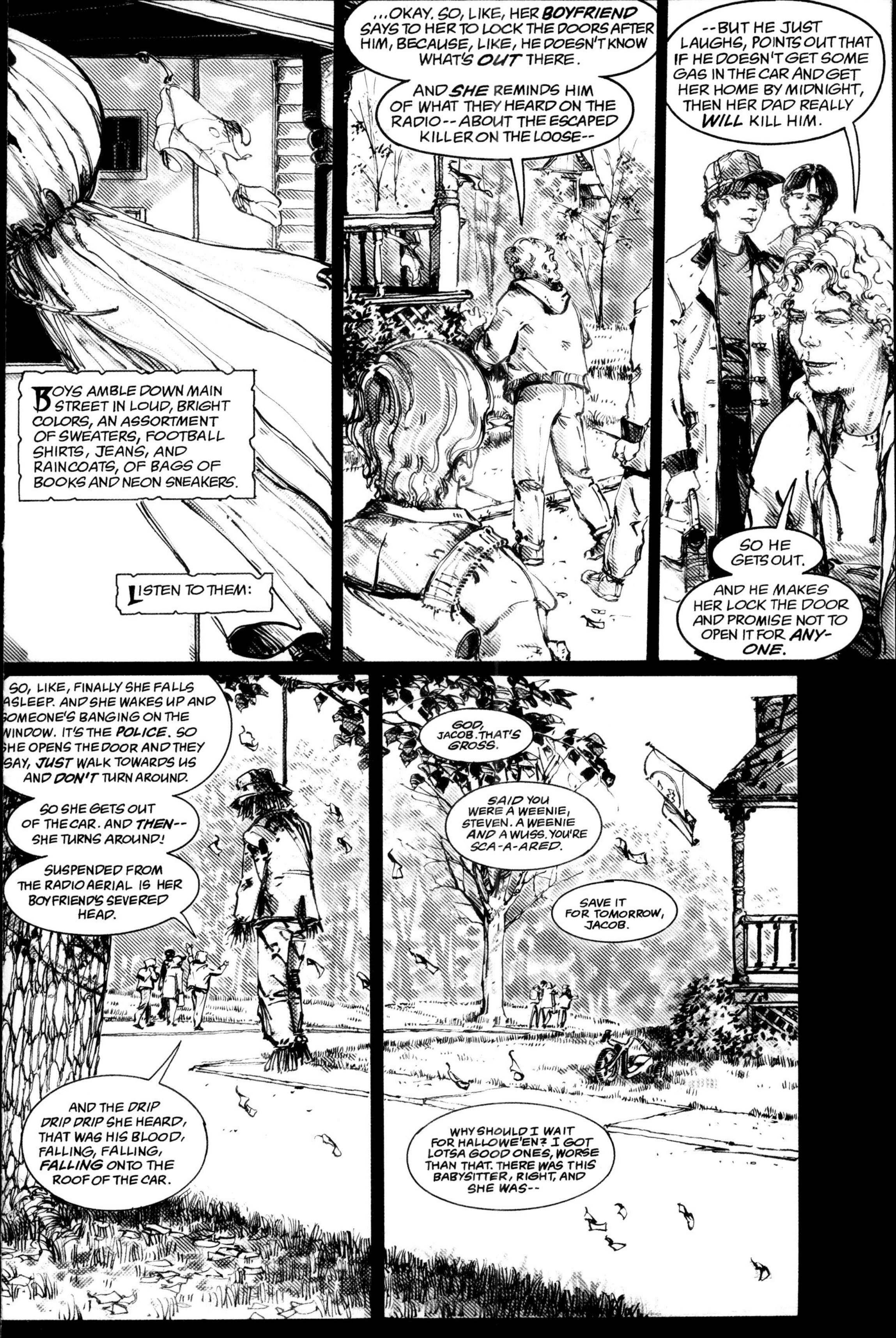
BOYS AMBLE DOWN MAIN STREET IN LOUD, BRIGHT COLORS, AN ASSORTMENT OF SWEATERS, FOOTBALL SHIRTS, JEANS, AND RAINCOATS, OF BAGS OF BOOKS AND NEON SNEAKERS.
LISTEN TO THEM:
...OKAY. SO, LIKE, HER BOYFRIEND SAYS TO HER TO LOCK THE DOORS AFTER HIM, BECAUSE, LIKE, HE DOESN'T KNOW WHAT'S OUT THERE.
AND SHE REMINDS HIM OF WHAT THEY HEARD ON THE RADIO--ABOUT THE ESCAPED KILLER ON THE LOOSE--
--BUT HE JUST LAUGHS, POINTS OUT THAT IF HE DOESN'T GET SOME GAS IN THE CAR AND GET HER HOME BY MIDNIGHT, THEN HER DAD REALLY WILL KILL HIM.
SO HE GETS OUT.
AND HE MAKES HER LOCK THE DOOR AND PROMISE NOT TO OPEN IT FOR ANY-ONE.
SO, LIKE, FINALLY SHE FALLS ASLEEP. AND SHE WAKES UP AND SOMEONE'S BANGING ON THE WINDOW. IT'S THE POLICE. SO SHE OPENS THE DOOR AND THEY SAY, JUST WALK TOWARDS US AND DON'T TURN AROUND.
SO SHE GETS OUT OF THE CAR. AND THEN--SHE TURNS AROUND!
SUSPENDED FROM THE RADIO AERIAL IS HER BOYFRIEND'S SEVERED HEAD.
AND THE DRIP DRIP DRIP SHE HEARD, THAT WAS HIS BLOOD, FALLING, FALLING, FALLING ONTO THE ROOF OF THE CAR.
GOD, JACOB. THAT'S GROSS.
SAID YOU WERE A WEENIE, STEVEN. A WEENIE AND A WUSS. YOU'RE SCA-A-ARED.
SAVE IT FOR TOMORROW, JACOB.
WHY SHOULD I WAIT FOR HALLOWE'EN? I GOT LOTSA GOOD ONES, WORSE THAN THAT. THERE WAS THIS BABYSITTER, RIGHT, AND SHE WAS--

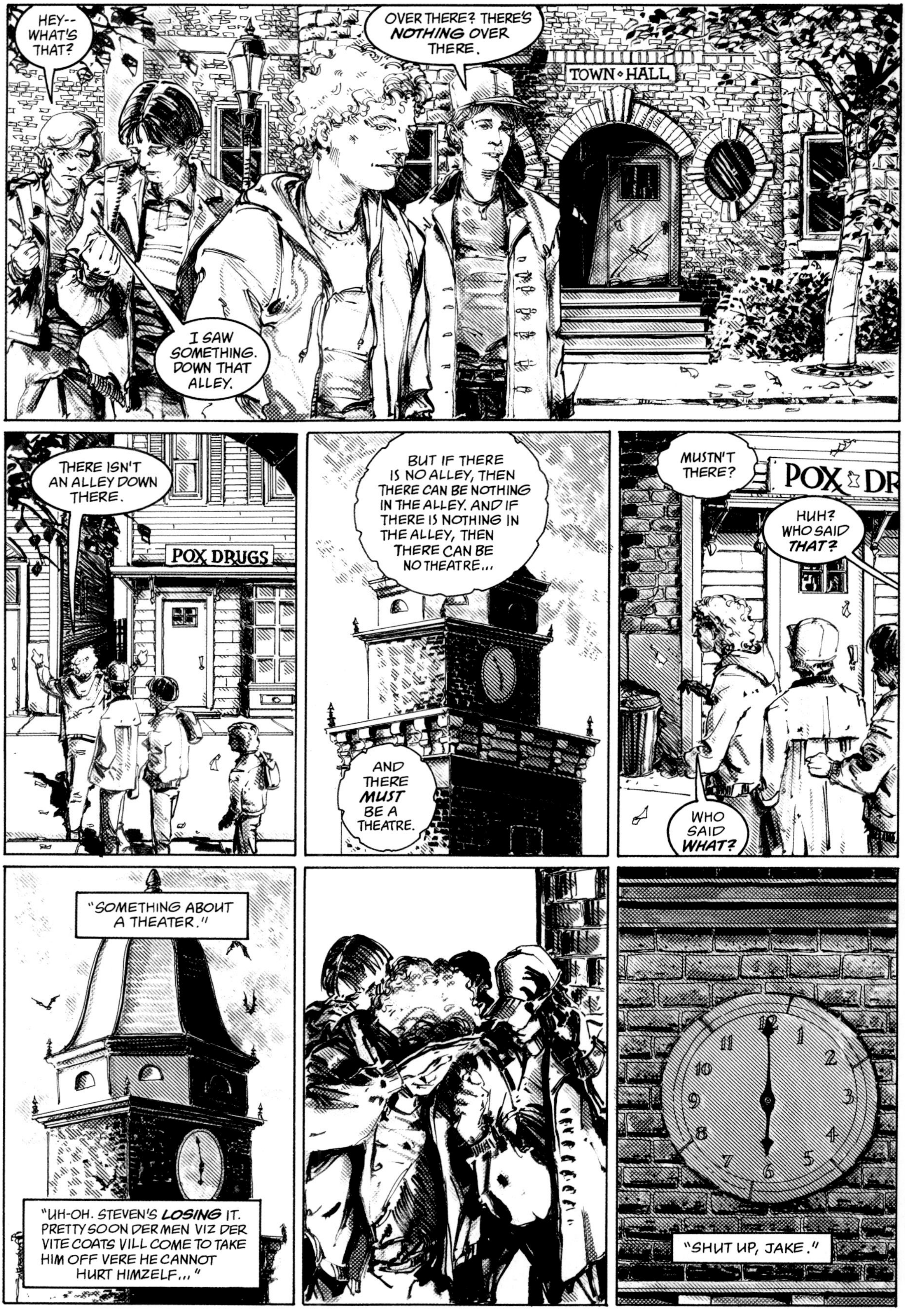
HEY-- WHAT'S THAT?
OVER THERE? THERE'S NOTHING OVER THERE.
TOWN HALL
I SAW SOMETHING. DOWN THAT ALLEY.
THERE ISN'T AN ALLEY DOWN THERE.
POX DRUGS
BUT IF THERE IS NO ALLEY, THEN THERE CAN BE NOTHING IN THE ALLEY. AND IF THERE IS NOTHING IN THE ALLEY, THEN THERE CAN BE NO THEATRE...
AND THERE MUST BE A THEATRE.
MUSTN'T THERE?
HUH? WHO SAID THAT?
WHO SAID WHAT?
"SOMETHING ABOUT A THEATER."
"UH-OH. STEVEN'S LOSING IT. PRETTY SOON DER MEN VIZ DER VITE COATS VILL COME TO TAKE HIM OFF VERE HE CANNOT HURT HIMZELF..."
"SHUT UP, JAKE."

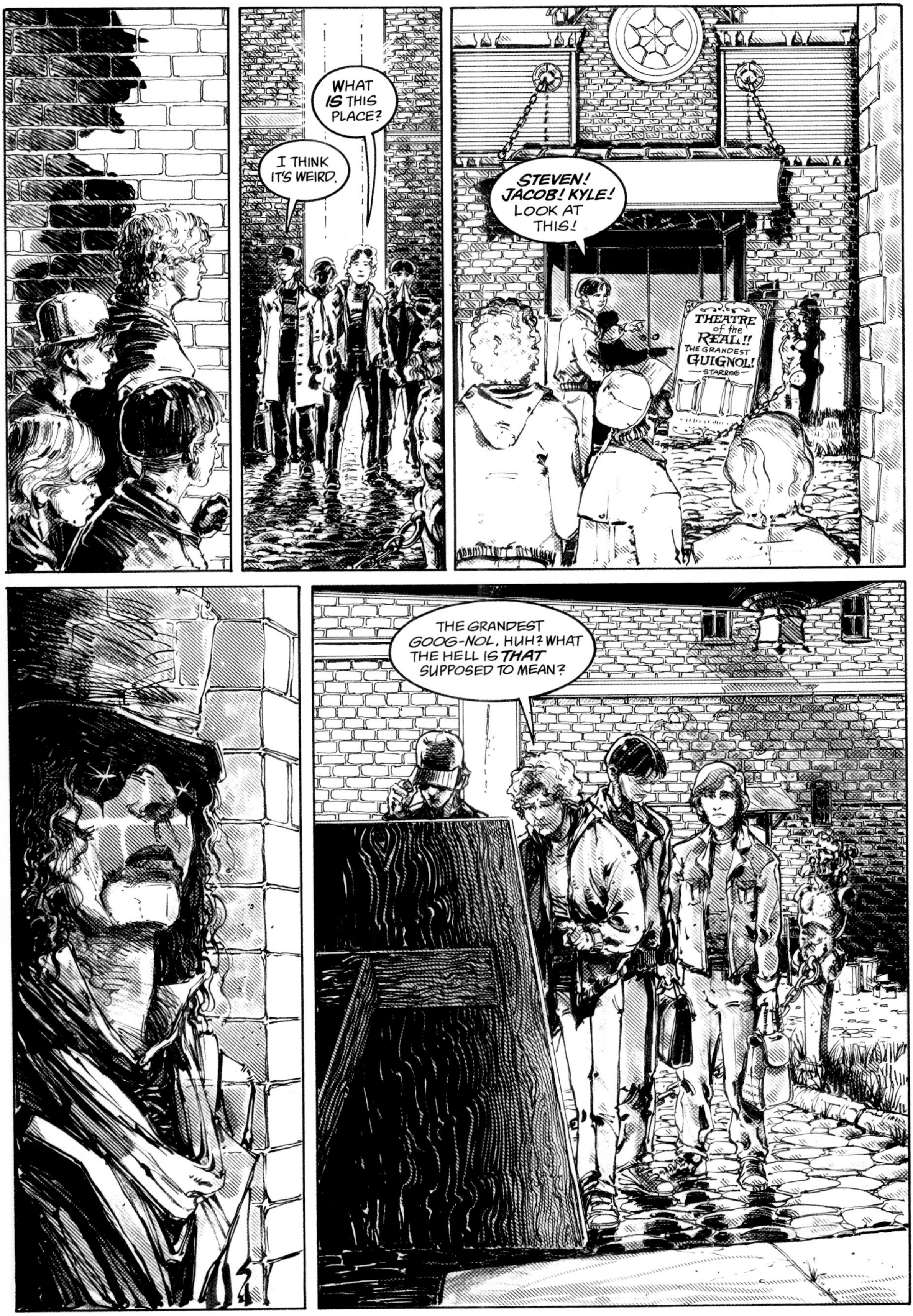

WHAT IS THIS PLACE?
I THINK IT'S WEIRD.
STEVEN! JACOB! KYLE! LOOK AT THIS!
THEATRE of the REAL!! THE GRANDEST GUIGNOL!
THE GRANDEST GOOG-NOL, HUH? WHAT THE HELL IS THAT SUPPOSED TO MEAN?

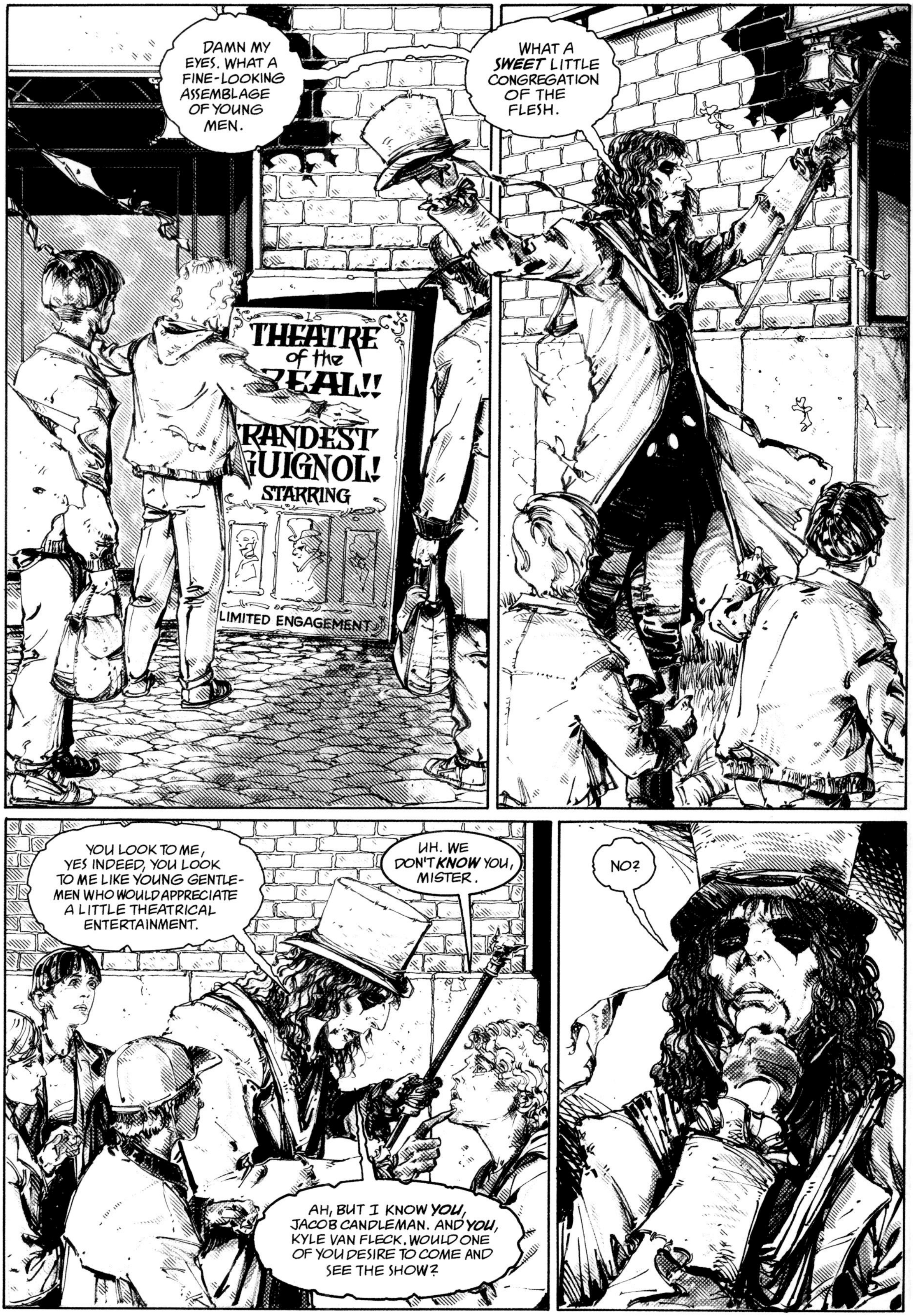
DAMN MY EYES. WHAT A FINE-LOOKING ASSEMBLAGE OF YOUNG MEN.
THEATRE of the REAL!! GRANDEST GUIGNOL! STARRING
LIMITED ENGAGEMENT
WHAT A SWEET LITTLE CONGREGATION OF THE FLESH.
YOU LOOK TO ME, YES INDEED, YOU LOOK TO ME LIKE YOUNG GENTLEMEN WHO WOULD APPRECIATE A LITTLE THEATRICAL ENTERTAINMENT.
UH. WE DON'T KNOW YOU, MISTER.
AH, BUT I KNOW YOU, JACOB CANDLEMAN. AND YOU, KYLE VAN FLECK. WOULD ONE OF YOU DESIRE TO COME AND SEE THE SHOW?
NO?

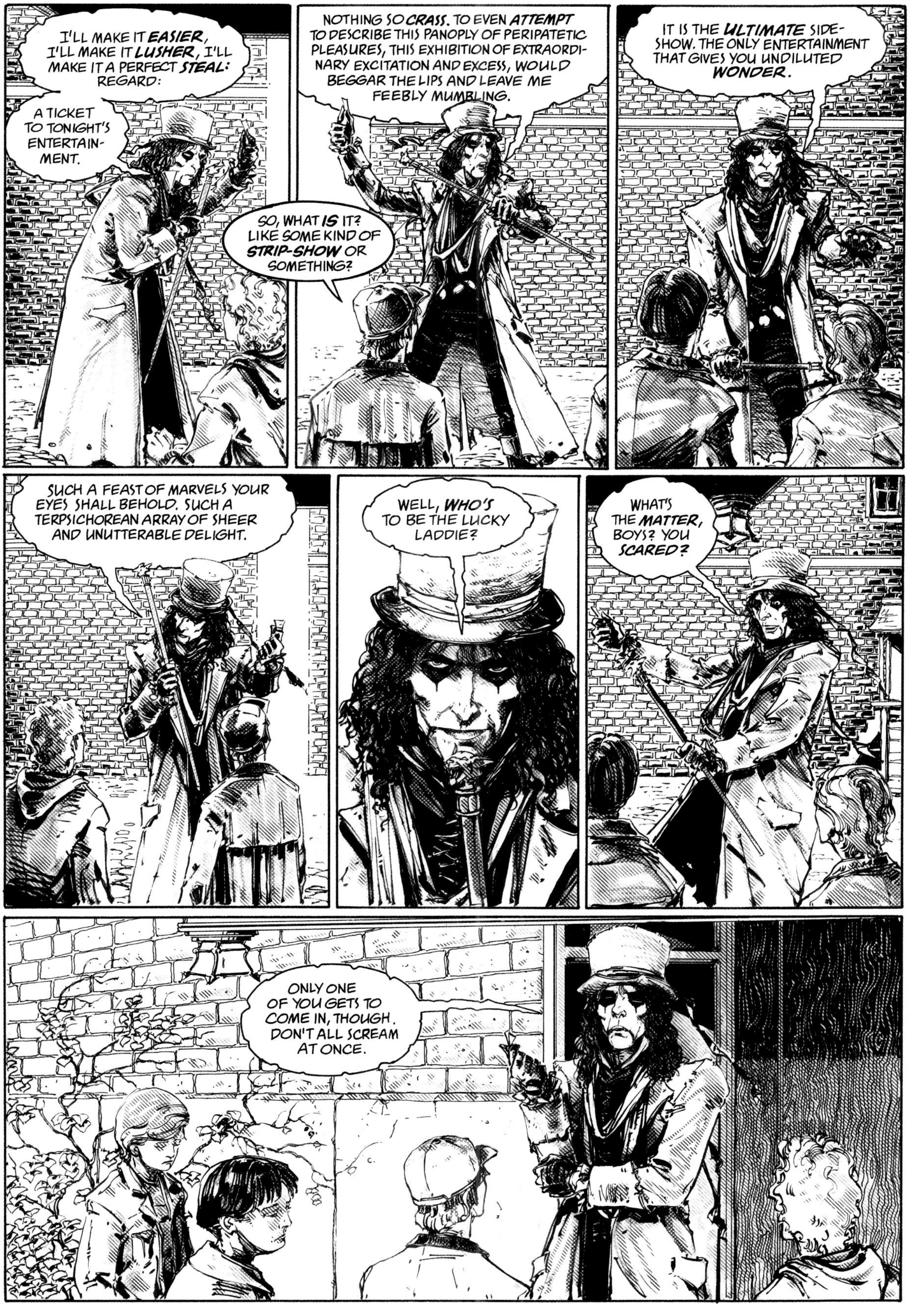
I'LL MAKE IT **EASIER**, I'LL MAKE IT **LUSHER**, I'LL MAKE IT A PERFECT **STEAL:** REGARD:
A TICKET TO TONIGHT'S ENTERTAINMENT.
SO, WHAT **IS** IT? LIKE SOME KIND OF **STRIP-SHOW** OR SOMETHING?
NOTHING SO **CRASS**. TO EVEN **ATTEMPT** TO DESCRIBE THIS PANOPLY OF PERIPATETIC PLEASURES, THIS EXHIBITION OF EXTRAORDINARY EXCITATION AND EXCESS, WOULD BEGGAR THE LIPS AND LEAVE ME FEEBLY MUMBLING.
IT IS THE **ULTIMATE** SIDE-SHOW. THE ONLY ENTERTAINMENT THAT GIVES YOU UNDILUTED **WONDER**.
SUCH A FEAST OF MARVELS YOUR EYES SHALL BEHOLD. SUCH A TERPSICHOREAN ARRAY OF SHEER AND UNUTTERABLE DELIGHT.
WELL, **WHO'S** TO BE THE LUCKY LADDIE?
WHAT'S THE **MATTER**, BOYS? YOU **SCARED?**
ONLY ONE OF YOU GETS TO COME IN, THOUGH. DON'T ALL SCREAM AT ONCE.

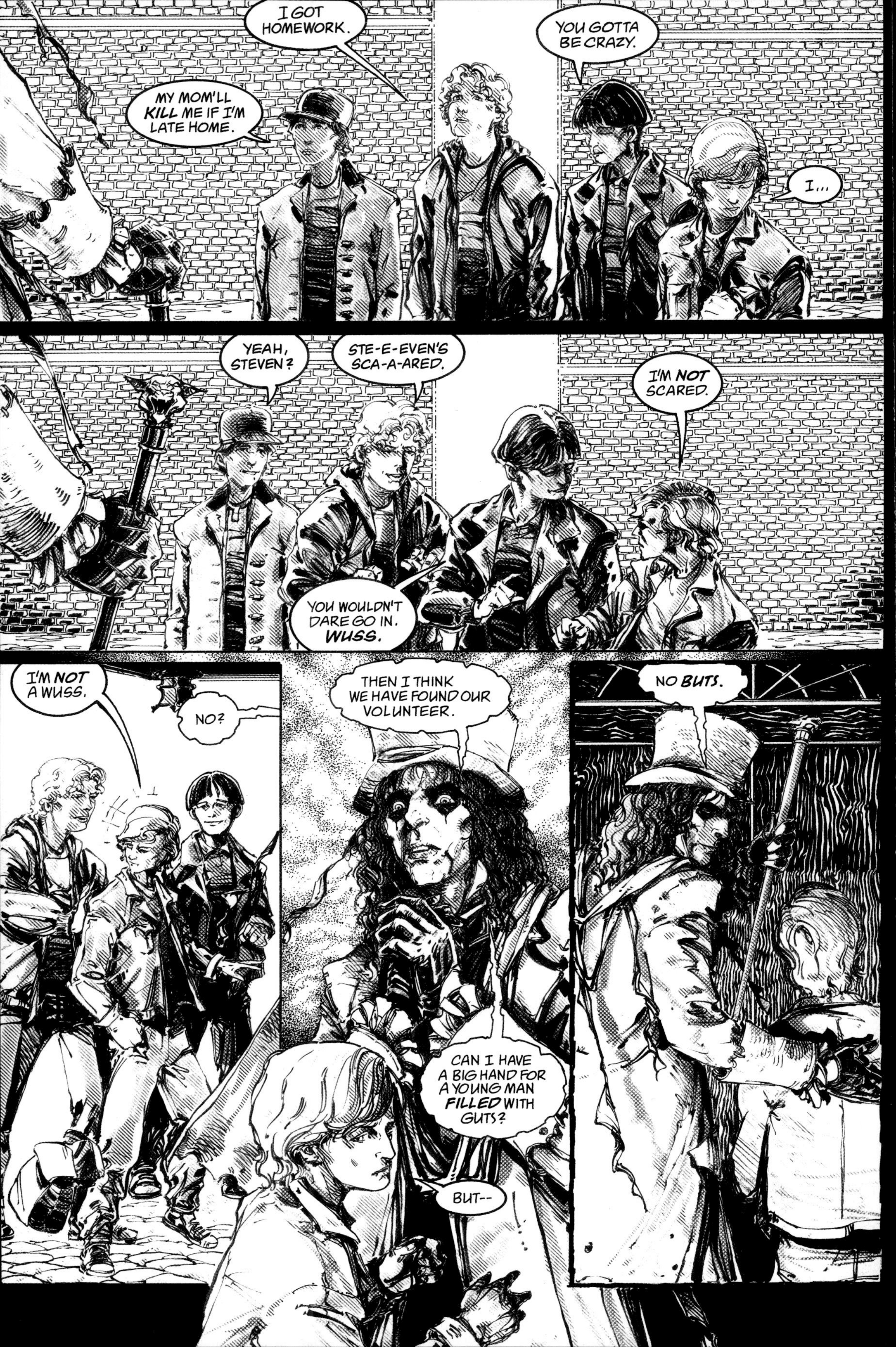
MY MOM'LL **KILL** ME IF I'M LATE HOME.
I GOT HOMEWORK.
YOU GOTTA BE CRAZY.
I...
YEAH, STEVEN?
STE-E-EVEN'S SCA-A-ARED.
YOU WOULDN'T DARE GO IN. **WUSS.**
I'M **NOT** SCARED.
I'M **NOT** A WUSS.
NO?
THEN I THINK WE HAVE FOUND OUR VOLUNTEER.
CAN I HAVE A BIG HAND FOR A YOUNG MAN **FILLED** WITH GUTS?
BUT--
NO **BUTS**.

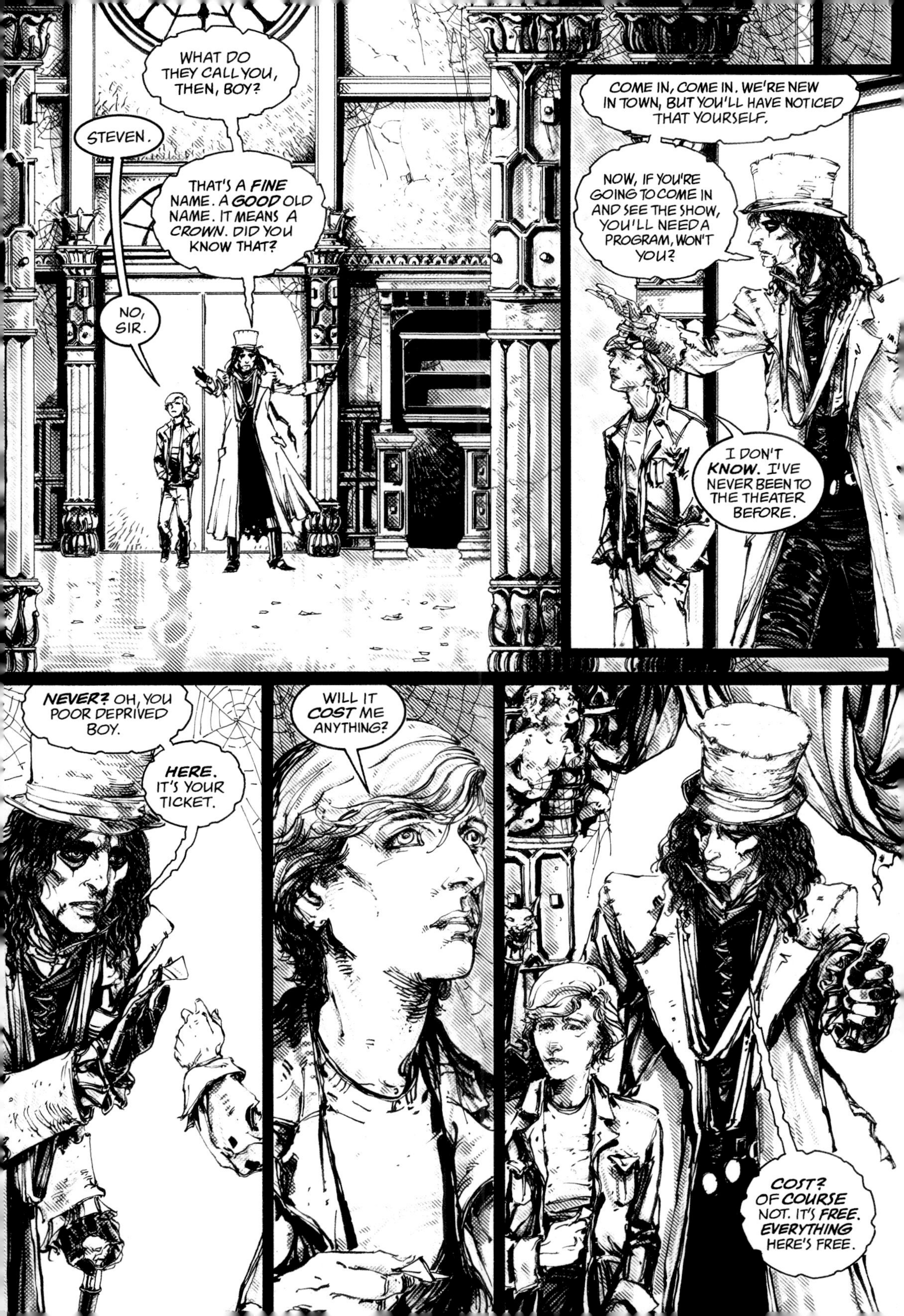
WHAT DO THEY CALL YOU, THEN, BOY?
STEVEN.
THAT'S A **FINE** NAME. A **GOOD** OLD NAME. IT MEANS A *CROWN*. DID YOU KNOW THAT?
NO, SIR.
COME IN, COME IN. WE'RE NEW IN TOWN, BUT YOU'LL HAVE NOTICED THAT YOURSELF.
NOW, IF YOU'RE GOING TO COME IN AND SEE THE SHOW, YOU'LL NEED A PROGRAM, WON'T YOU?
I DON'T **KNOW**. I'VE NEVER BEEN TO THE THEATER BEFORE.
NEVER? OH, YOU POOR DEPRIVED BOY.
HERE. IT'S YOUR TICKET.
WILL IT *COST* ME ANYTHING?
COST? OF **COURSE** NOT. IT'S **FREE**. **EVERYTHING** HERE'S FREE.

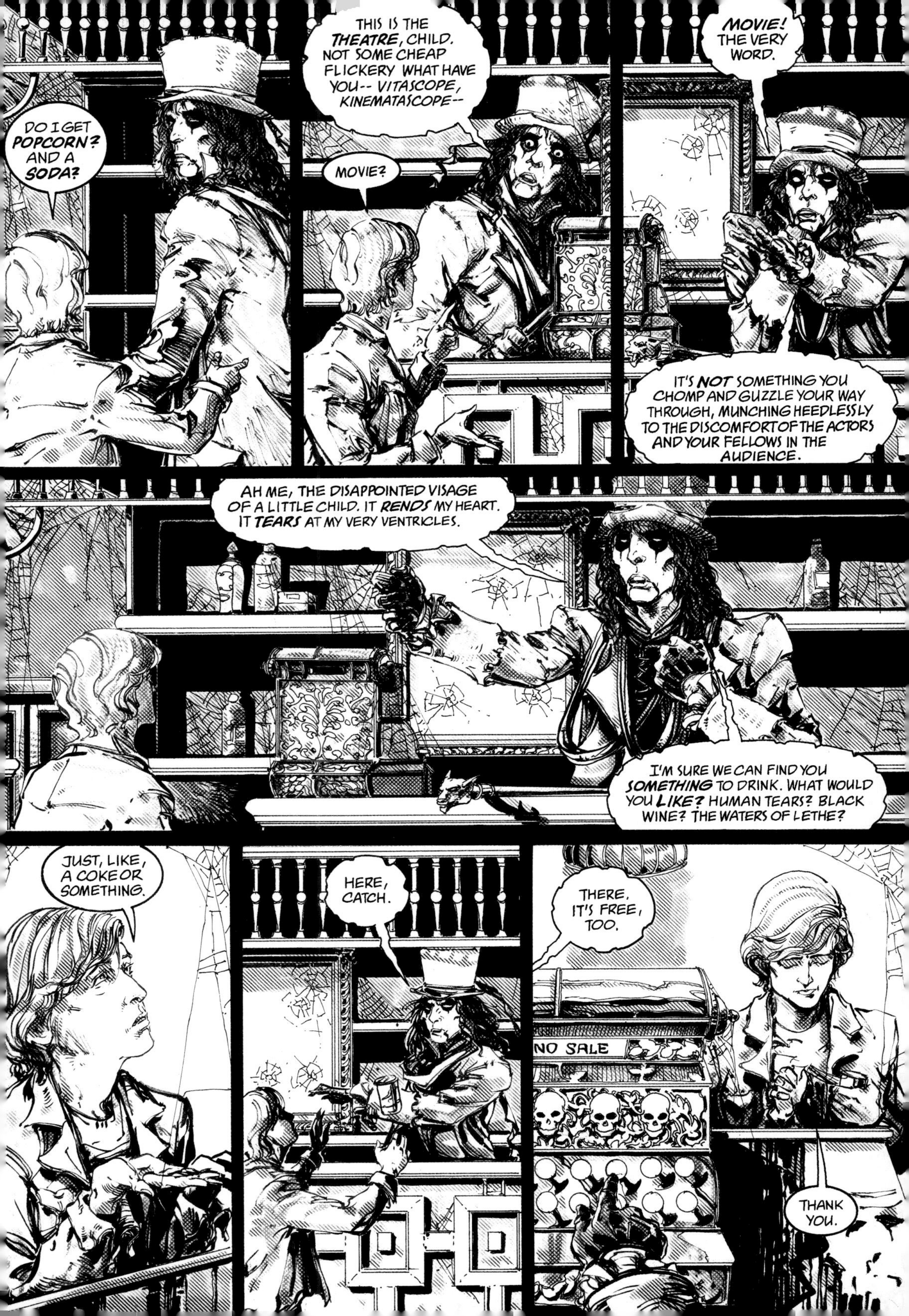
DO I GET POPCORN? AND A SODA?
THIS IS THE THEATRE, CHILD. NOT SOME CHEAP FLICKERY WHAT HAVE YOU-- VITASCOPE, KINEMATASCOPE--
MOVIE?
MOVIE! THE VERY WORD.
IT'S NOT SOMETHING YOU CHOMP AND GUZZLE YOUR WAY THROUGH, MUNCHING HEEDLESSLY TO THE DISCOMFORT OF THE ACTORS AND YOUR FELLOWS IN THE AUDIENCE.
AH ME, THE DISAPPOINTED VISAGE OF A LITTLE CHILD. IT RENDS MY HEART. IT TEARS AT MY VERY VENTRICLES.
I'M SURE WE CAN FIND YOU SOMETHING TO DRINK. WHAT WOULD YOU LIKE? HUMAN TEARS? BLACK WINE? THE WATERS OF LETHE?
JUST, LIKE, A COKE OR SOMETHING.
HERE, CATCH.
THERE. IT'S FREE, TOO.
NO SALE
THANK YOU.

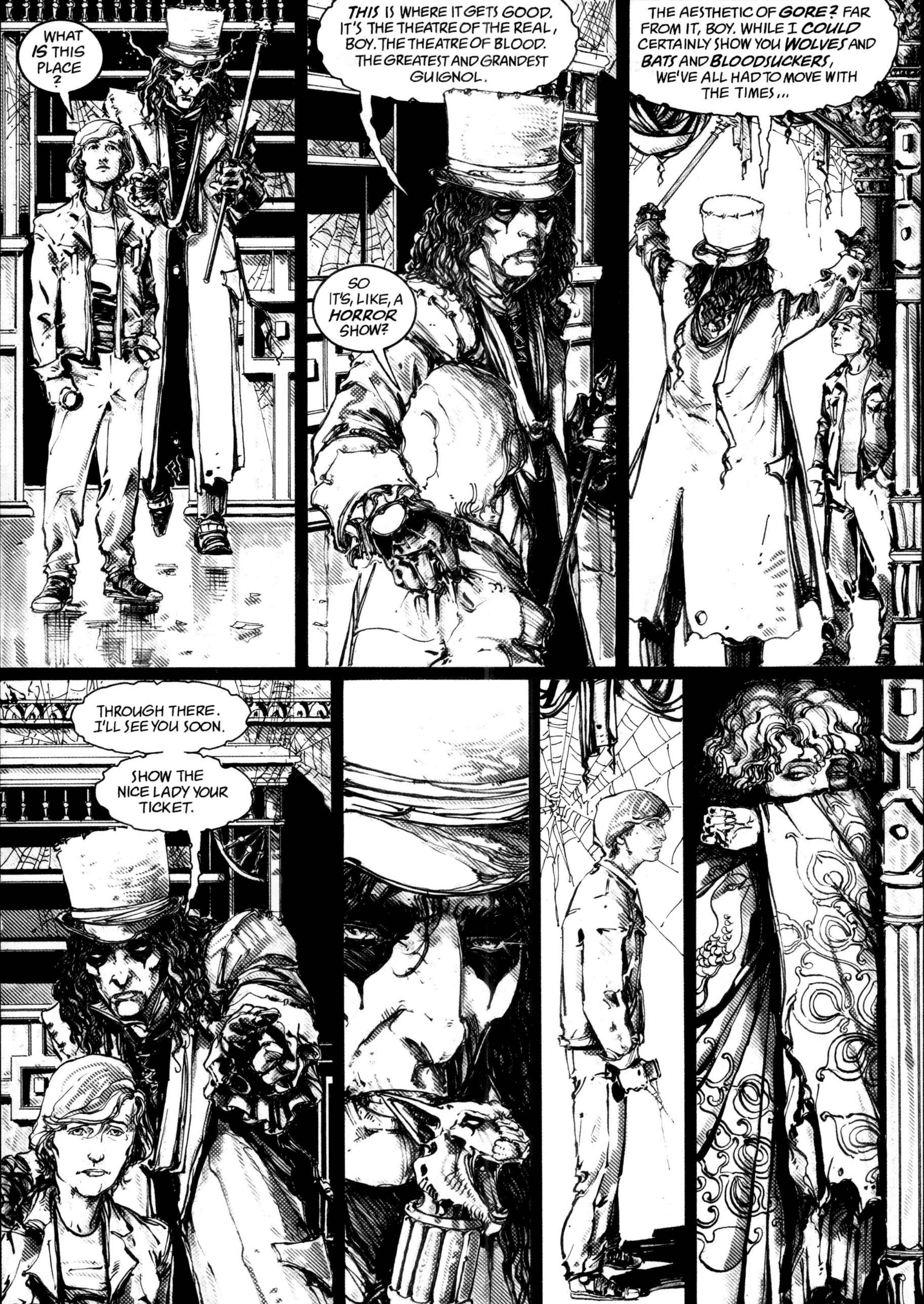
WHAT IS THIS PLACE ?
THIS IS WHERE IT GETS GOOD. IT'S THE THEATRE OF THE REAL, BOY. THE THEATRE OF BLOOD. THE GREATEST AND GRANDEST GUIGNOL.
SO IT'S, LIKE, A HORROR SHOW?
THE AESTHETIC OF GORE? FAR FROM IT, BOY. WHILE I COULD CERTAINLY SHOW YOU WOLVES AND BATS AND BLOODSUCKERS, WE'VE ALL HAD TO MOVE WITH THE TIMES...
THROUGH THERE. I'LL SEE YOU SOON.
SHOW THE NICE LADY YOUR TICKET.

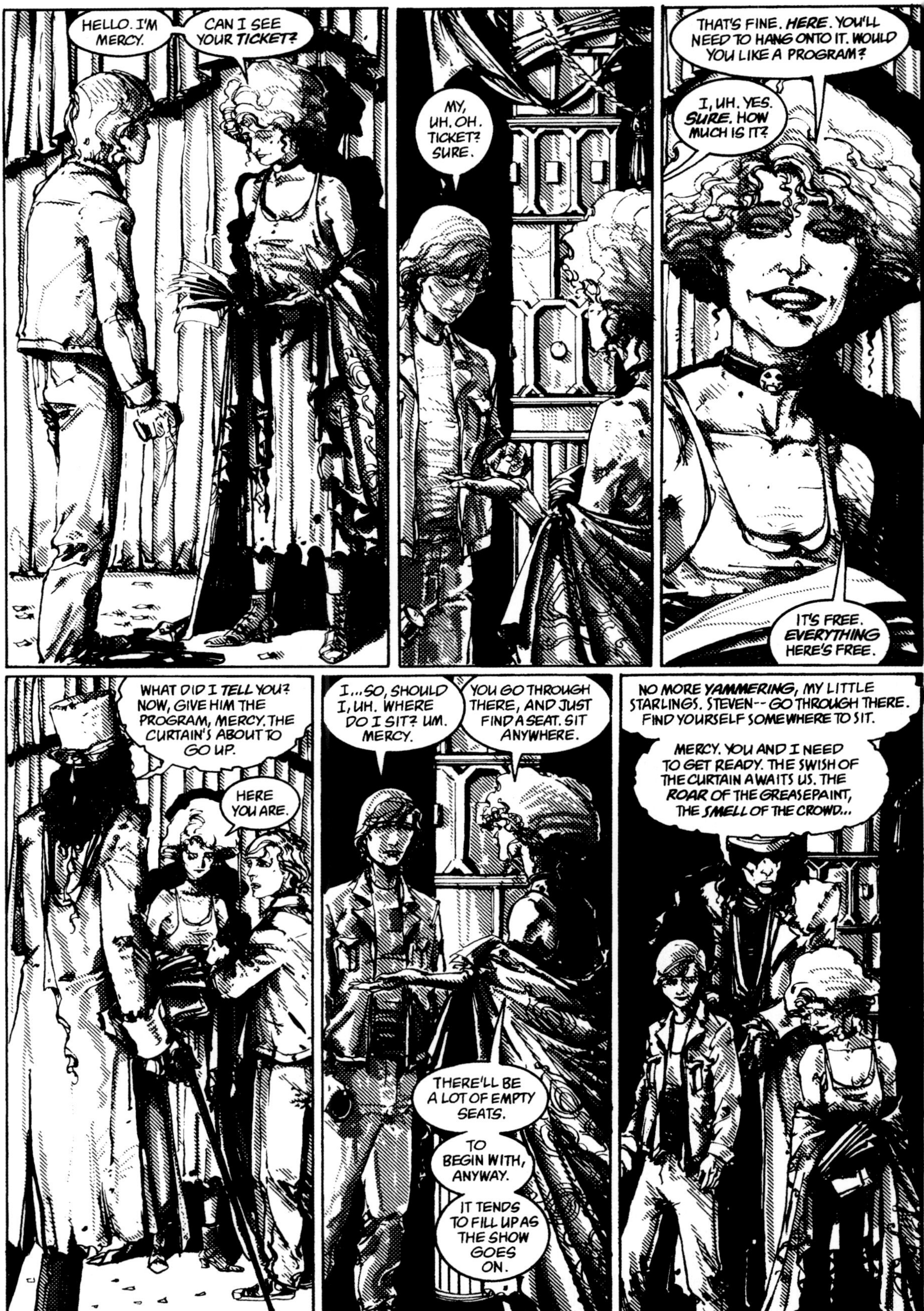
HELLO. I'M MERCY.
CAN I SEE YOUR TICKET?
MY, UH. OH. TICKET? SURE.
THAT'S FINE. HERE. YOU'LL NEED TO HANG ONTO IT. WOULD YOU LIKE A PROGRAM?
I, UH. YES. SURE. HOW MUCH IS IT?
IT'S FREE. EVERYTHING HERE'S FREE.
WHAT DID I TELL YOU? NOW, GIVE HIM THE PROGRAM, MERCY. THE CURTAIN'S ABOUT TO GO UP.
HERE YOU ARE.
I...SO, SHOULD I, UH. WHERE DO I SIT? UM. MERCY.
YOU GO THROUGH THERE, AND JUST FIND A SEAT. SIT ANYWHERE.
THERE'LL BE A LOT OF EMPTY SEATS.
TO BEGIN WITH, ANYWAY.
IT TENDS TO FILL UP AS THE SHOW GOES ON.
NO MORE YAMMERING, MY LITTLE STARLINGS. STEVEN-- GO THROUGH THERE. FIND YOURSELF SOMEWHERE TO SIT.
MERCY. YOU AND I NEED TO GET READY. THE SWISH OF THE CURTAIN AWAITS US. THE ROAR OF THE GREASEPAINT, THE SMELL OF THE CROWD...

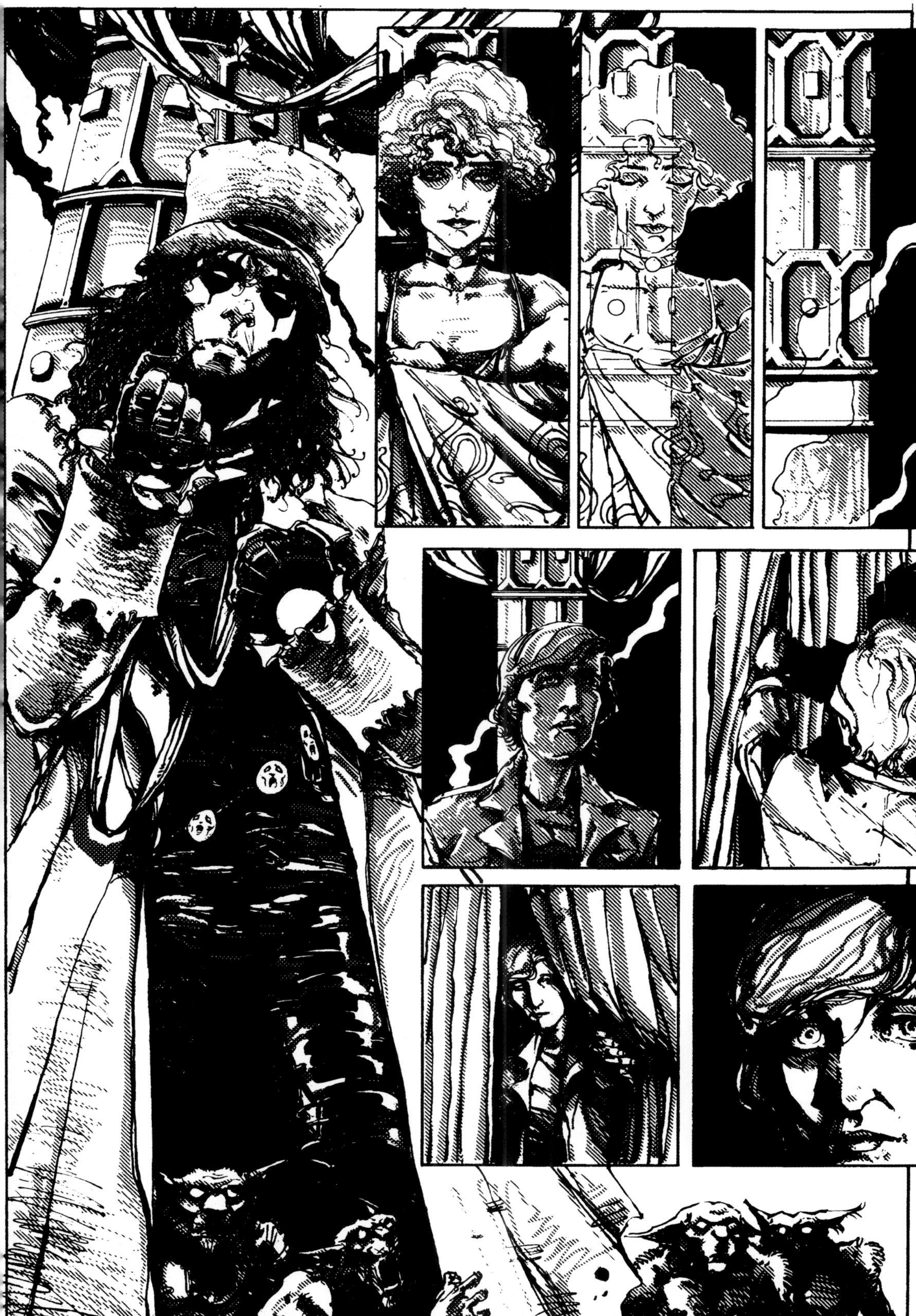

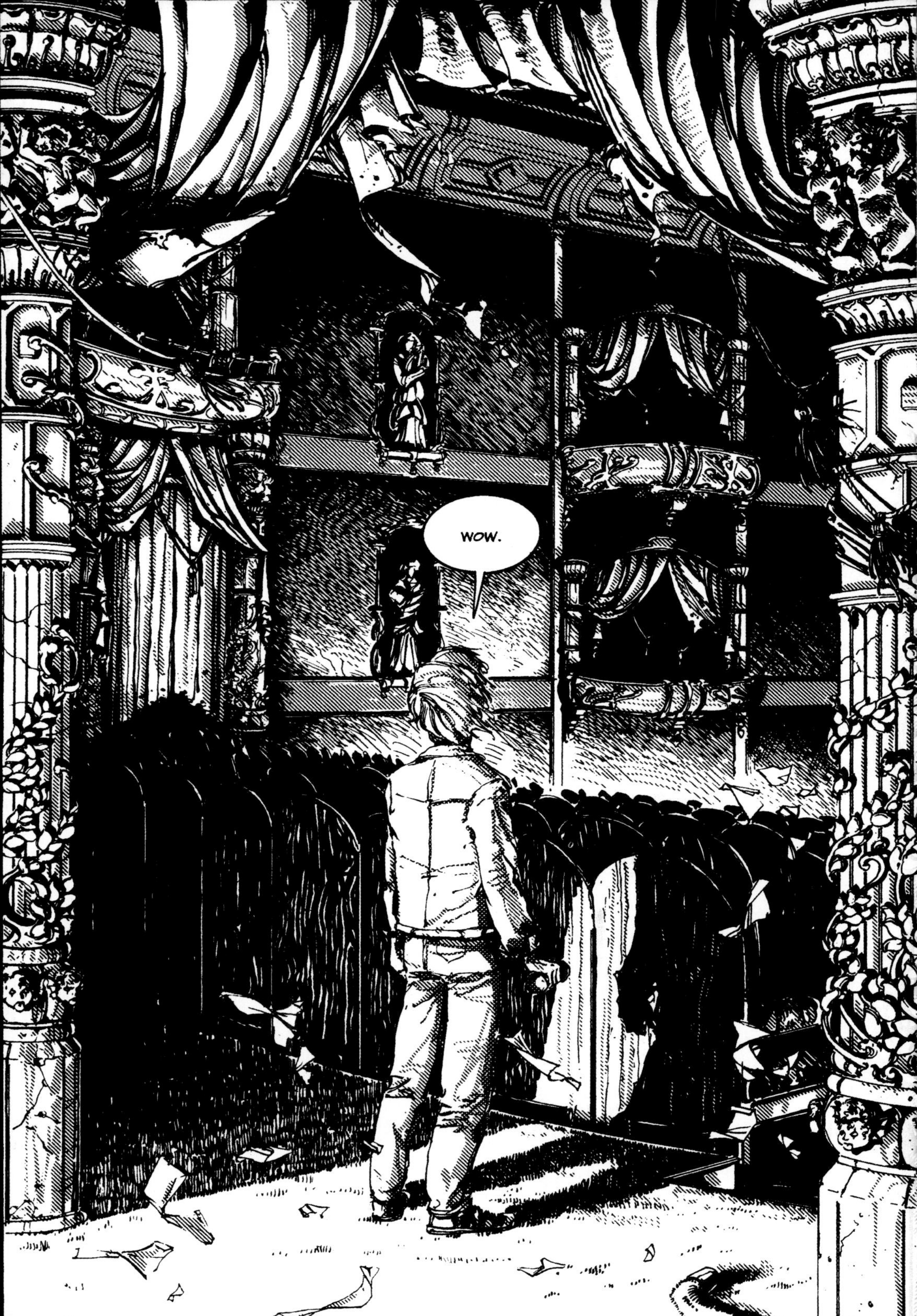
WOW.

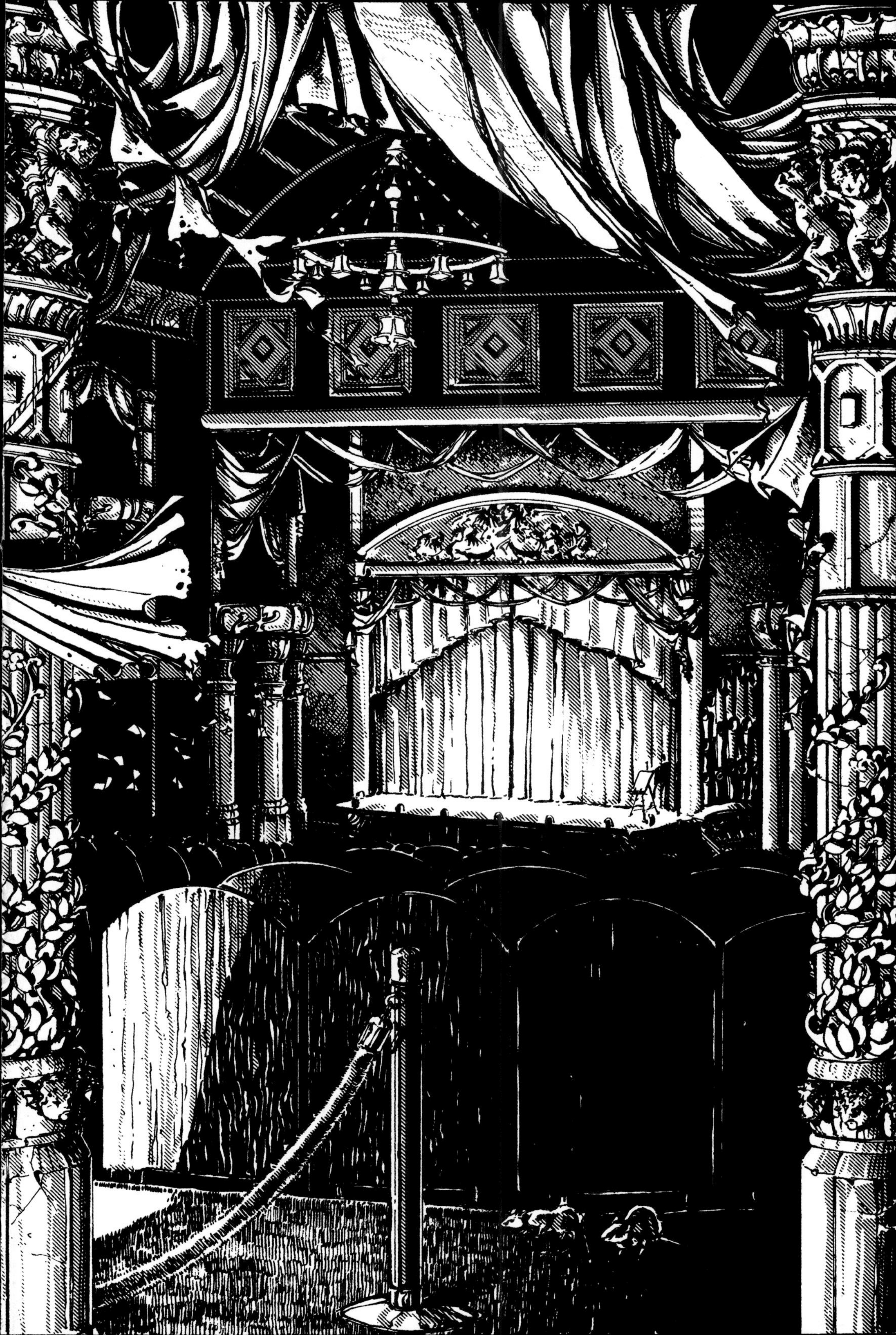

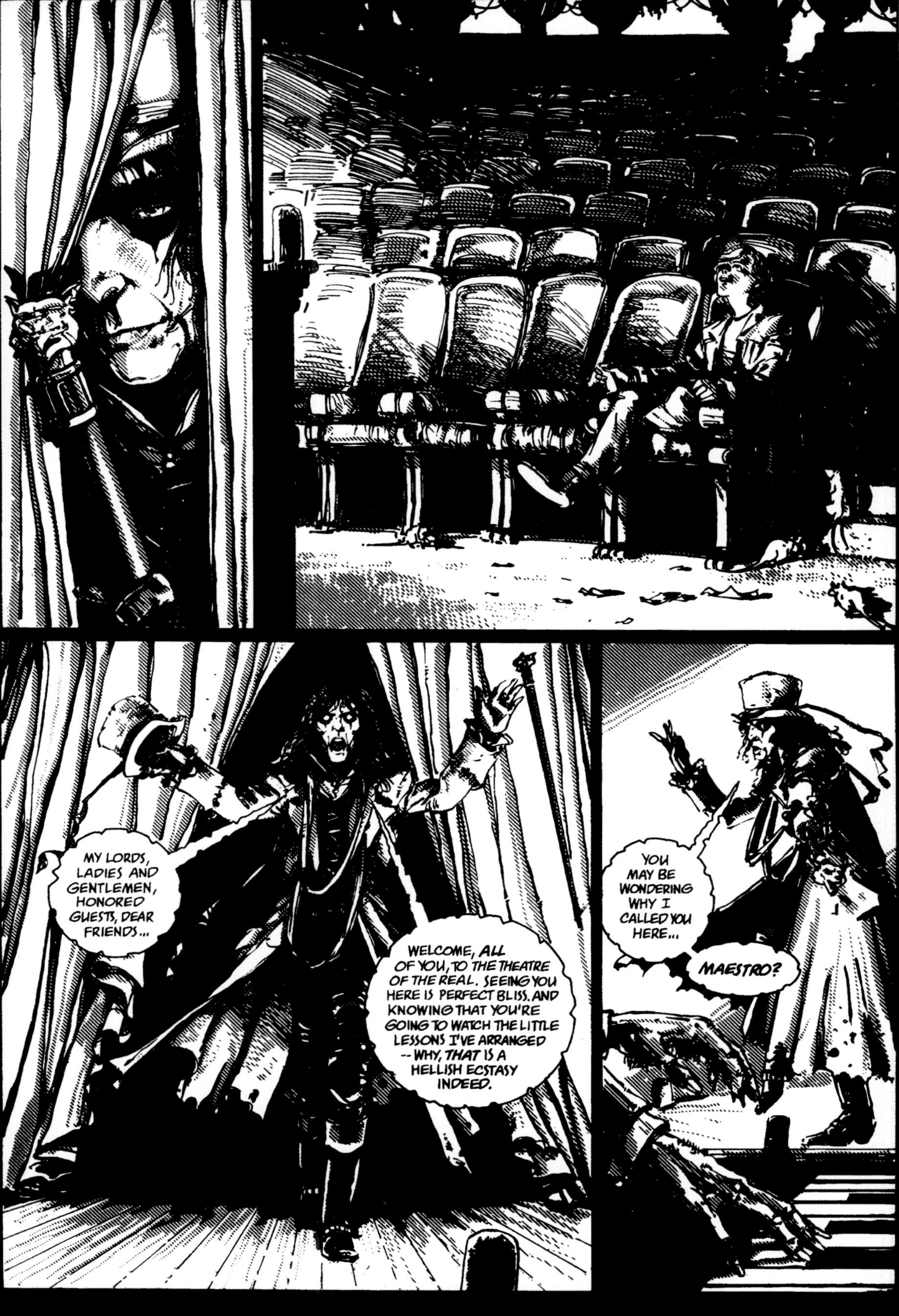
MY LORDS, LADIES AND GENTLEMEN, HONORED GUESTS, DEAR FRIENDS...
WELCOME, ALL OF YOU, TO THE THEATRE OF THE REAL. SEEING YOU HERE IS PERFECT BLISS. AND KNOWING THAT YOU'RE GOING TO WATCH THE LITTLE LESSONS I'VE ARRANGED --WHY, THAT IS A HELLISH ECSTASY INDEED.
YOU MAY BE WONDERING WHY I CALLED YOU HERE...
MAESTRO?

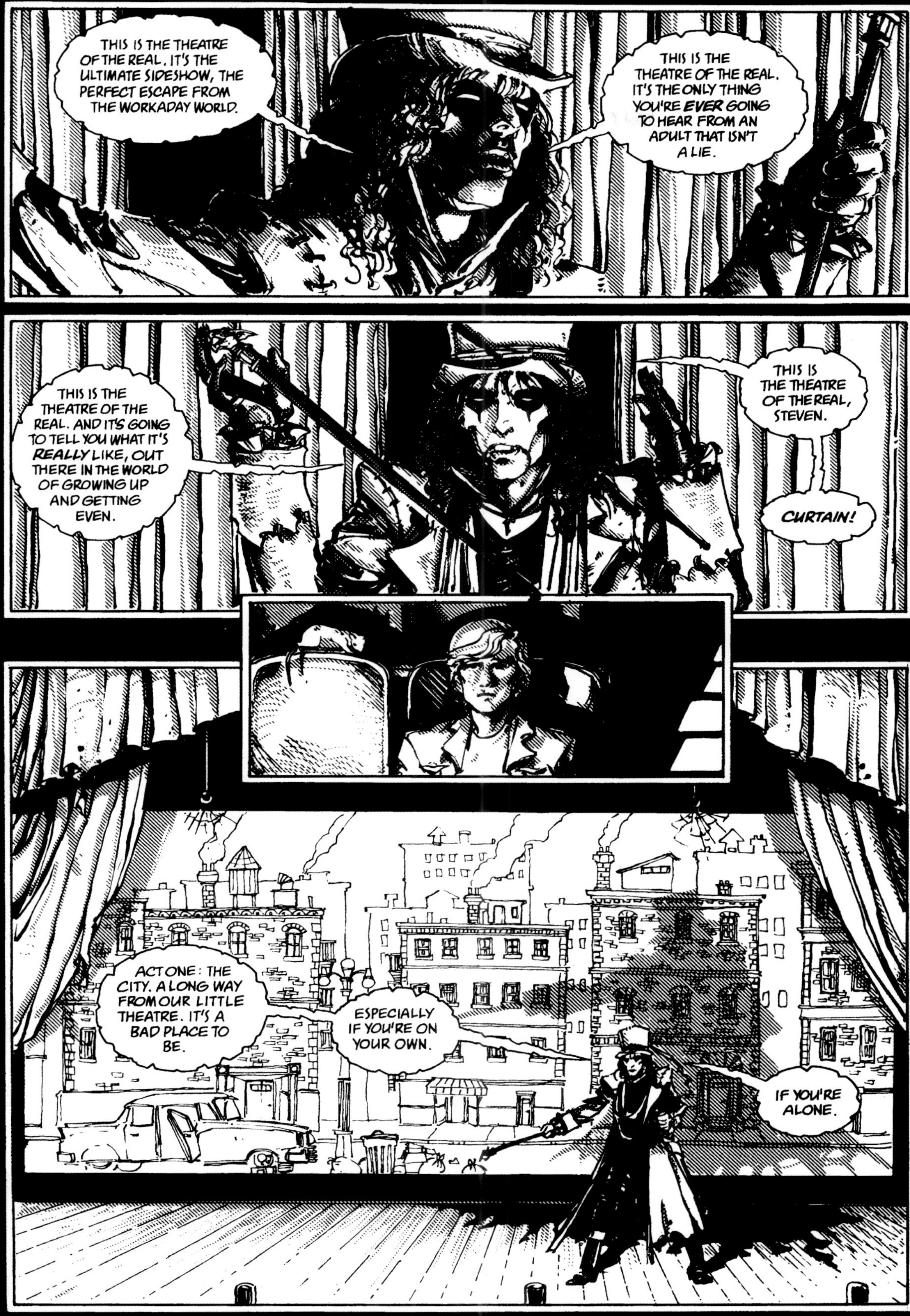
THIS IS THE THEATRE OF THE REAL. IT'S THE ULTIMATE SIDESHOW, THE PERFECT ESCAPE FROM THE WORKADAY WORLD.
THIS IS THE THEATRE OF THE REAL. IT'S THE ONLY THING YOU'RE EVER GOING TO HEAR FROM AN ADULT THAT ISN'T A LIE.
THIS IS THE THEATRE OF THE REAL. AND IT'S GOING TO TELL YOU WHAT IT'S REALLY LIKE, OUT THERE IN THE WORLD OF GROWING UP AND GETTING EVEN.
THIS IS THE THEATRE OF THE REAL, STEVEN.
CURTAIN!
ACT ONE: THE CITY. A LONG WAY FROM OUR LITTLE THEATRE. IT'S A BAD PLACE TO BE.
ESPECIALLY IF YOU'RE ON YOUR OWN.
IF YOU'RE ALONE.

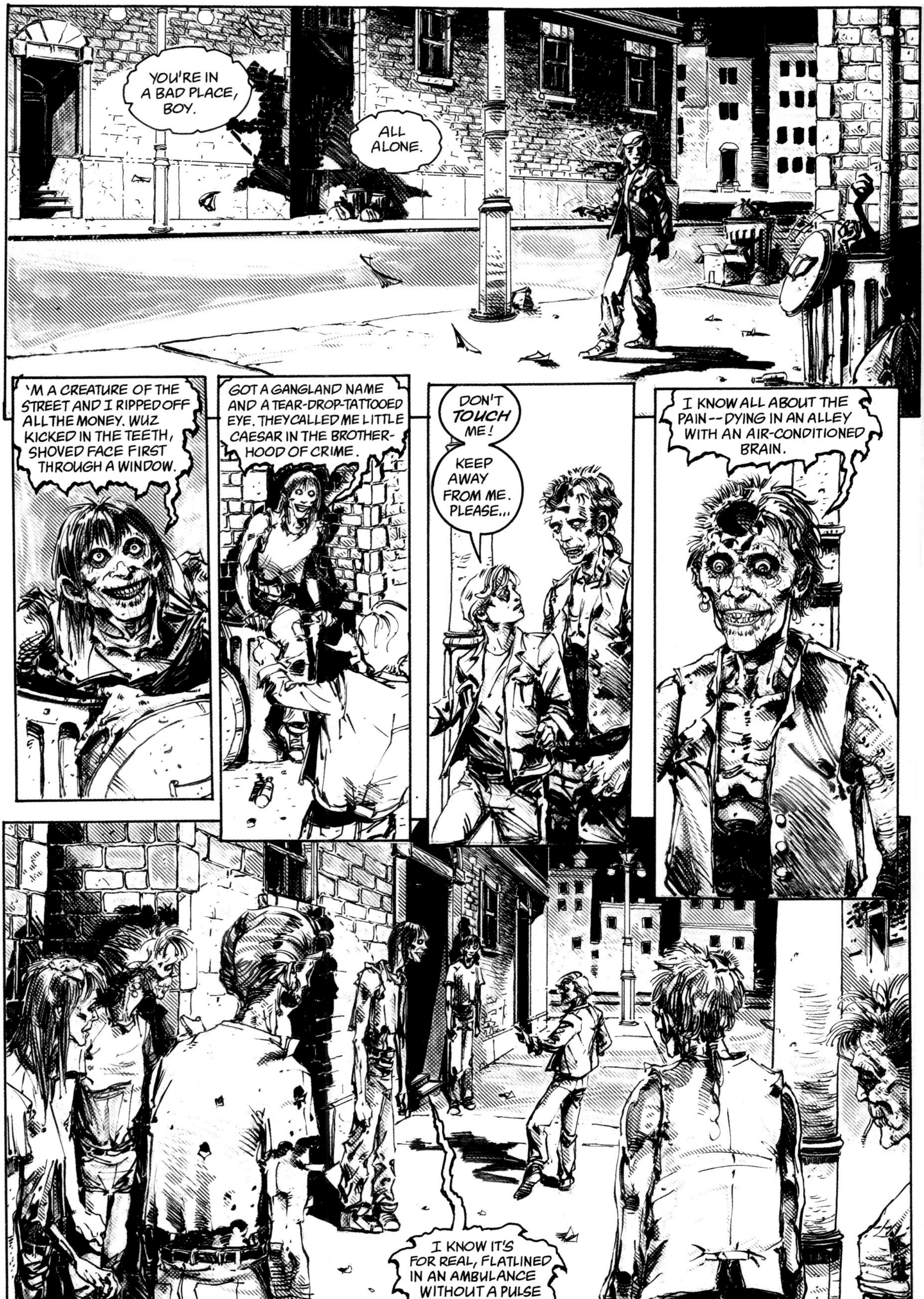
YOU'RE IN A BAD PLACE, BOY.
ALL ALONE.
'M A CREATURE OF THE STREET AND I RIPPED OFF ALL THE MONEY. WUZ KICKED IN THE TEETH, SHOVED FACE FIRST THROUGH A WINDOW.
GOT A GANGLAND NAME AND A TEAR-DROP-TATTOOED EYE. THEY CALLED ME LITTLE CAESAR IN THE BROTHER-HOOD OF CRIME.
DON'T TOUCH ME!
KEEP AWAY FROM ME. PLEASE...
I KNOW ALL ABOUT THE PAIN--DYING IN AN ALLEY WITH AN AIR-CONDITIONED BRAIN.
I KNOW IT'S FOR REAL, FLATLINED IN AN AMBULANCE WITHOUT A PULSE TO FEEL.

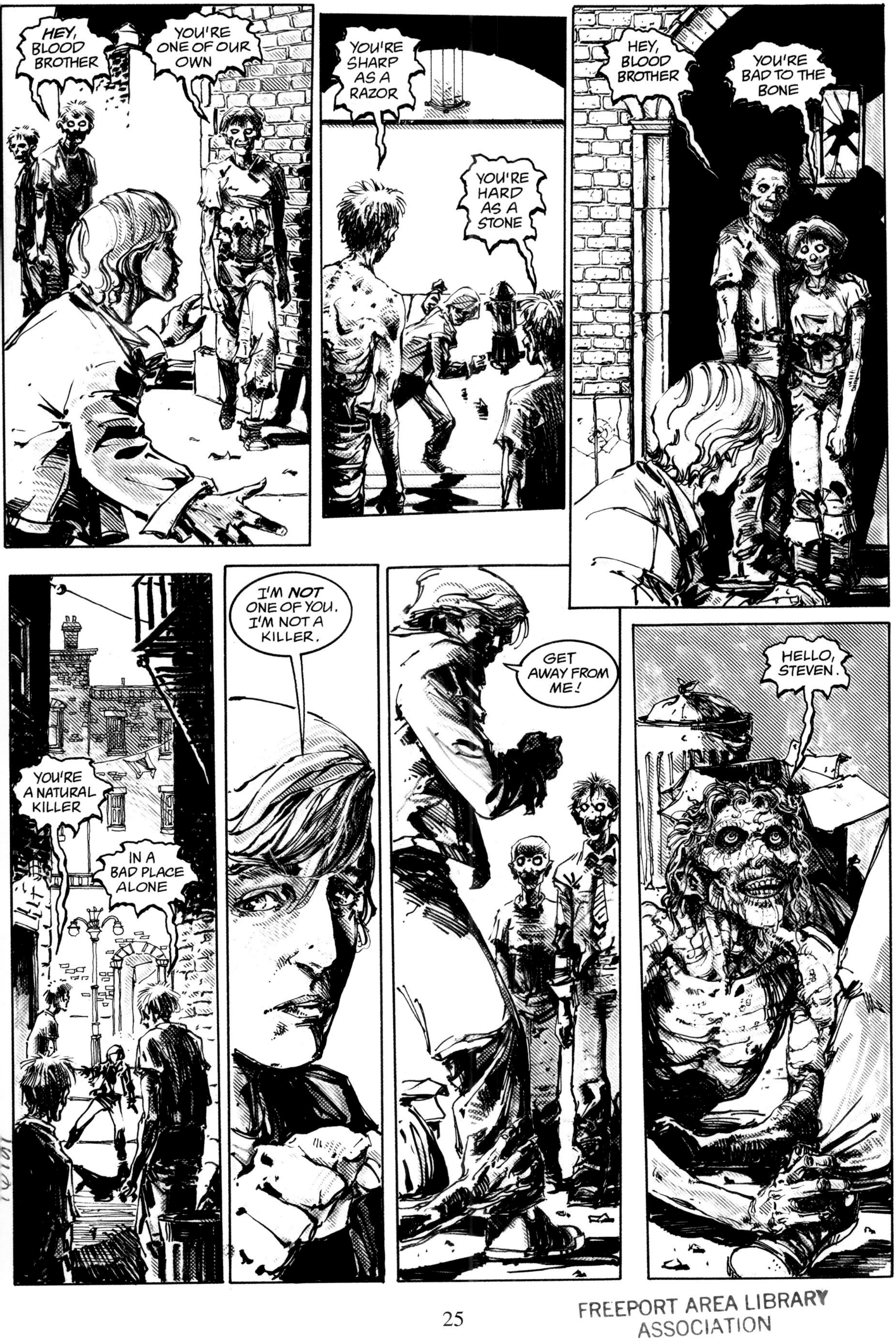
HEY, BLOOD BROTHER
YOU'RE ONE OF OUR OWN
YOU'RE SHARP AS A RAZOR
YOU'RE HARD AS A STONE
HEY, BLOOD BROTHER
YOU'RE BAD TO THE BONE
YOU'RE A NATURAL KILLER
IN A BAD PLACE ALONE
I'M NOT ONE OF YOU. I'M NOT A KILLER.
GET AWAY FROM ME!
HELLO, STEVEN.

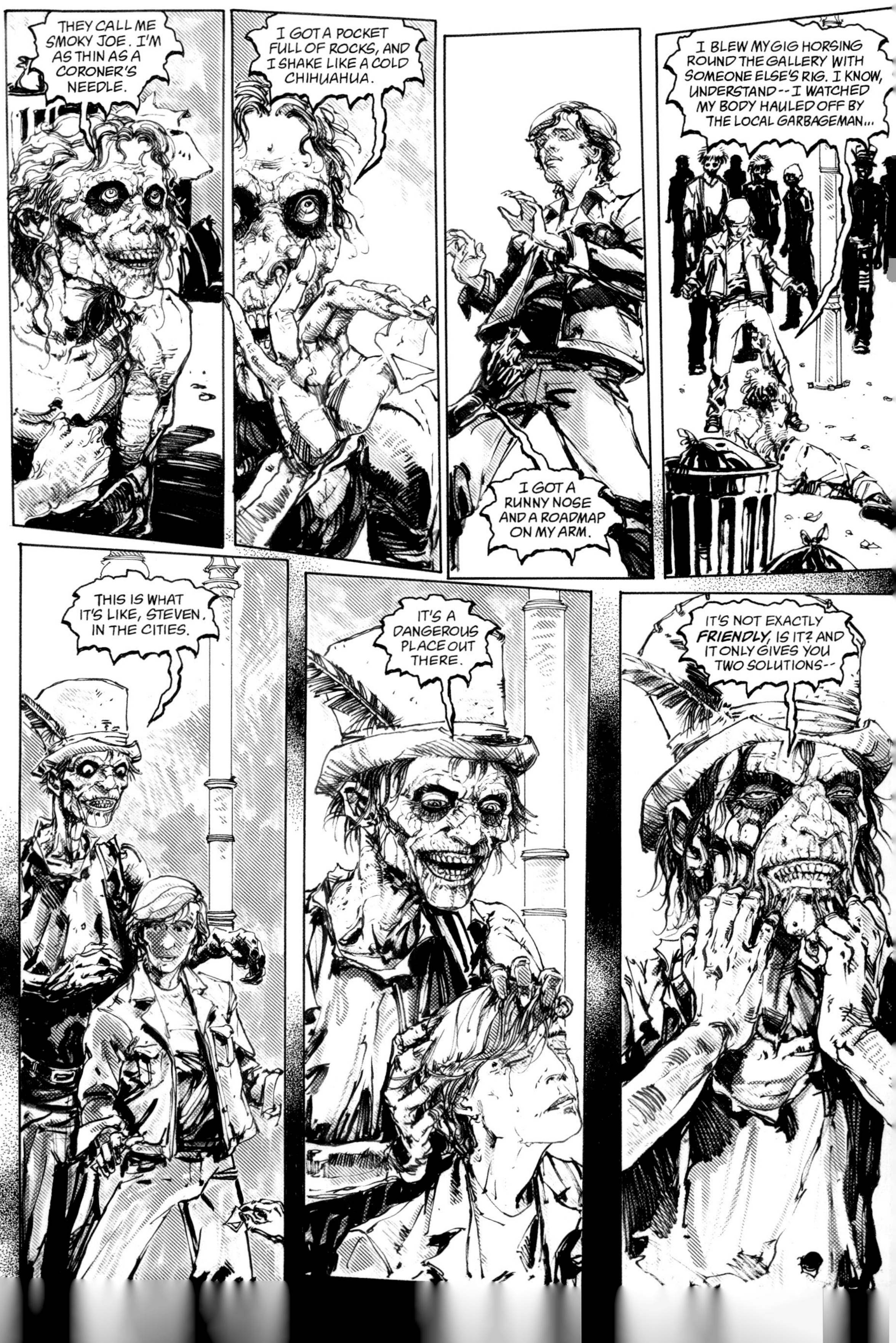
THEY CALL ME SMOKY JOE. I'M AS THIN AS A CORONER'S NEEDLE.
I GOT A POCKET FULL OF ROCKS, AND I SHAKE LIKE A COLD CHIHUAHUA.
I GOT A RUNNY NOSE AND A ROADMAP ON MY ARM.
I BLEW MY GIG HORSING ROUND THE GALLERY WITH SOMEONE ELSE'S RIG. I KNOW, UNDERSTAND -- I WATCHED MY BODY HAULED OFF BY THE LOCAL GARBAGEMAN...
THIS IS WHAT IT'S LIKE, STEVEN, IN THE CITIES.
IT'S A DANGEROUS PLACE OUT THERE.
IT'S NOT EXACTLY FRIENDLY, IS IT? AND IT ONLY GIVES YOU TWO SOLUTIONS--

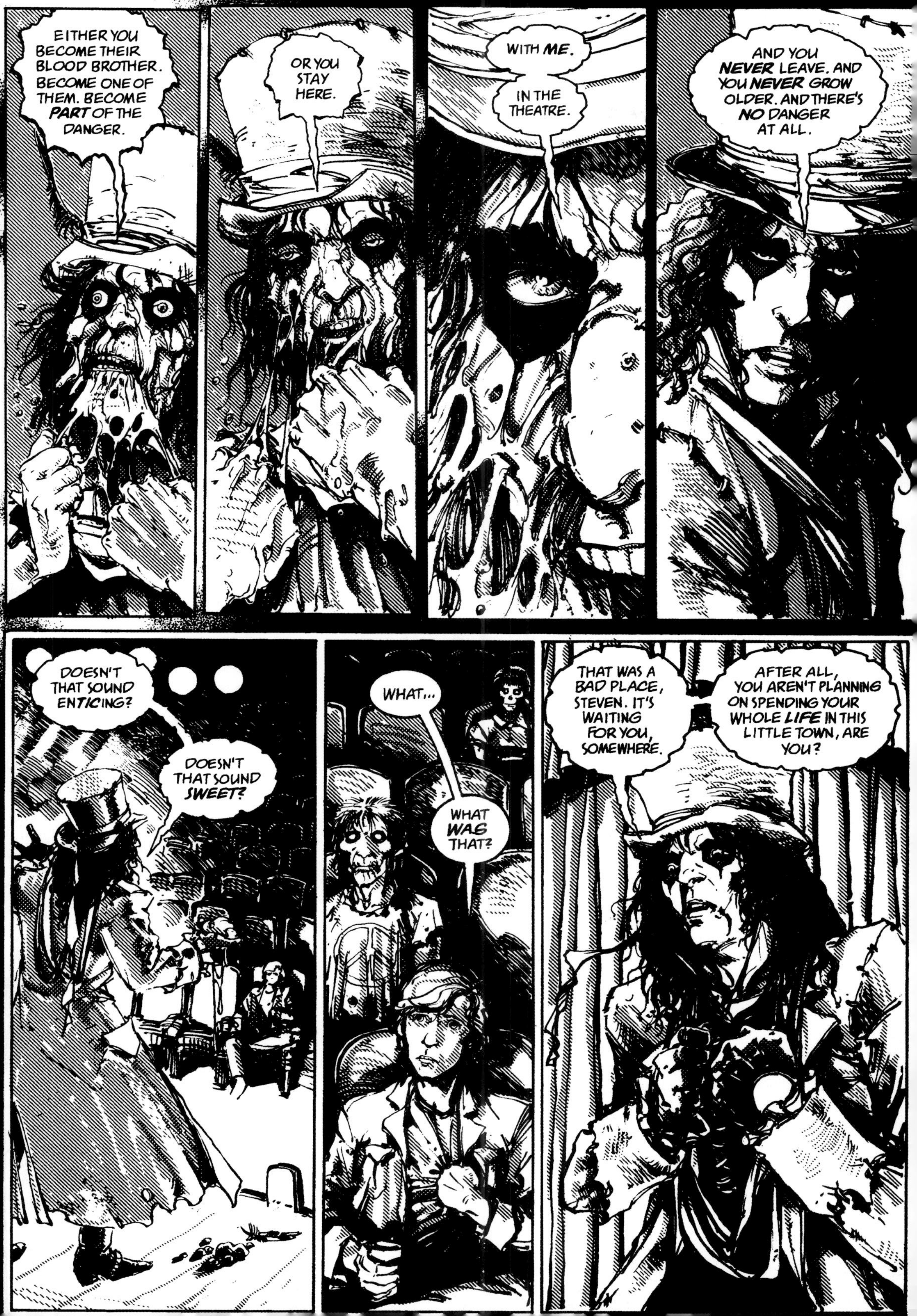
EITHER YOU BECOME THEIR BLOOD BROTHER. BECOME ONE OF THEM. BECOME PART OF THE DANGER.
OR YOU STAY HERE.
WITH ME.
IN THE THEATRE.
AND YOU NEVER LEAVE. AND YOU NEVER GROW OLDER. AND THERE'S NO DANGER AT ALL.
DOESN'T THAT SOUND ENTICING?
DOESN'T THAT SOUND SWEET?
WHAT...
WHAT WAS THAT?
THAT WAS A BAD PLACE, STEVEN. IT'S WAITING FOR YOU, SOMEWHERE.
AFTER ALL, YOU AREN'T PLANNING ON SPENDING YOUR WHOLE LIFE IN THIS LITTLE TOWN, ARE YOU?

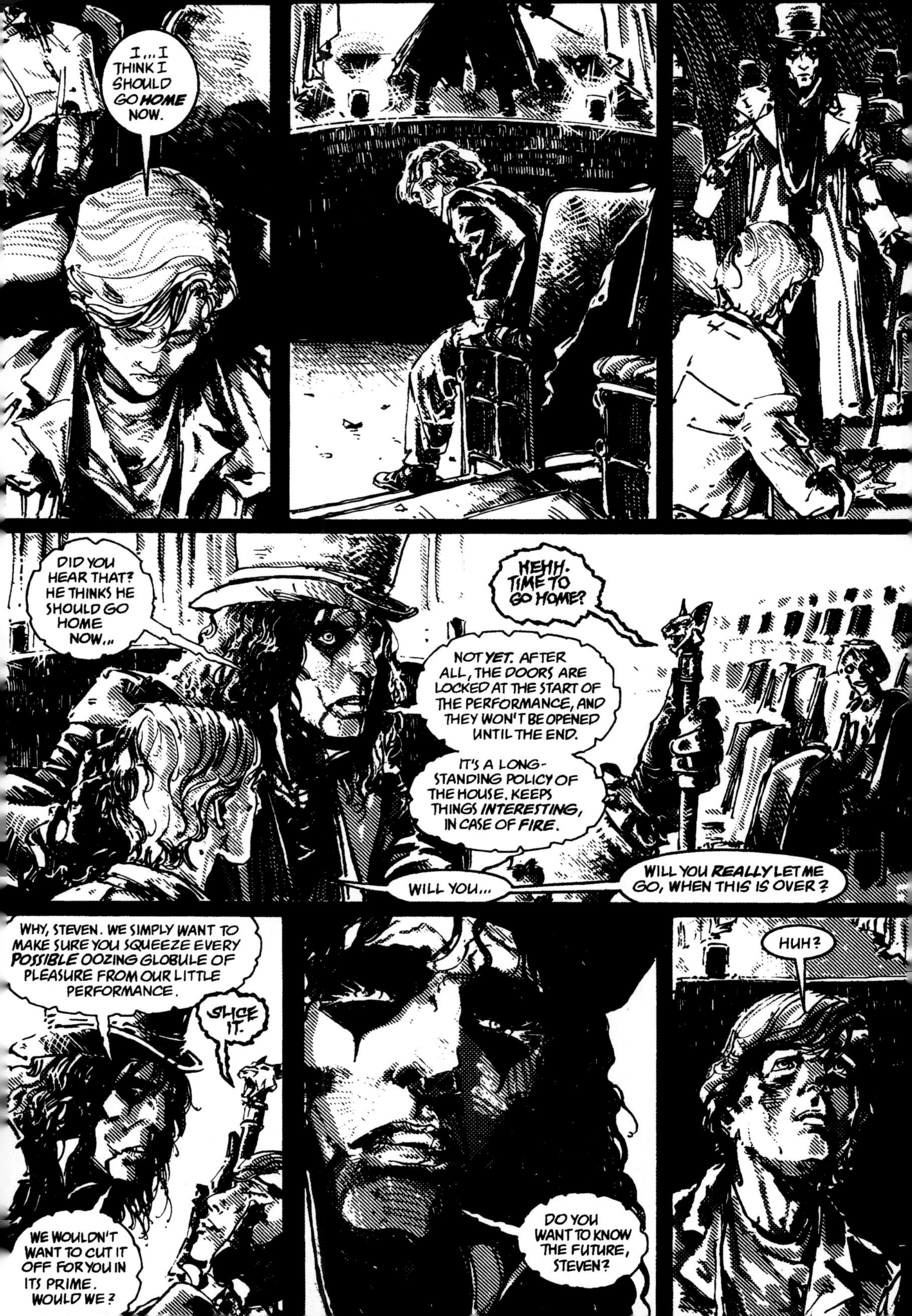

I... I THINK I SHOULD GO HOME NOW.
DID YOU HEAR THAT? HE THINKS HE SHOULD GO HOME NOW...
HEHH. TIME TO GO HOME?
NOT YET. AFTER ALL, THE DOORS ARE LOCKED AT THE START OF THE PERFORMANCE, AND THEY WON'T BE OPENED UNTIL THE END.
IT'S A LONG-STANDING POLICY OF THE HOUSE. KEEPS THINGS INTERESTING, IN CASE OF FIRE.
WILL YOU...
WILL YOU REALLY LET ME GO, WHEN THIS IS OVER?
WHY, STEVEN. WE SIMPLY WANT TO MAKE SURE YOU SQUEEZE EVERY POSSIBLE OOZING GLOBULE OF PLEASURE FROM OUR LITTLE PERFORMANCE.
SLICE IT.
WE WOULDN'T WANT TO CUT IT OFF FOR YOU IN ITS PRIME. WOULD WE?
DO YOU WANT TO KNOW THE FUTURE, STEVEN?
HUH?

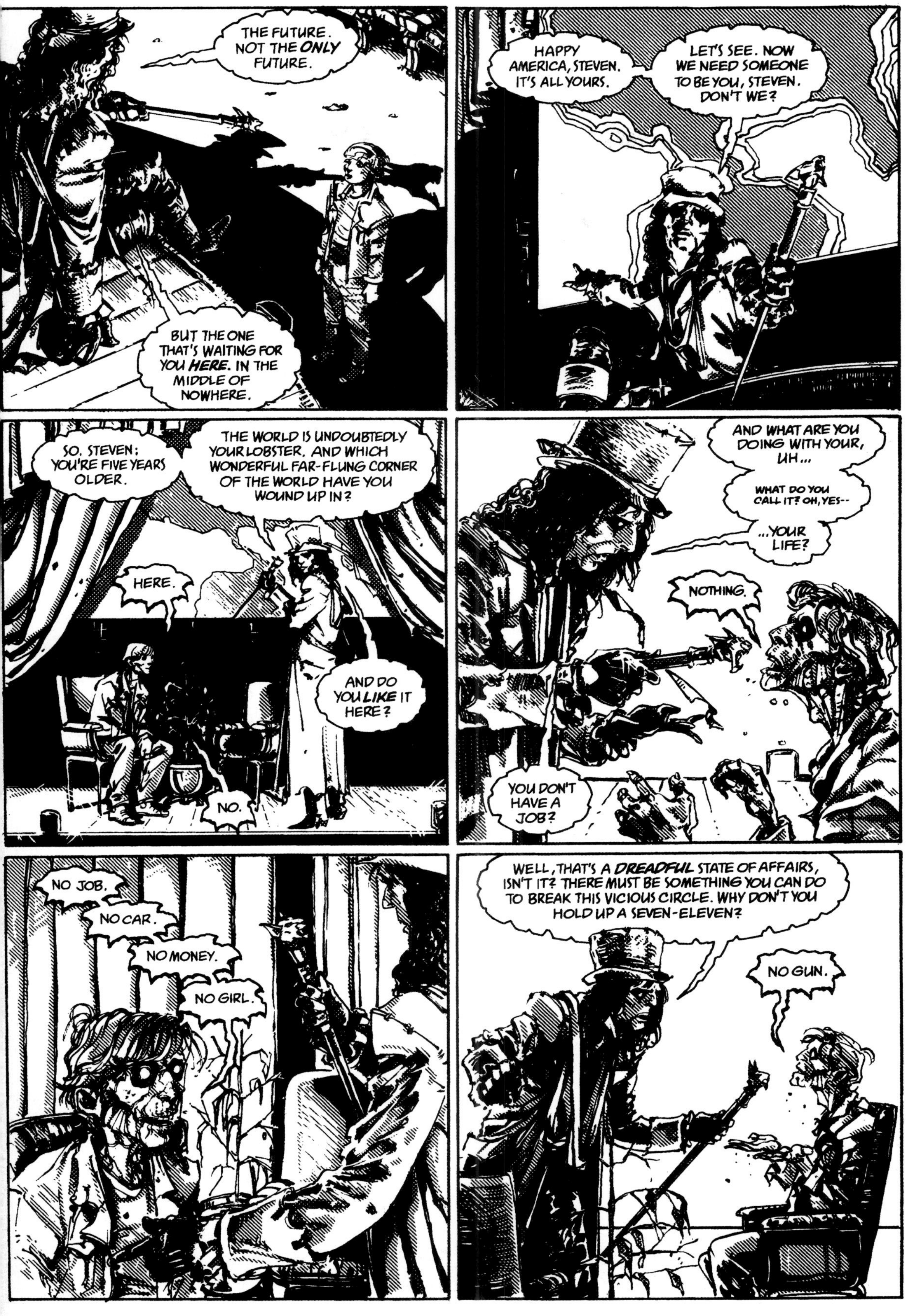
THE FUTURE. NOT THE ONLY FUTURE.
BUT THE ONE THAT'S WAITING FOR YOU HERE. IN THE MIDDLE OF NOWHERE.
HAPPY AMERICA, STEVEN. IT'S ALL YOURS.
LET'S SEE. NOW WE NEED SOMEONE TO BE YOU, STEVEN. DON'T WE?
SO, STEVEN: YOU'RE FIVE YEARS OLDER.
THE WORLD IS UNDOUBTEDLY YOUR LOBSTER. AND WHICH WONDERFUL FAR-FLUNG CORNER OF THE WORLD HAVE YOU WOUND UP IN?
HERE.
AND DO YOU LIKE IT HERE?
NO.
AND WHAT ARE YOU DOING WITH YOUR, UH...
WHAT DO YOU CALL IT? OH, YES--
...YOUR LIFE?
NOTHING.
YOU DON'T HAVE A JOB?
NO JOB.
NO CAR.
NO MONEY.
NO GIRL.
WELL, THAT'S A DREADFUL STATE OF AFFAIRS, ISN'T IT? THERE MUST BE SOMETHING YOU CAN DO TO BREAK THIS VICIOUS CIRCLE. WHY DON'T YOU HOLD UP A SEVEN-ELEVEN?
NO GUN.

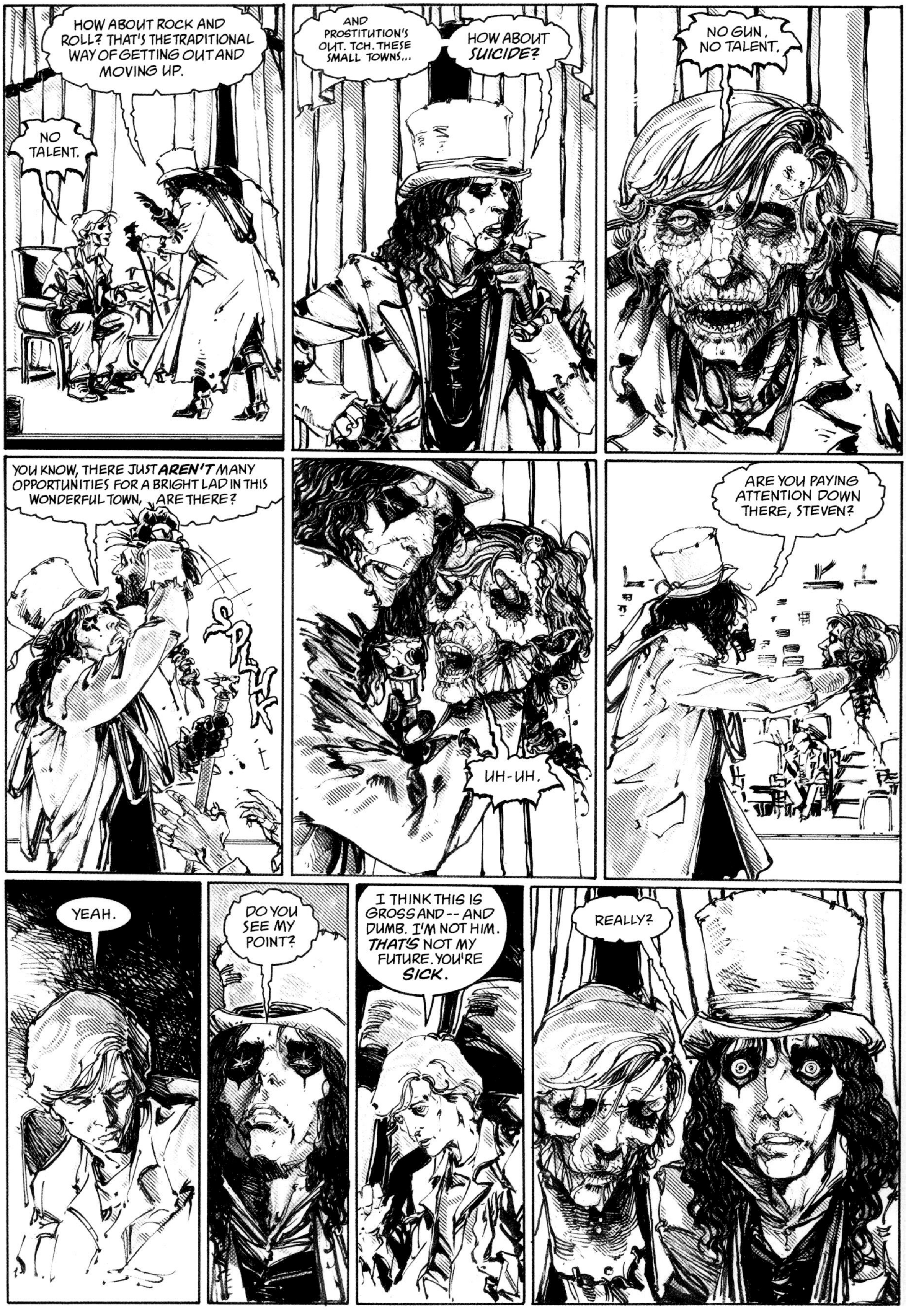
HOW ABOUT ROCK AND ROLL? THAT'S THE TRADITIONAL WAY OF GETTING OUT AND MOVING UP.
NO TALENT.
AND PROSTITUTION'S OUT. TCH. THESE SMALL TOWNS...
HOW ABOUT SUICIDE?
NO GUN, NO TALENT.
YOU KNOW, THERE JUST AREN'T MANY OPPORTUNITIES FOR A BRIGHT LAD IN THIS WONDERFUL TOWN, ARE THERE?
SPLUK
UH-UH.
ARE YOU PAYING ATTENTION DOWN THERE, STEVEN?
YEAH.
DO YOU SEE MY POINT?
I THINK THIS IS GROSS AND -- AND DUMB. I'M NOT HIM. THAT'S NOT MY FUTURE. YOU'RE SICK.
REALLY?

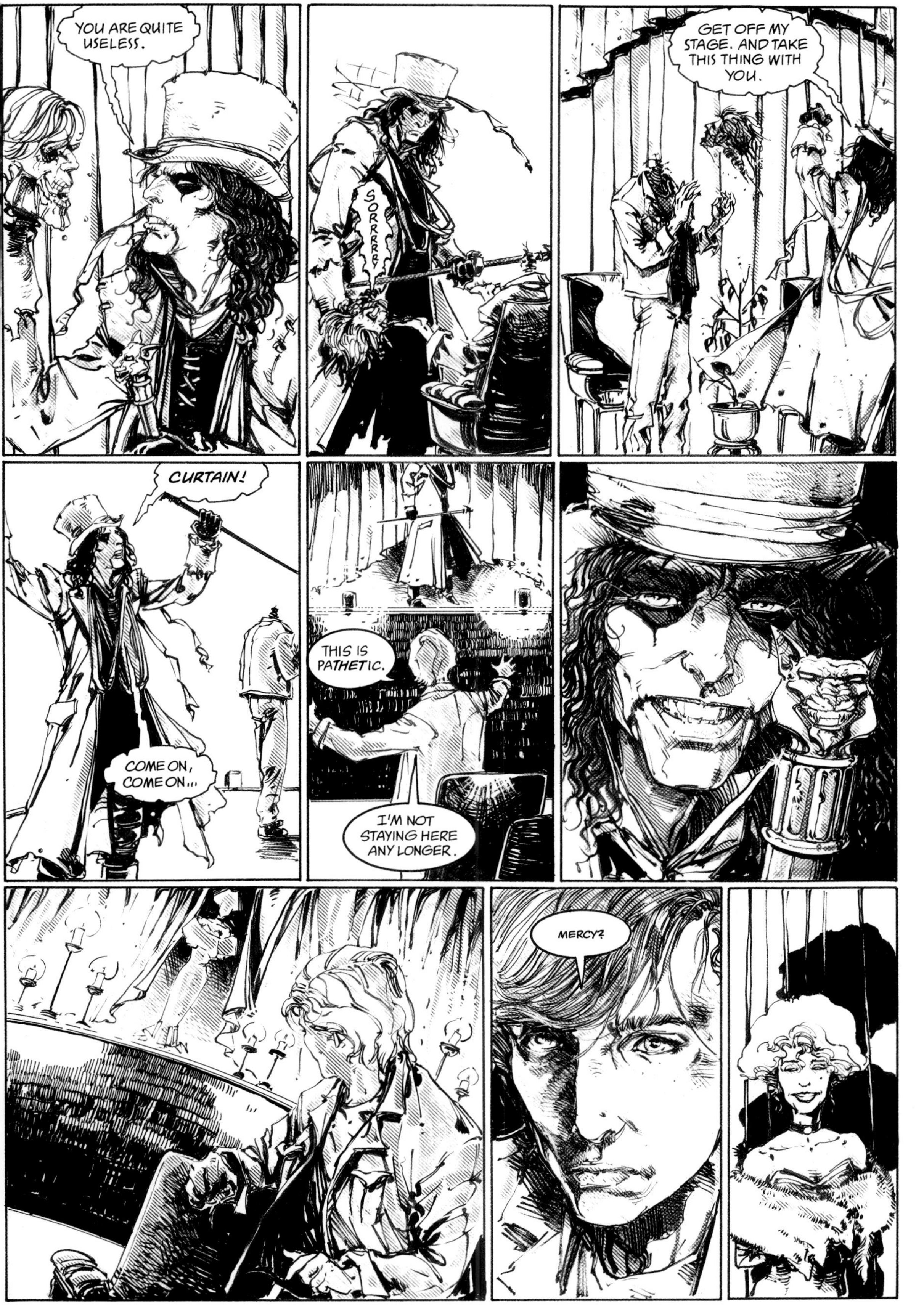

YOU ARE QUITE USELESS.
SORRRRRY
GET OFF MY STAGE. AND TAKE THIS THING WITH YOU.
CURTAIN!
COME ON, COME ON...
THIS IS PATHETIC.
I'M NOT STAYING HERE ANY LONGER.
MERCY?

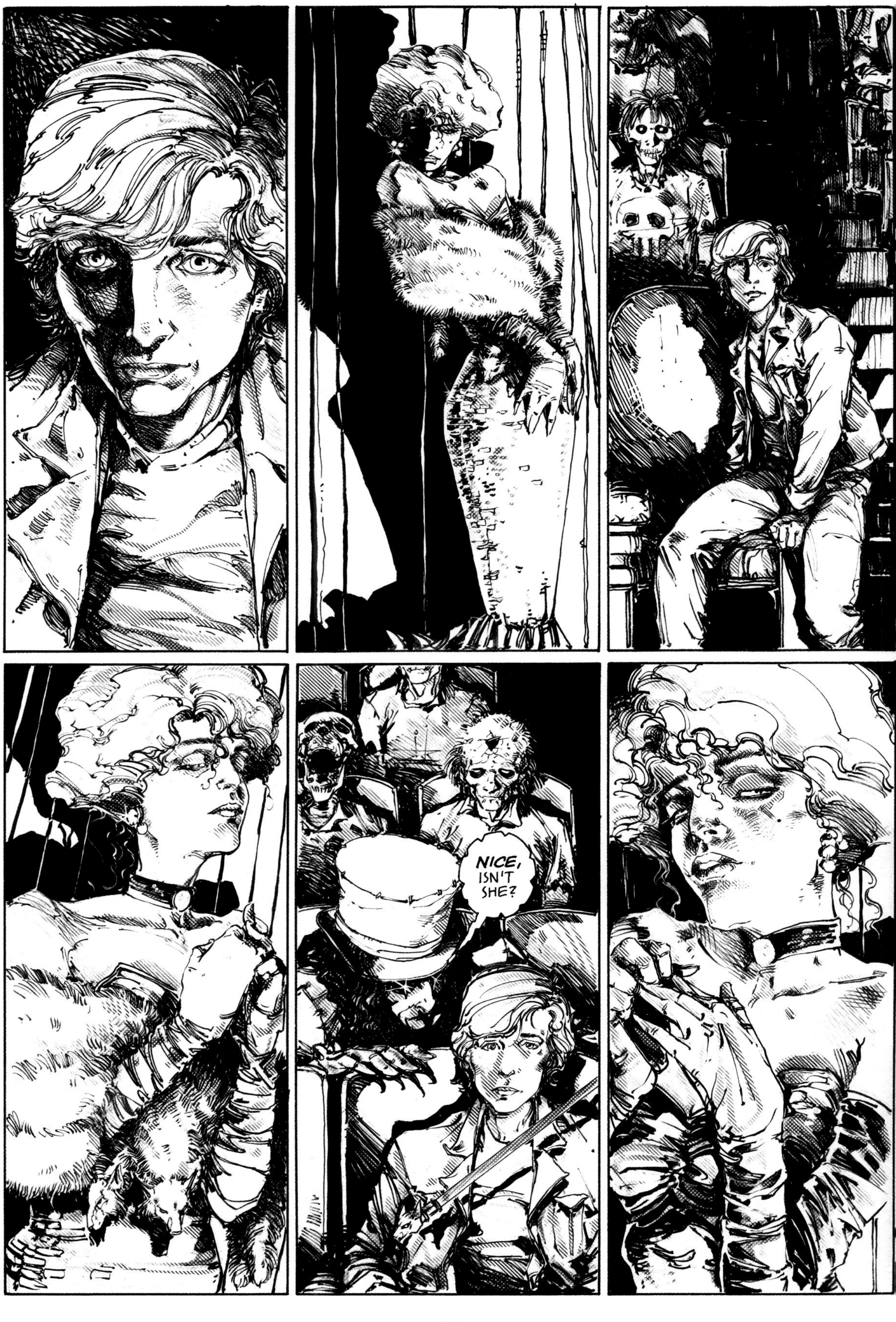
NICE, ISN'T SHE?

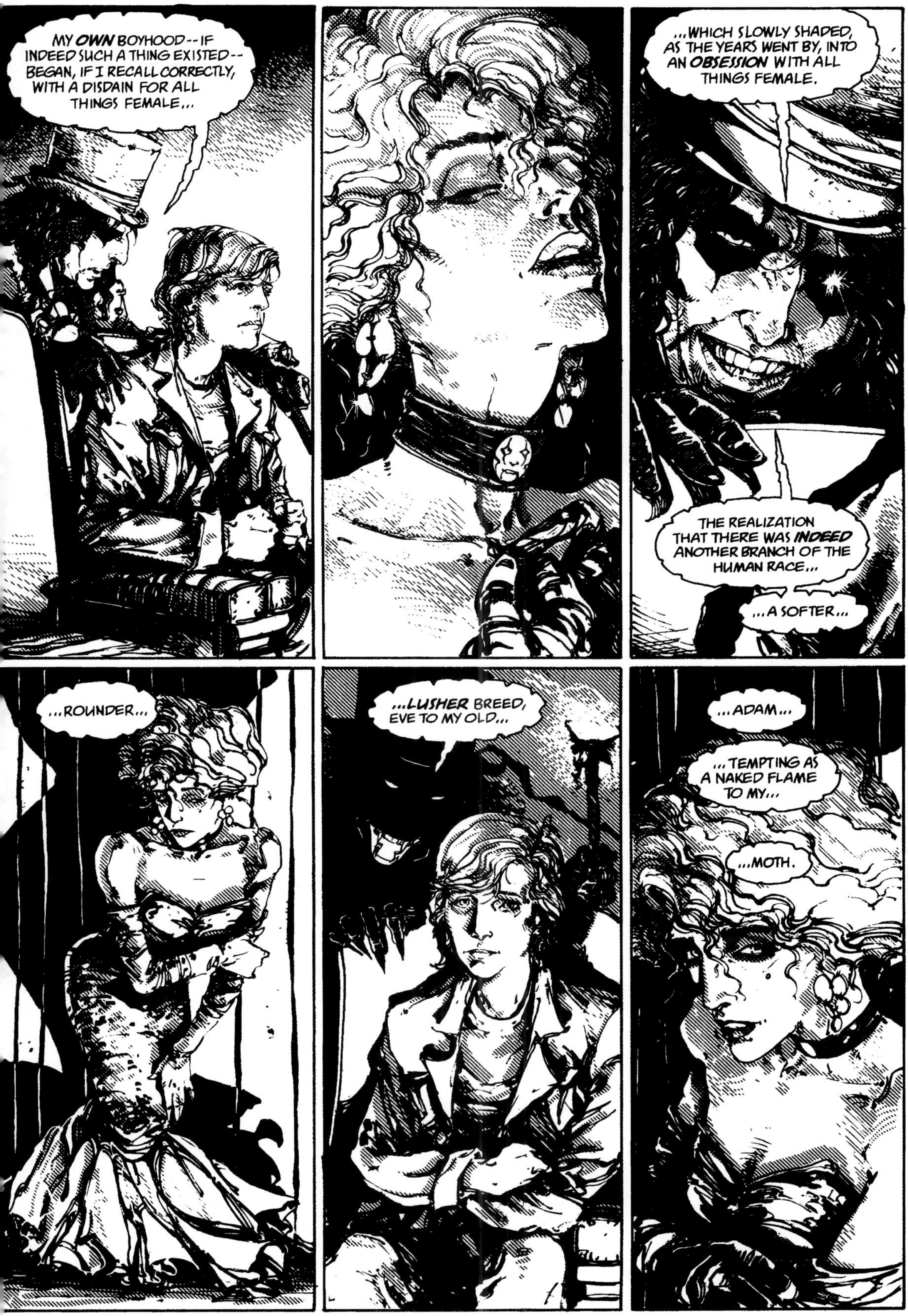
MY OWN BOYHOOD--IF INDEED SUCH A THING EXISTED--BEGAN, IF I RECALL CORRECTLY, WITH A DISDAIN FOR ALL THINGS FEMALE...
...WHICH SLOWLY SHADED, AS THE YEARS WENT BY, INTO AN OBSESSION WITH ALL THINGS FEMALE.
THE REALIZATION THAT THERE WAS INDEED ANOTHER BRANCH OF THE HUMAN RACE...
...A SOFTER...
...ROUNDER...
...LUSHER BREED, EVE TO MY OLD...
...ADAM...
...TEMPTING AS A NAKED FLAME TO MY...
...MOTH.

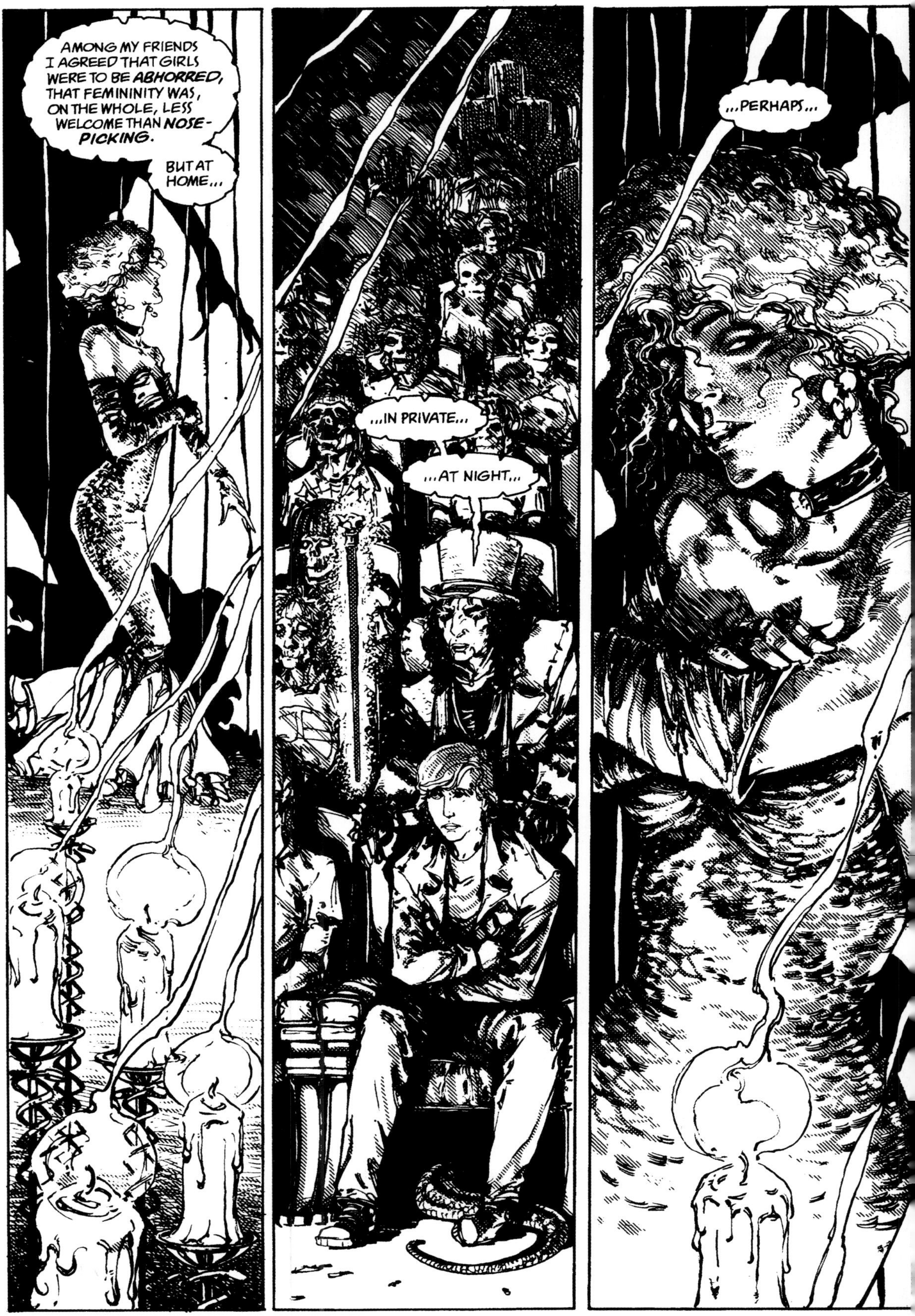
AMONG MY FRIENDS I AGREED THAT GIRLS WERE TO BE ABHORRED, THAT FEMININITY WAS, ON THE WHOLE, LESS WELCOME THAN NOSE-PICKING.
BUT AT HOME...
...IN PRIVATE...
...AT NIGHT...
...PERHAPS...

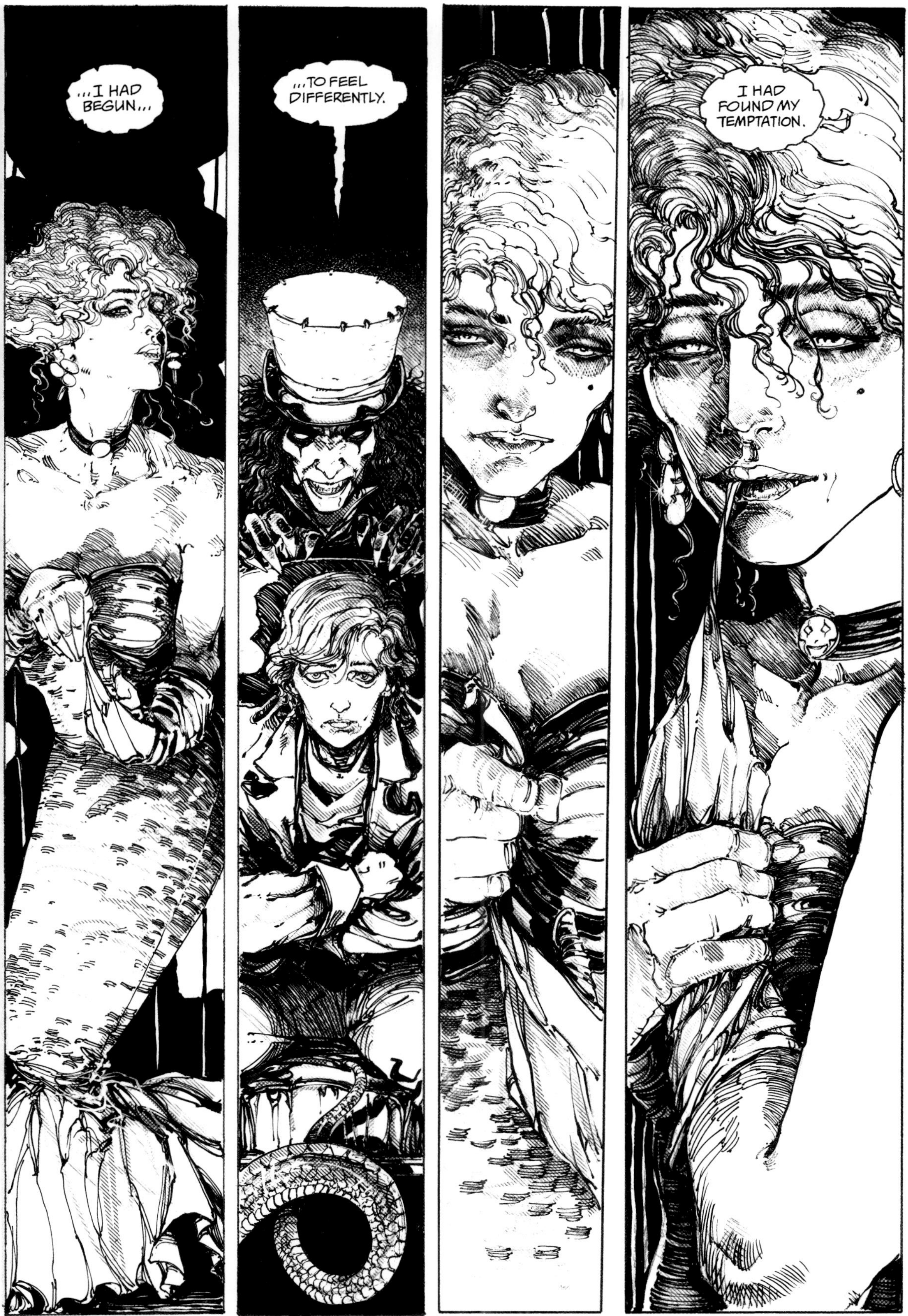
...I HAD BEGUN...
...TO FEEL DIFFERENTLY.
I HAD FOUND MY TEMPTATION.

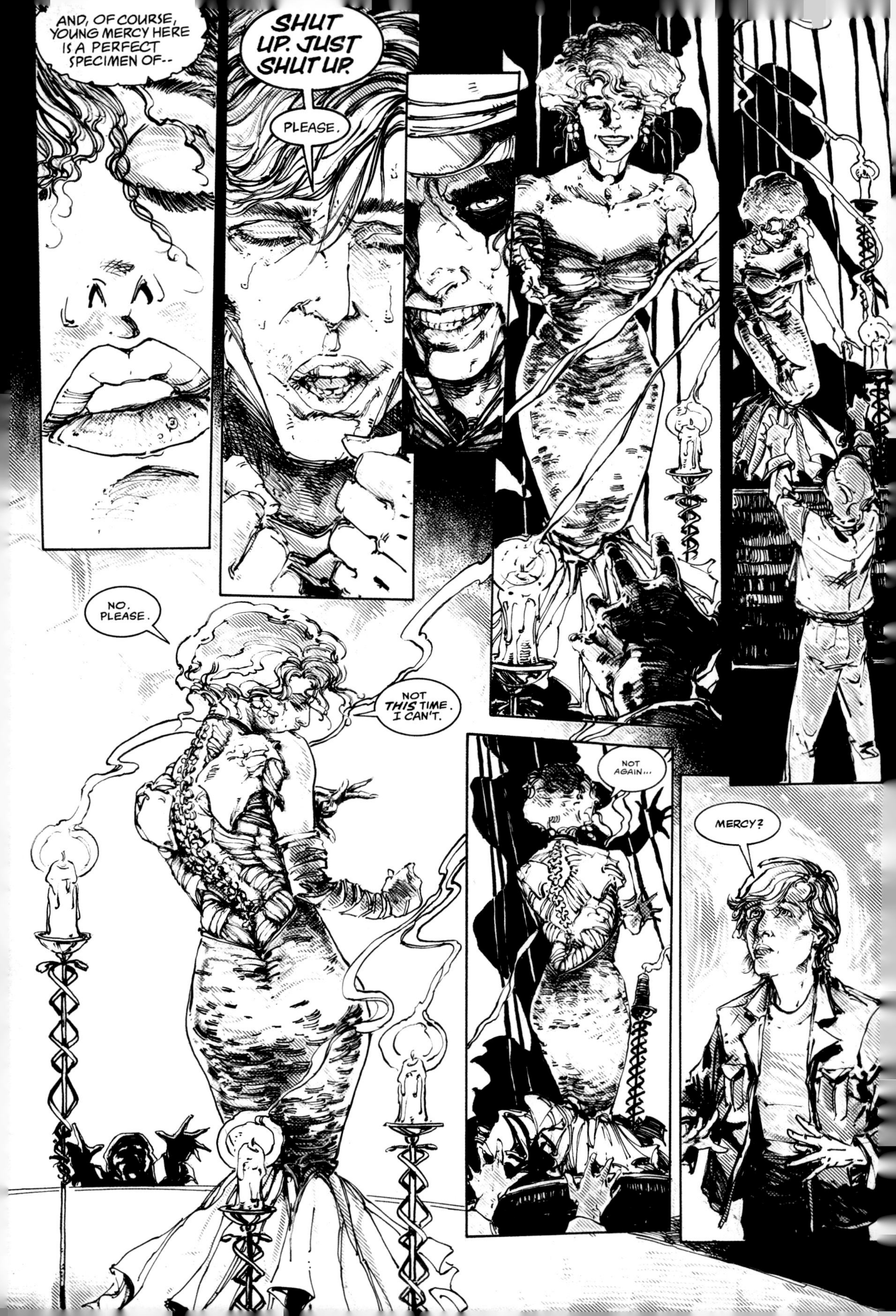
AND, OF COURSE, YOUNG MERCY HERE IS A PERFECT SPECIMEN OF--
SHUT UP. JUST SHUT UP.
PLEASE.
NO. PLEASE.
NOT THIS TIME. I CAN'T.
NOT AGAIN...
MERCY?

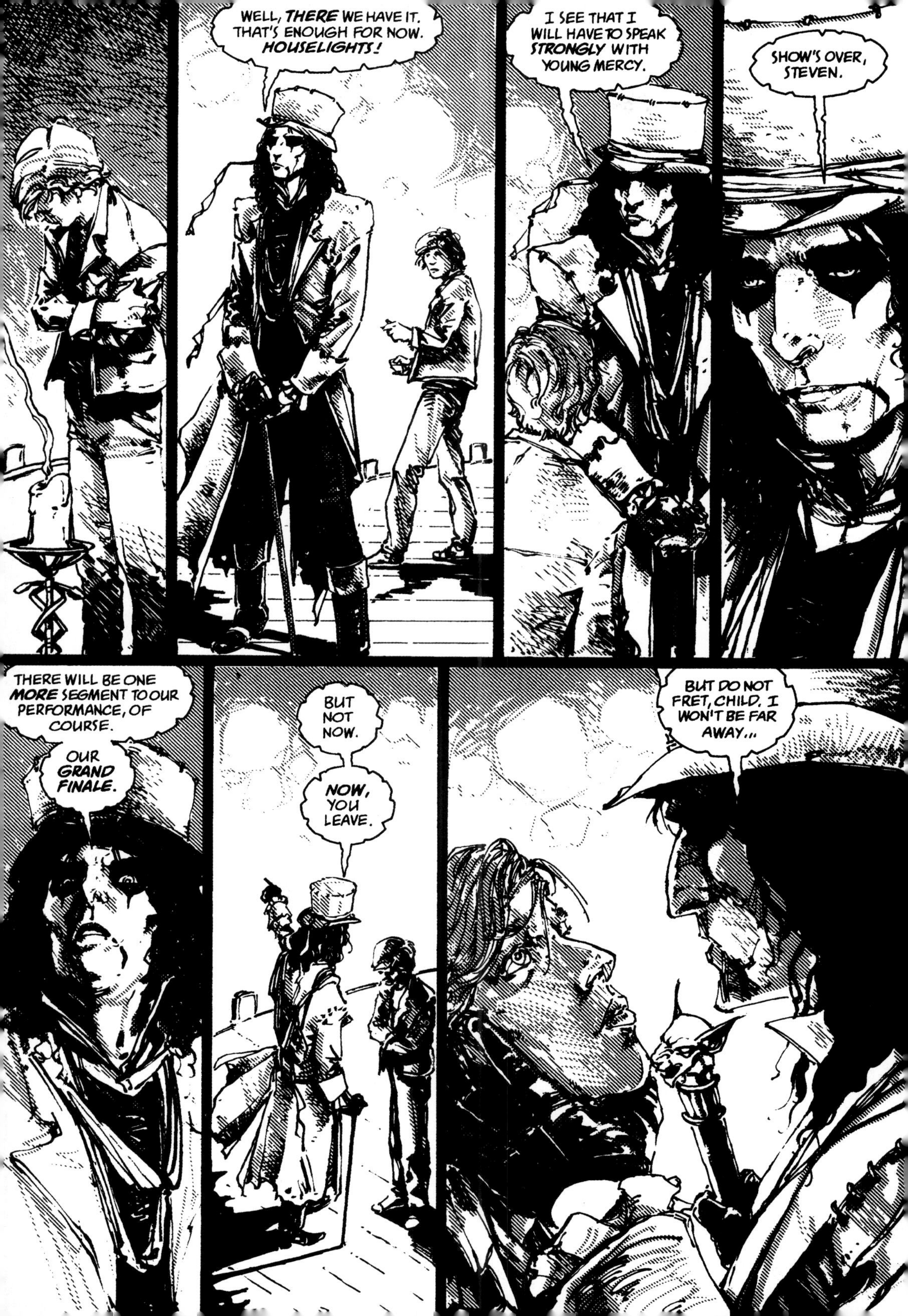
WELL, THERE WE HAVE IT. THAT'S ENOUGH FOR NOW. HOUSELIGHTS!
I SEE THAT I WILL HAVE TO SPEAK STRONGLY WITH YOUNG MERCY.
SHOW'S OVER, STEVEN.
THERE WILL BE ONE MORE SEGMENT TO OUR PERFORMANCE, OF COURSE.
OUR GRAND FINALE.
BUT NOT NOW.
NOW, YOU LEAVE.
BUT DO NOT FRET, CHILD. I WON'T BE FAR AWAY...

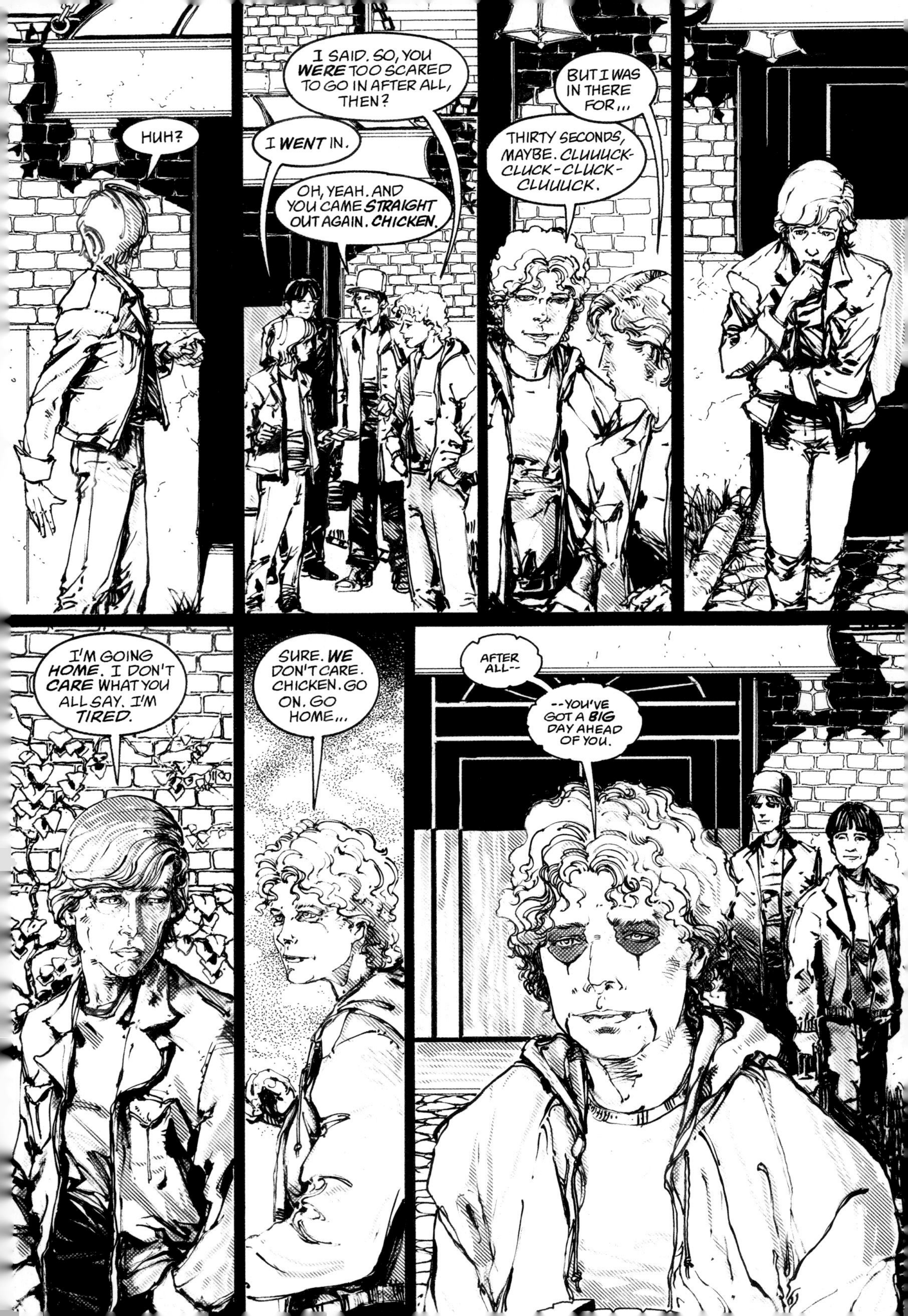
HUH?
I SAID. SO, YOU WERE TOO SCARED TO GO IN AFTER ALL, THEN?
I WENT IN.
OH, YEAH. AND YOU CAME STRAIGHT OUT AGAIN. CHICKEN.
BUT I WAS IN THERE FOR...
THIRTY SECONDS, MAYBE. CLUUUCK-CLUCK-CLUCK-CLUUUCK.
I'M GOING HOME. I DON'T CARE WHAT YOU ALL SAY. I'M TIRED.
SURE. WE DON'T CARE. CHICKEN. GO ON. GO HOME...
AFTER ALL--
--YOU'VE GOT A BIG DAY AHEAD OF YOU.

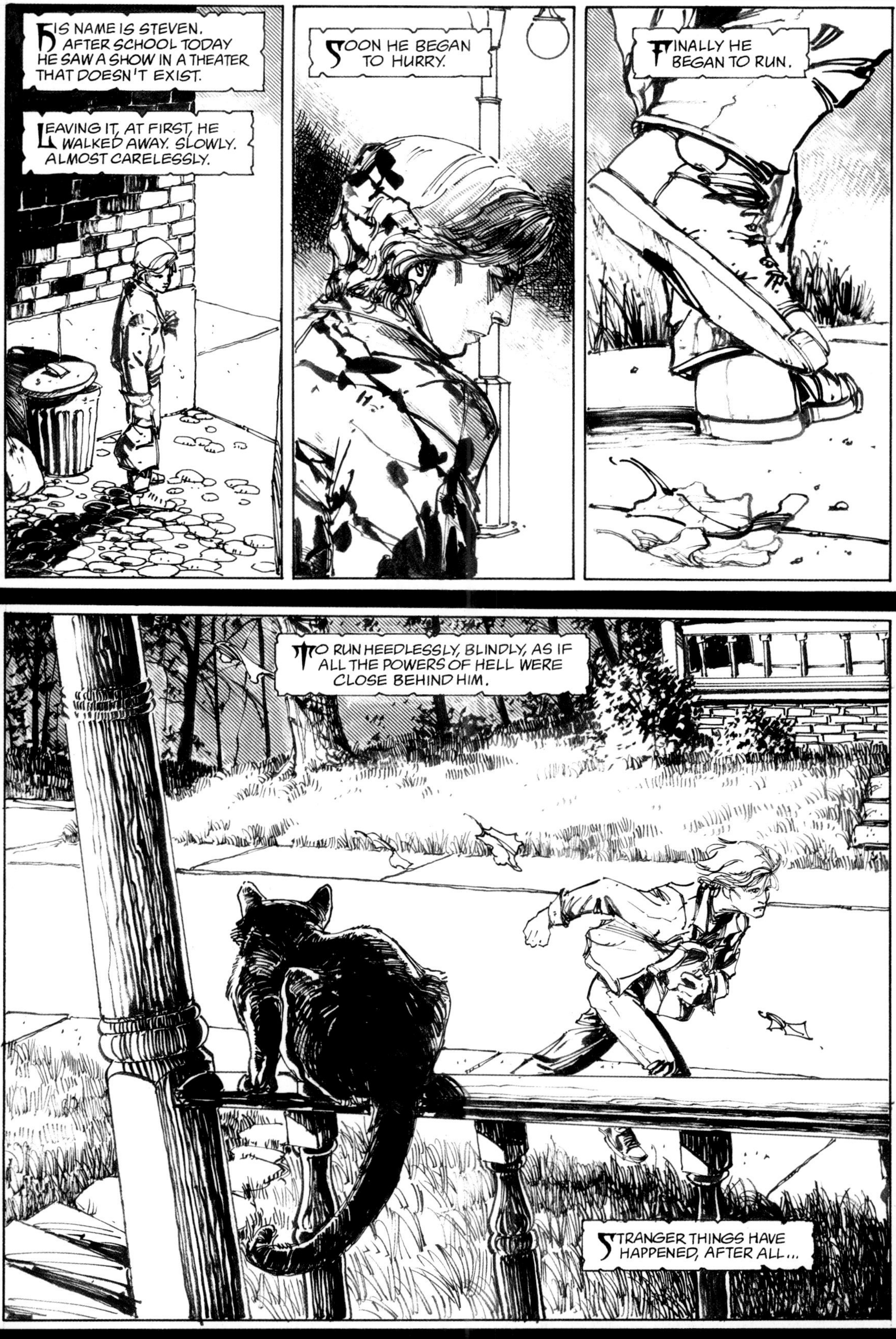
HIS NAME IS STEVEN. AFTER SCHOOL TODAY HE SAW A SHOW IN A THEATER THAT DOESN'T EXIST.
LEAVING IT, AT FIRST, HE WALKED AWAY. SLOWLY. ALMOST CARELESSLY.
SOON HE BEGAN TO HURRY.
FINALLY HE BEGAN TO RUN.
TO RUN HEEDLESSLY, BLINDLY, AS IF ALL THE POWERS OF HELL WERE CLOSE BEHIND HIM.
STRANGER THINGS HAVE HAPPENED, AFTER ALL...

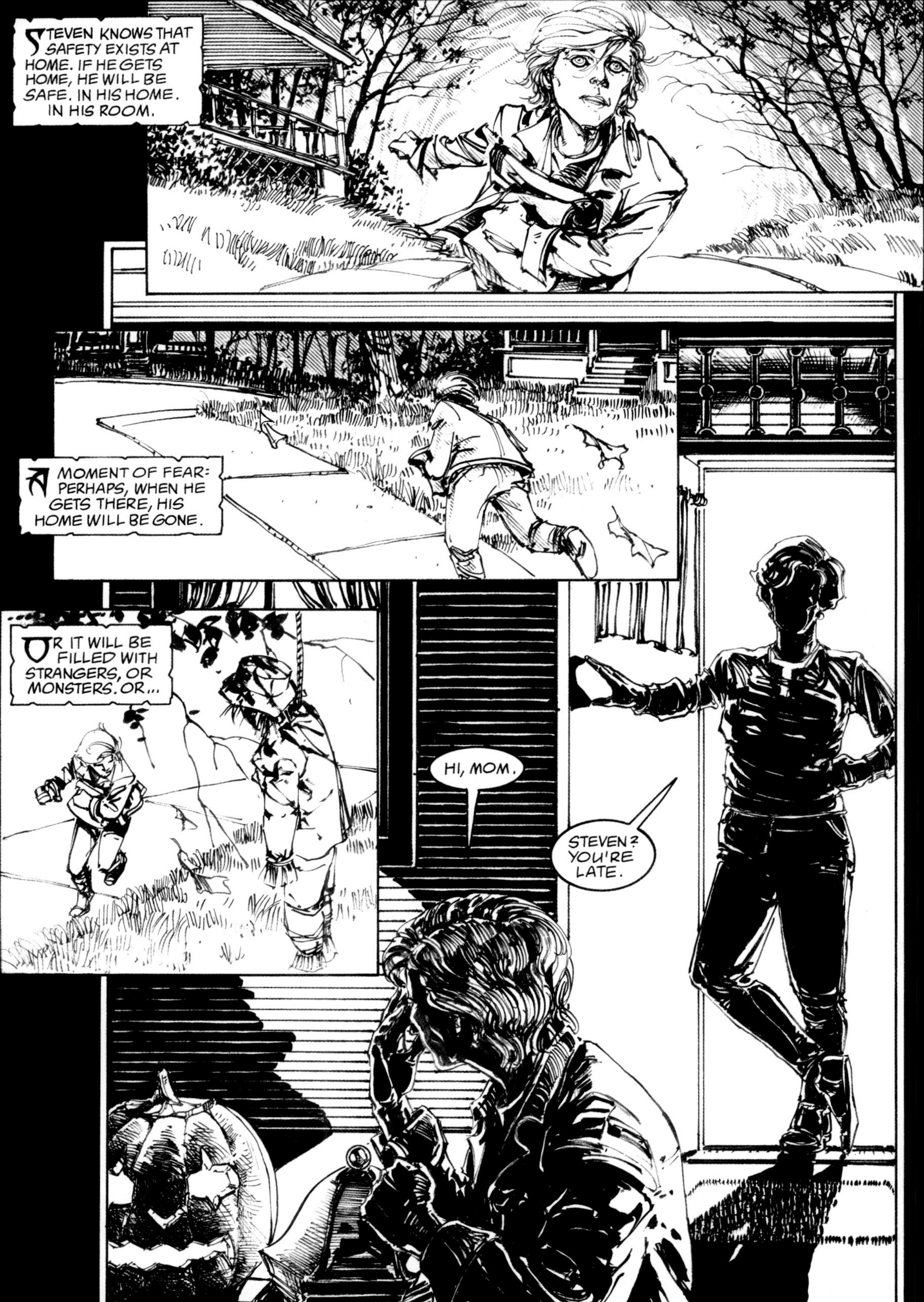
STEVEN KNOWS THAT SAFETY EXISTS AT HOME. IF HE GETS HOME, HE WILL BE SAFE. IN HIS HOME. IN HIS ROOM.
A MOMENT OF FEAR: PERHAPS, WHEN HE GETS THERE, HIS HOME WILL BE GONE.
OR IT WILL BE FILLED WITH STRANGERS, OR MONSTERS. OR...
HI, MOM.
STEVEN? YOU'RE LATE.

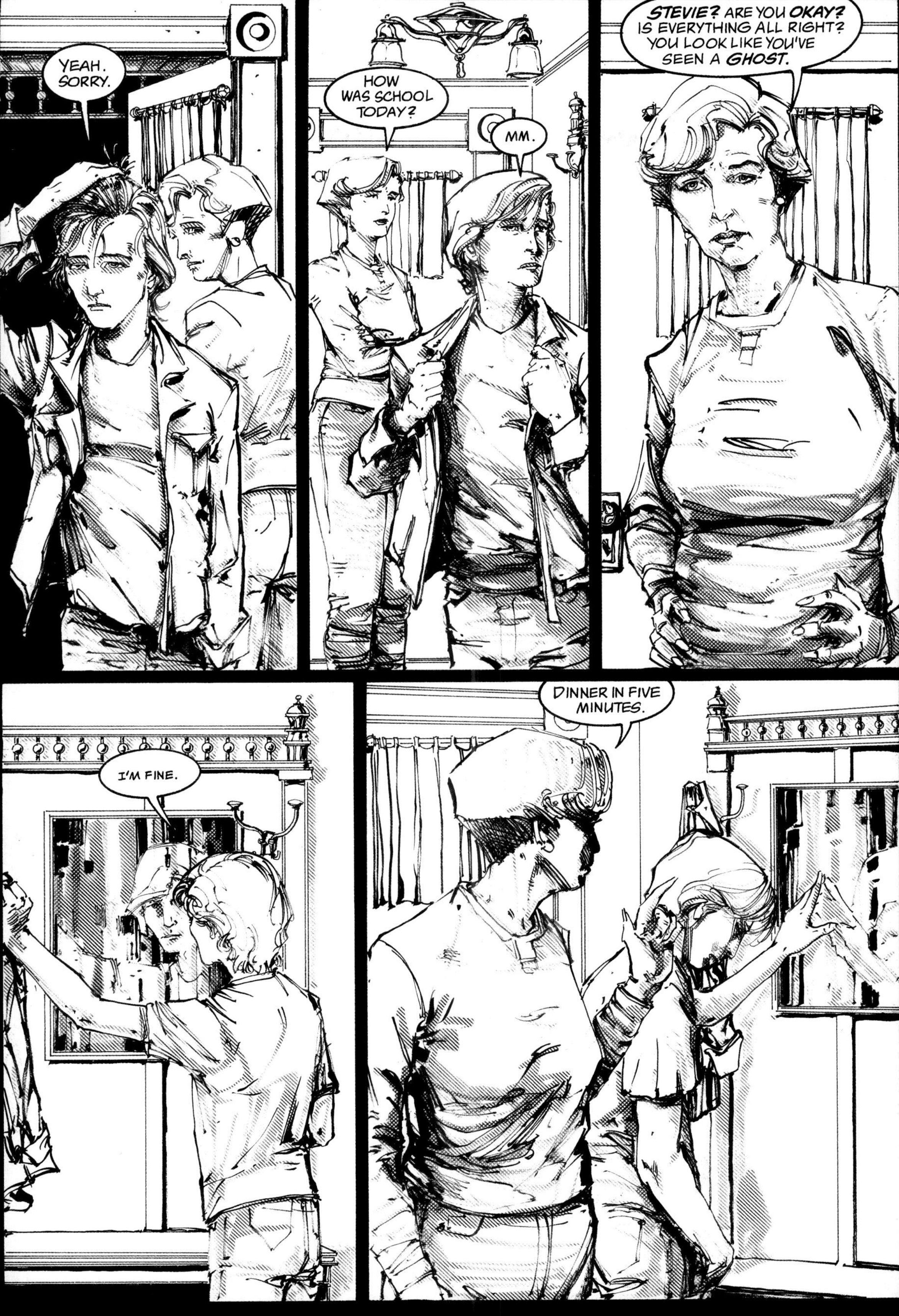
YEAH. SORRY.
HOW WAS SCHOOL TODAY?
MM.
STEVIE? ARE YOU OKAY? IS EVERYTHING ALL RIGHT? YOU LOOK LIKE YOU'VE SEEN A GHOST.
I'M FINE.
DINNER IN FIVE MINUTES.

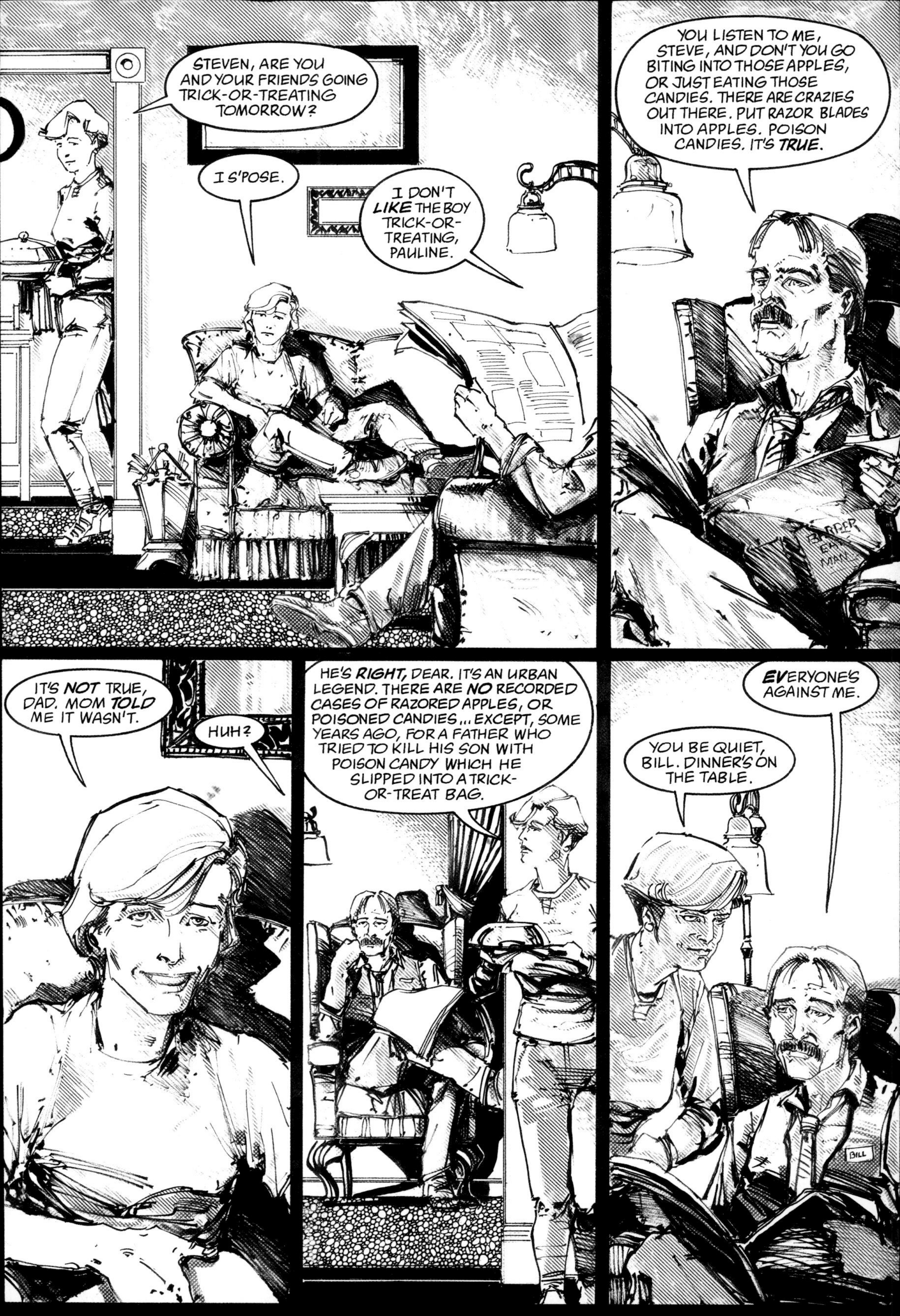
STEVEN, ARE YOU AND YOUR FRIENDS GOING TRICK-OR-TREATING TOMORROW?
I S'POSE.
I DON'T ***LIKE*** THE BOY TRICK-OR-TREATING, PAULINE.
YOU LISTEN TO ME, STEVE, AND DON'T YOU GO BITING INTO THOSE APPLES, OR JUST EATING THOSE CANDIES. THERE ARE CRAZIES OUT THERE. PUT RAZOR BLADES INTO APPLES. POISON CANDIES. IT'S ***TRUE***.
IT'S ***NOT*** TRUE, DAD. MOM ***TOLD*** ME IT WASN'T.
HUH?
HE'S ***RIGHT,*** DEAR. IT'S AN URBAN LEGEND. THERE ARE ***NO*** RECORDED CASES OF RAZORED APPLES, OR POISONED CANDIES... EXCEPT, SOME YEARS AGO, FOR A FATHER WHO TRIED TO KILL HIS SON WITH POISON CANDY WHICH HE SLIPPED INTO A TRICK-OR-TREAT BAG.
EVERYONE'S AGAINST ME.
YOU BE QUIET, BILL. DINNER'S ON THE TABLE.
BILL

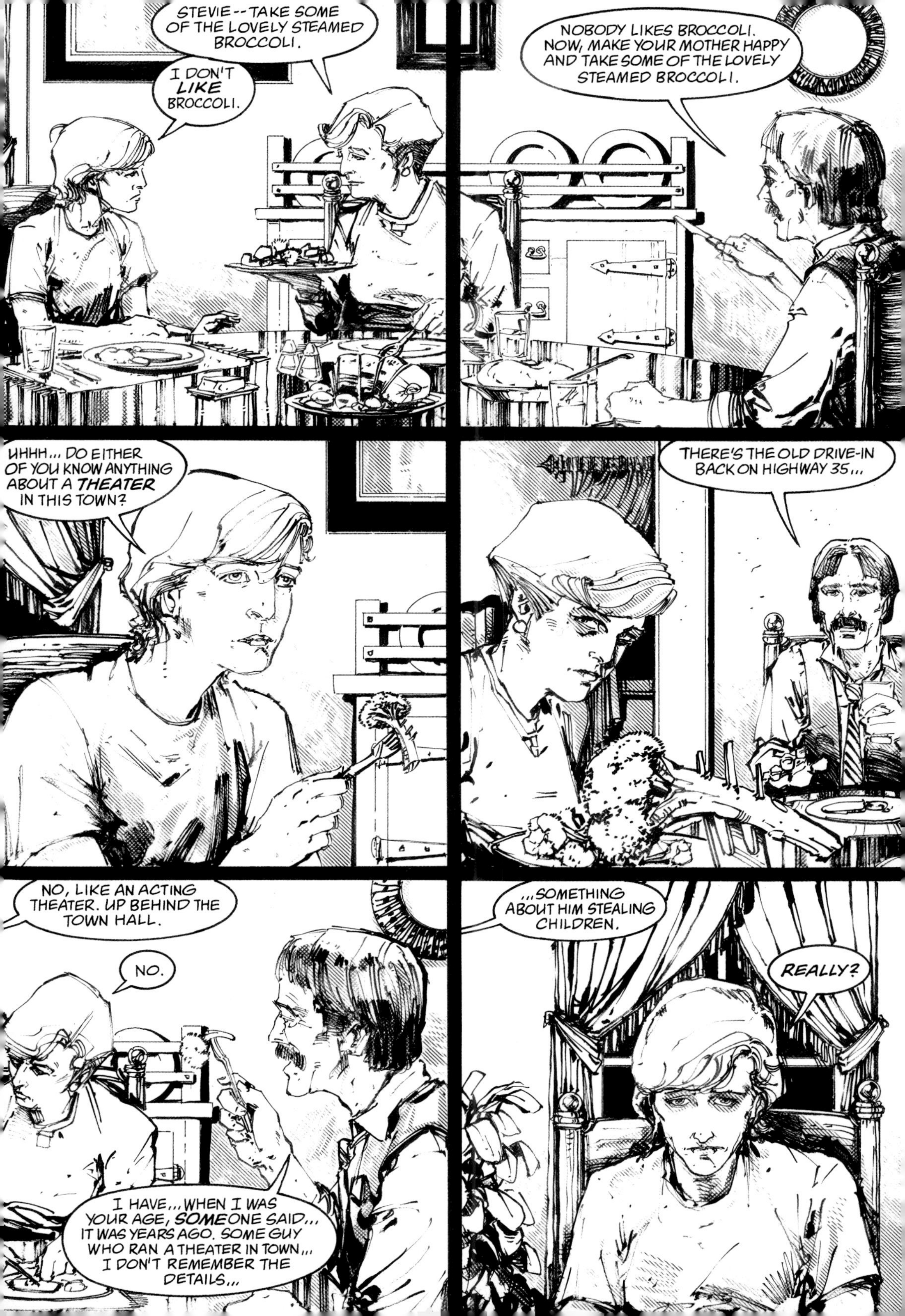
STEVIE--TAKE SOME OF THE LOVELY STEAMED BROCCOLI.
I DON'T LIKE BROCCOLI.
NOBODY LIKES BROCCOLI. NOW, MAKE YOUR MOTHER HAPPY AND TAKE SOME OF THE LOVELY STEAMED BROCCOLI.
UHHH... DO EITHER OF YOU KNOW ANYTHING ABOUT A THEATER IN THIS TOWN?
THERE'S THE OLD DRIVE-IN BACK ON HIGHWAY 35...
NO, LIKE AN ACTING THEATER. UP BEHIND THE TOWN HALL.
NO.
I HAVE... WHEN I WAS YOUR AGE, SOMEONE SAID... IT WAS YEARS AGO. SOME GUY WHO RAN A THEATER IN TOWN... I DON'T REMEMBER THE DETAILS...
...SOMETHING ABOUT HIM STEALING CHILDREN.
REALLY?

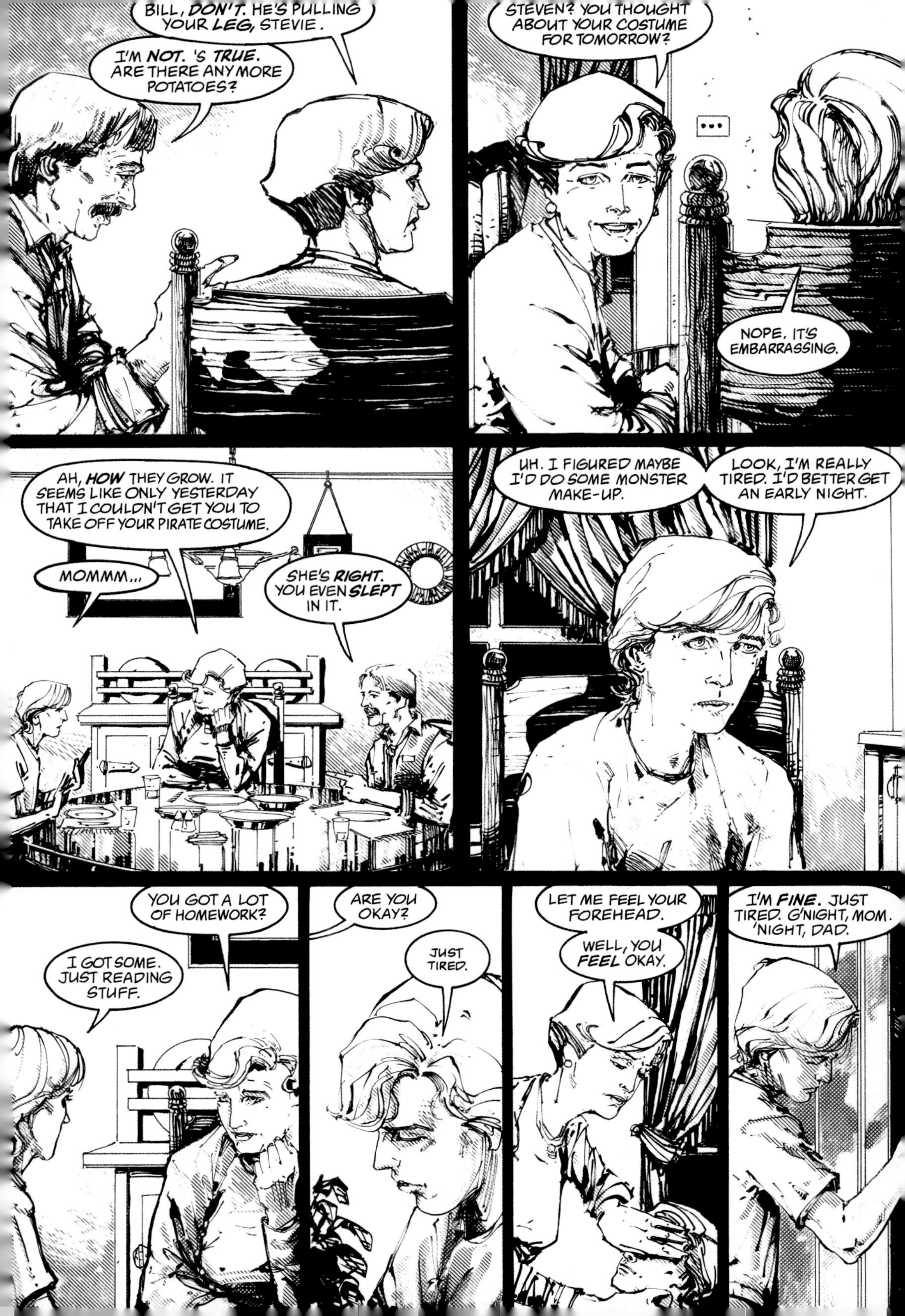
BILL, DON'T. HE'S PULLING YOUR LEG, STEVIE.
I'M NOT. 'S TRUE. ARE THERE ANY MORE POTATOES?
STEVEN? YOU THOUGHT ABOUT YOUR COSTUME FOR TOMORROW?
...
NOPE. IT'S EMBARRASSING.
AH, HOW THEY GROW. IT SEEMS LIKE ONLY YESTERDAY THAT I COULDN'T GET YOU TO TAKE OFF YOUR PIRATE COSTUME.
MOMMM...
SHE'S RIGHT. YOU EVEN SLEPT IN IT.
UH. I FIGURED MAYBE I'D DO SOME MONSTER MAKE-UP.
LOOK, I'M REALLY TIRED. I'D BETTER GET AN EARLY NIGHT.
YOU GOT A LOT OF HOMEWORK?
I GOT SOME. JUST READING STUFF.
ARE YOU OKAY?
JUST TIRED.
LET ME FEEL YOUR FOREHEAD.
WELL, YOU FEEL OKAY.
I'M FINE. JUST TIRED. G'NIGHT, MOM. 'NIGHT, DAD.

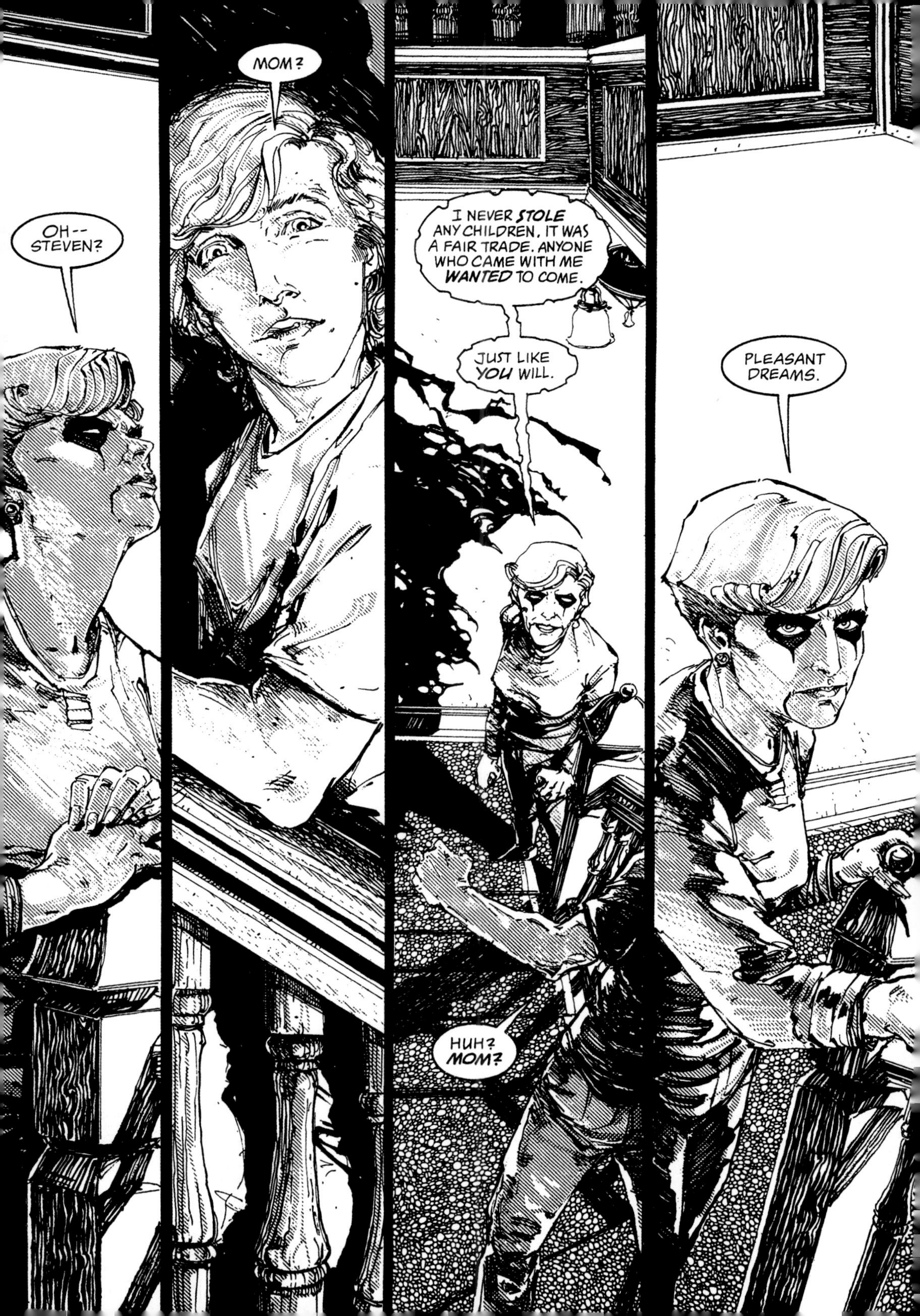
OH-- STEVEN?
MOM?
I NEVER STOLE ANY CHILDREN. IT WAS A FAIR TRADE. ANYONE WHO CAME WITH ME WANTED TO COME.
JUST LIKE YOU WILL.
HUH? MOM?
PLEASANT DREAMS.

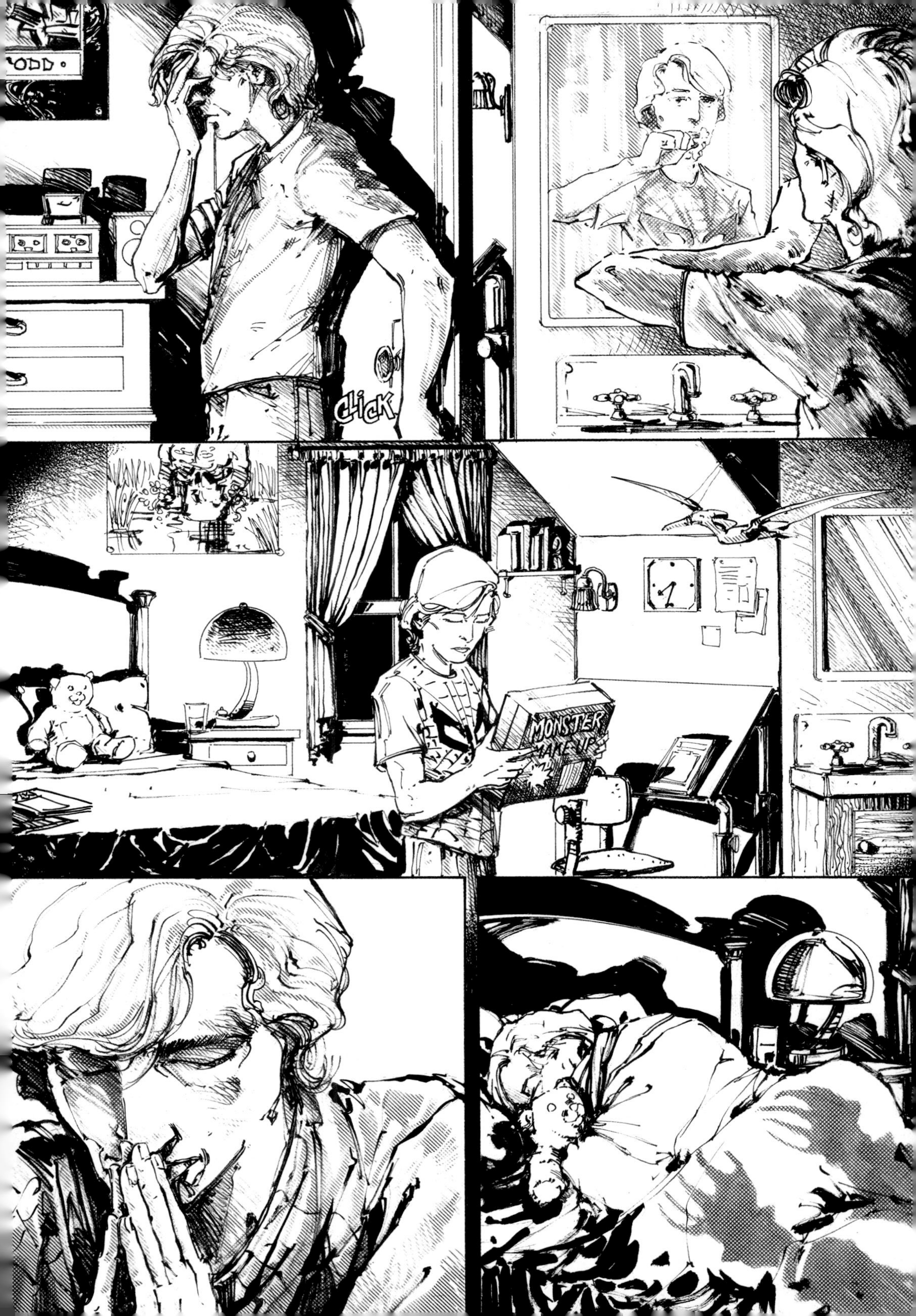
CLICK
MONSTER MAKE-UP

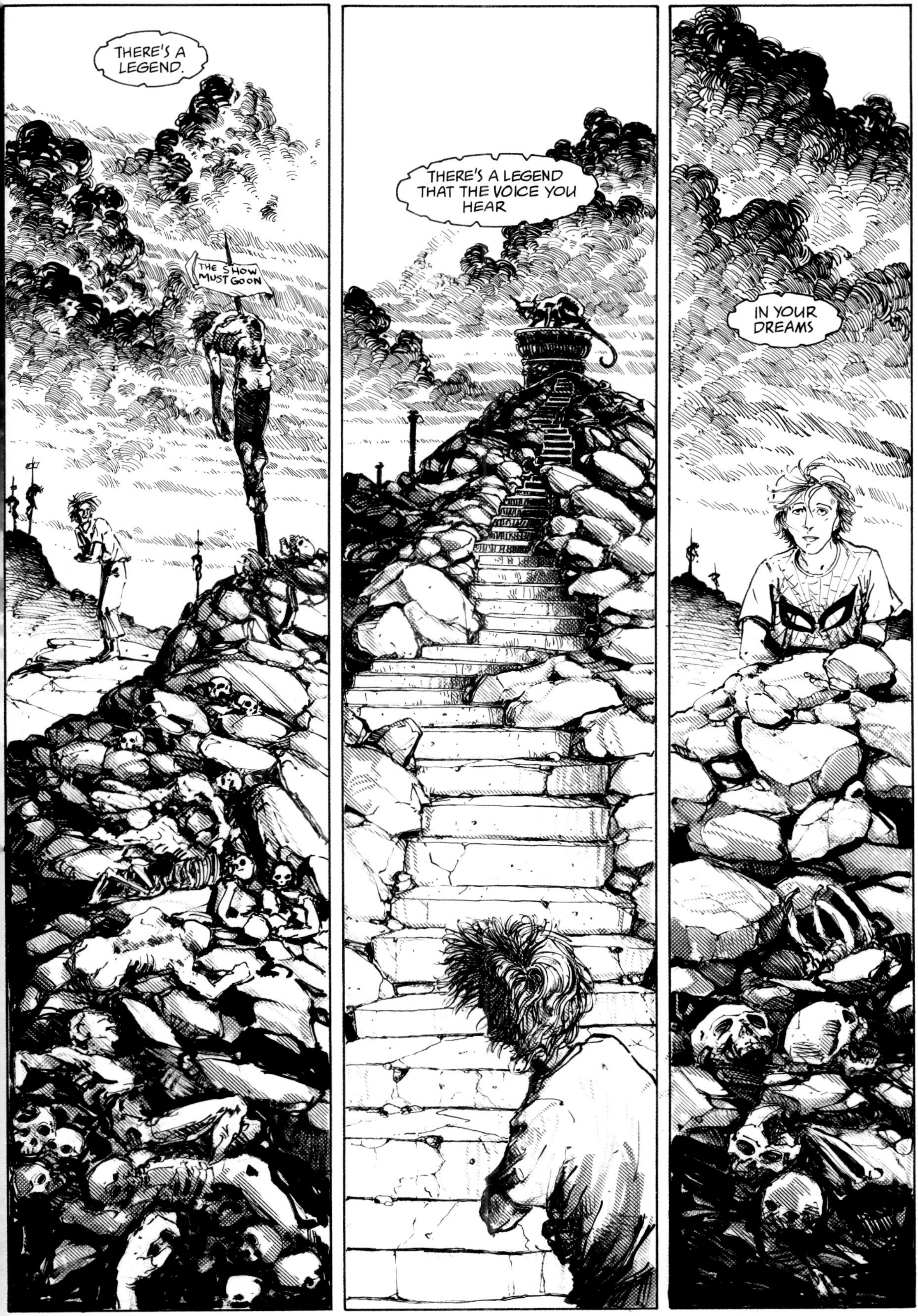
THERE'S A LEGEND.
THE SHOW MUST GO ON
THERE'S A LEGEND THAT THE VOICE YOU HEAR
IN YOUR DREAMS

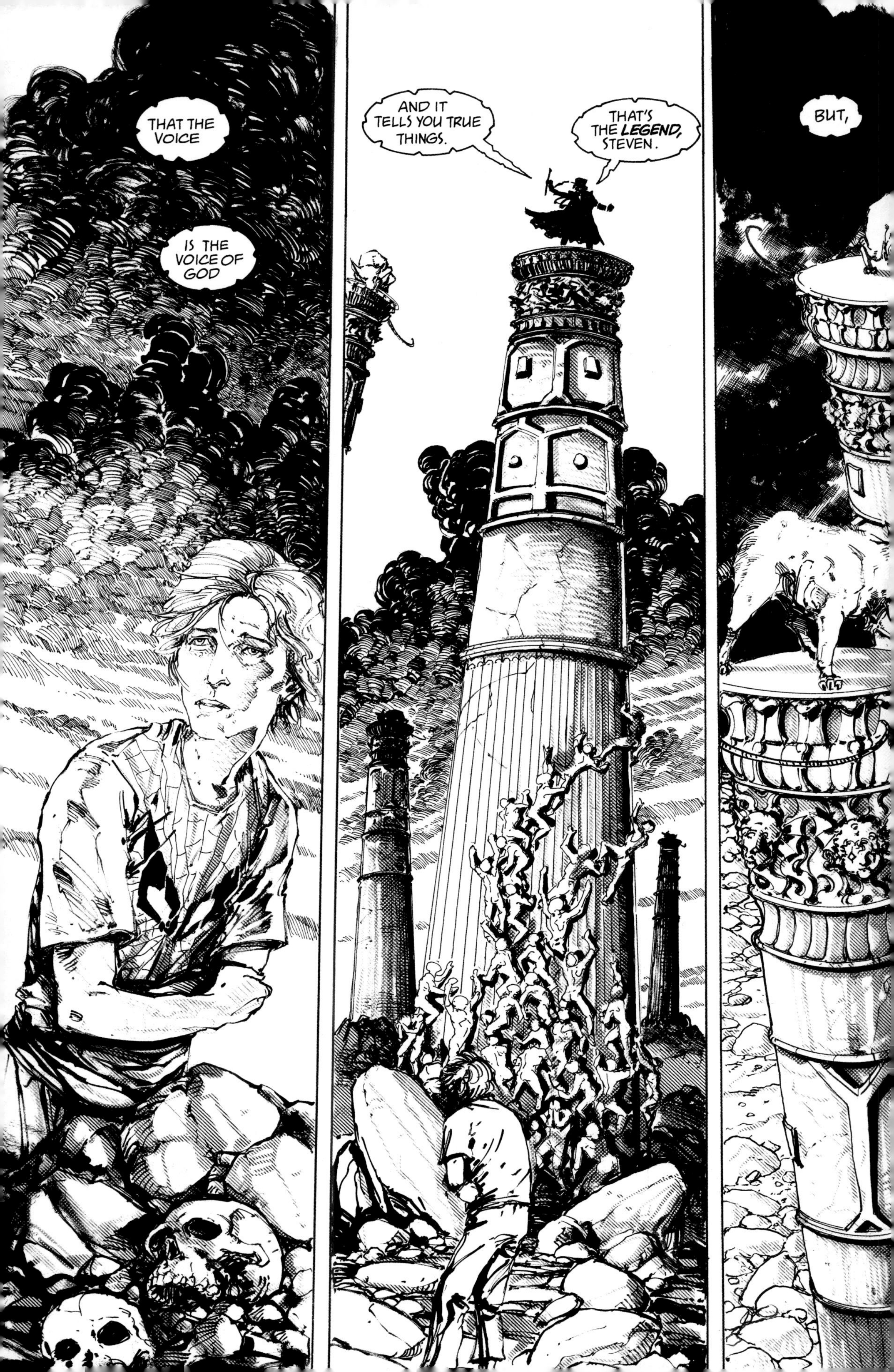
THAT THE VOICE
IS THE VOICE OF GOD
AND IT TELLS YOU TRUE THINGS.
THAT'S THE ***LEGEND,*** STEVEN.
BUT,

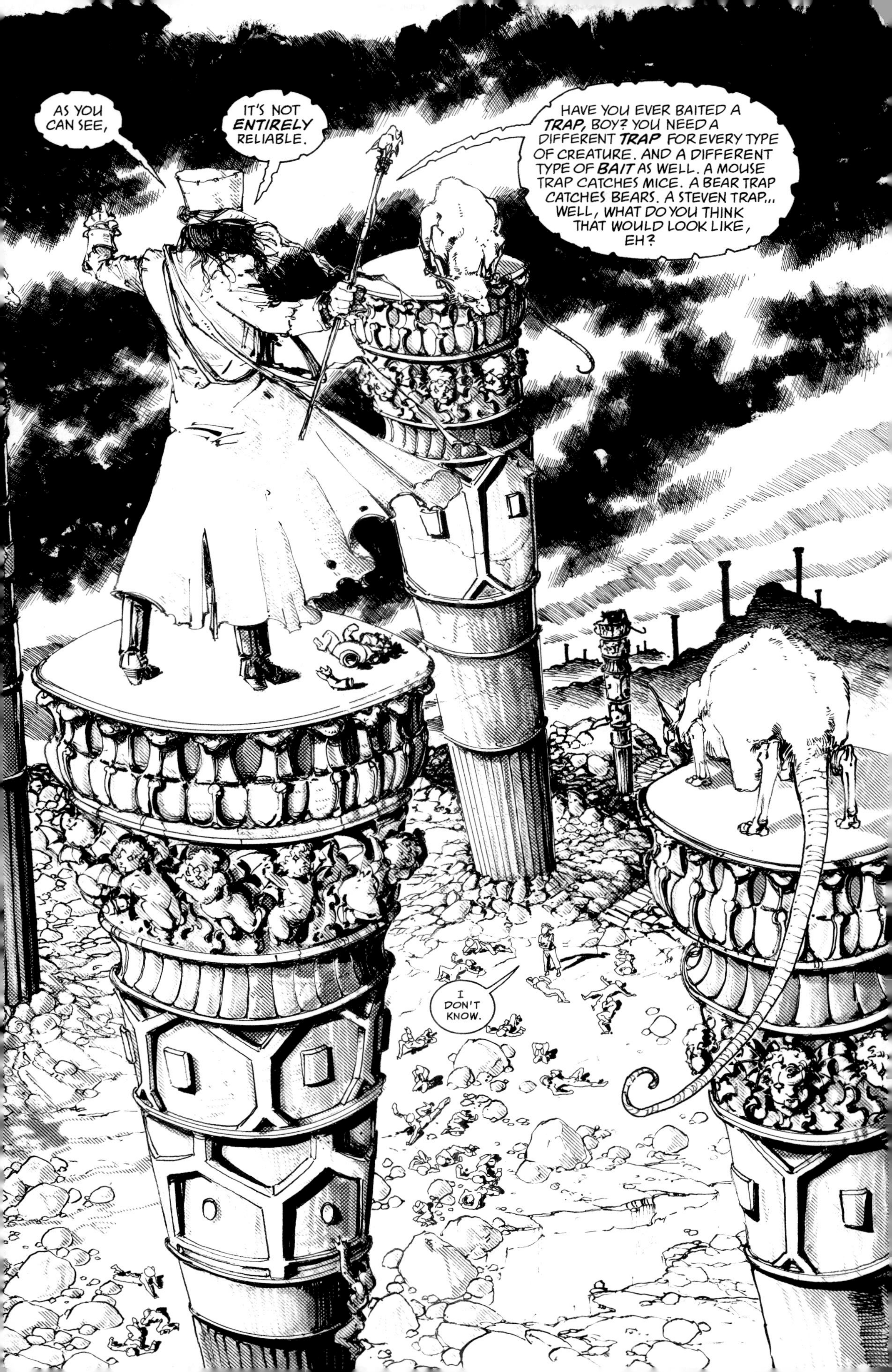
AS YOU CAN SEE,
IT'S NOT ENTIRELY RELIABLE.
HAVE YOU EVER BAITED A TRAP, BOY? YOU NEED A DIFFERENT TRAP FOR EVERY TYPE OF CREATURE. AND A DIFFERENT TYPE OF BAIT AS WELL. A MOUSE TRAP CATCHES MICE. A BEAR TRAP CATCHES BEARS. A STEVEN TRAP... WELL, WHAT DO YOU THINK THAT WOULD LOOK LIKE, EH?
I DON'T KNOW.

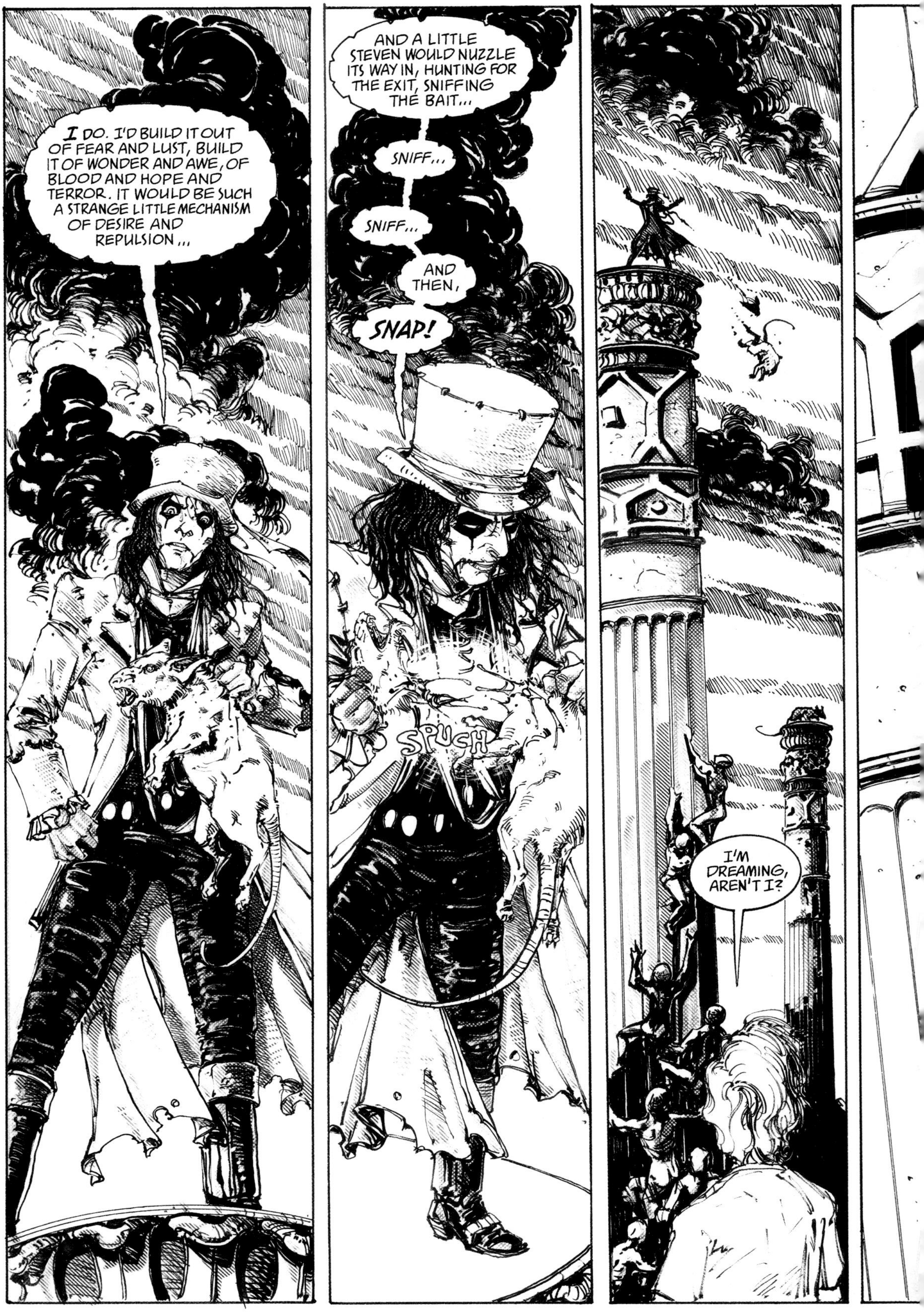
I DO. I'D BUILD IT OUT OF FEAR AND LUST, BUILD IT OF WONDER AND AWE, OF BLOOD AND HOPE AND TERROR. IT WOULD BE SUCH A STRANGE LITTLE MECHANISM OF DESIRE AND REPULSION...
AND A LITTLE STEVEN WOULD NUZZLE ITS WAY IN, HUNTING FOR THE EXIT, SNIFFING THE BAIT...
SNIFF...
SNIFF...
AND THEN,
SNAP!
SPUCH
I'M DREAMING, AREN'T I?

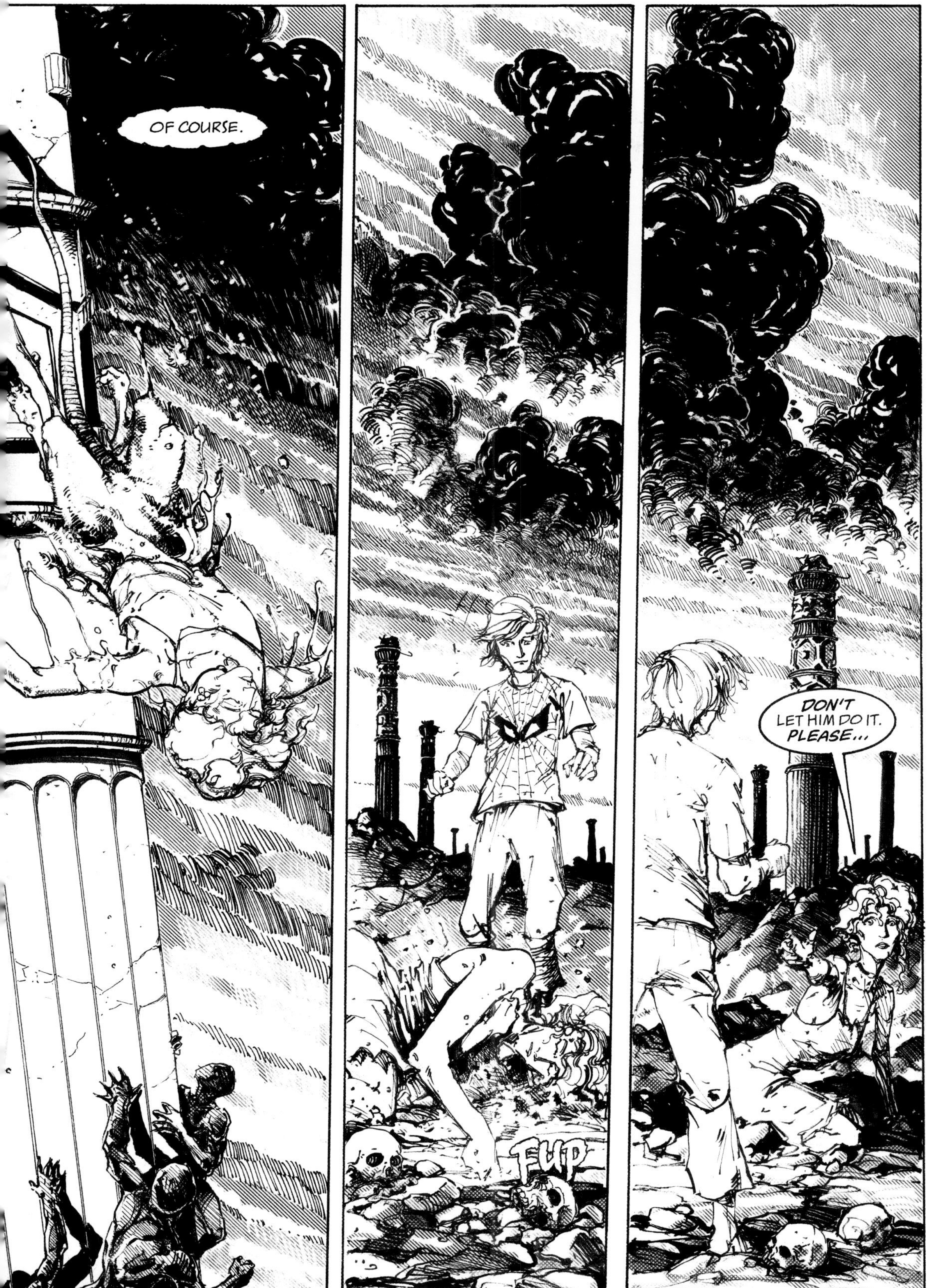
OF COURSE.
FUP
DON'T LET HIM DO IT. PLEASE...

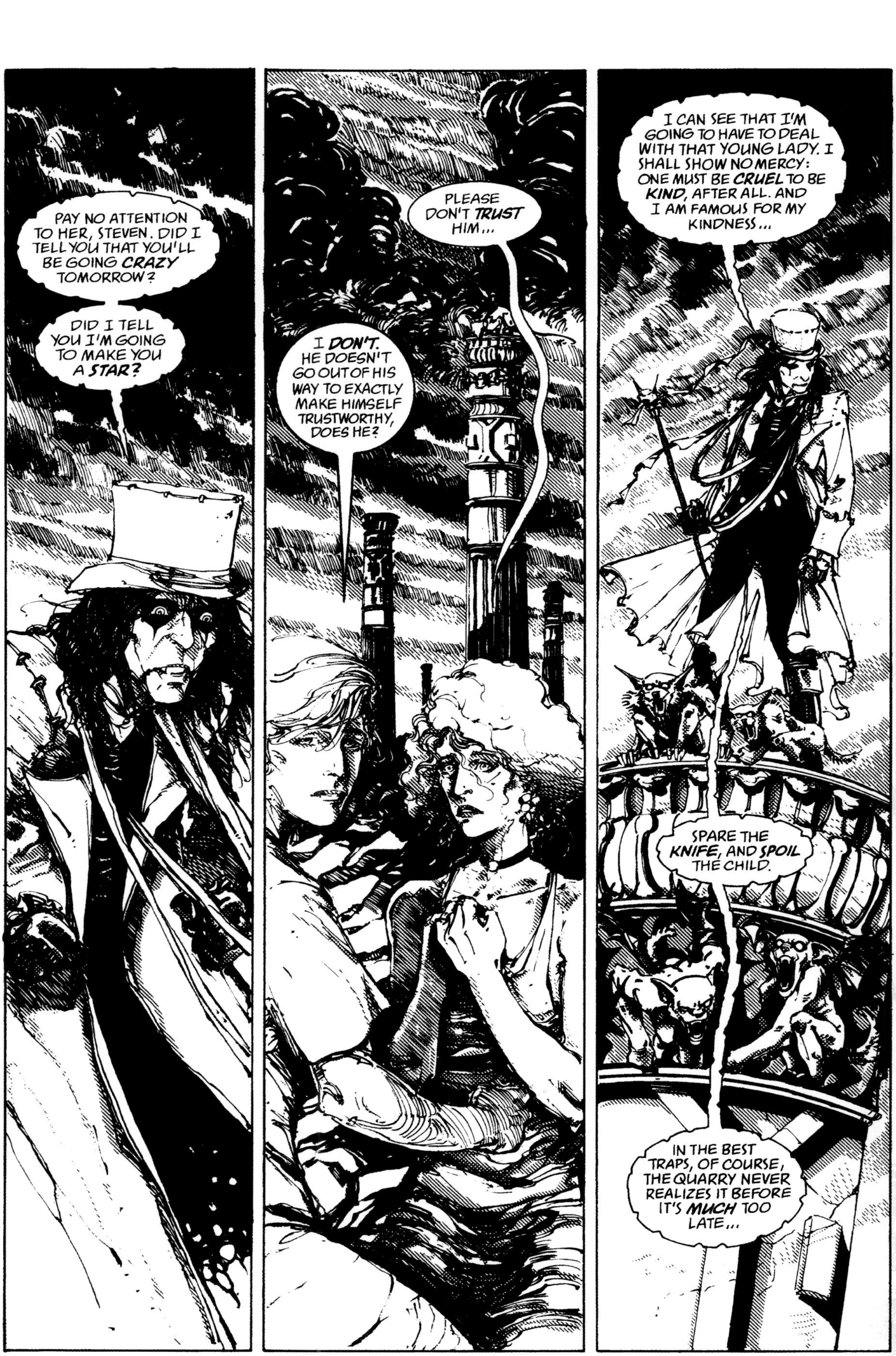
PAY NO ATTENTION TO HER, STEVEN. DID I TELL YOU THAT YOU'LL BE GOING CRAZY TOMORROW?
DID I TELL YOU I'M GOING TO MAKE YOU A STAR?
PLEASE DON'T TRUST HIM...
I DON'T. HE DOESN'T GO OUT OF HIS WAY TO EXACTLY MAKE HIMSELF TRUSTWORTHY, DOES HE?
I CAN SEE THAT I'M GOING TO HAVE TO DEAL WITH THAT YOUNG LADY. I SHALL SHOW NO MERCY: ONE MUST BE CRUEL TO BE KIND, AFTER ALL. AND I AM FAMOUS FOR MY KINDNESS...
SPARE THE KNIFE, AND SPOIL THE CHILD.
IN THE BEST TRAPS, OF COURSE, THE QUARRY NEVER REALIZES IT BEFORE IT'S MUCH TOO LATE...

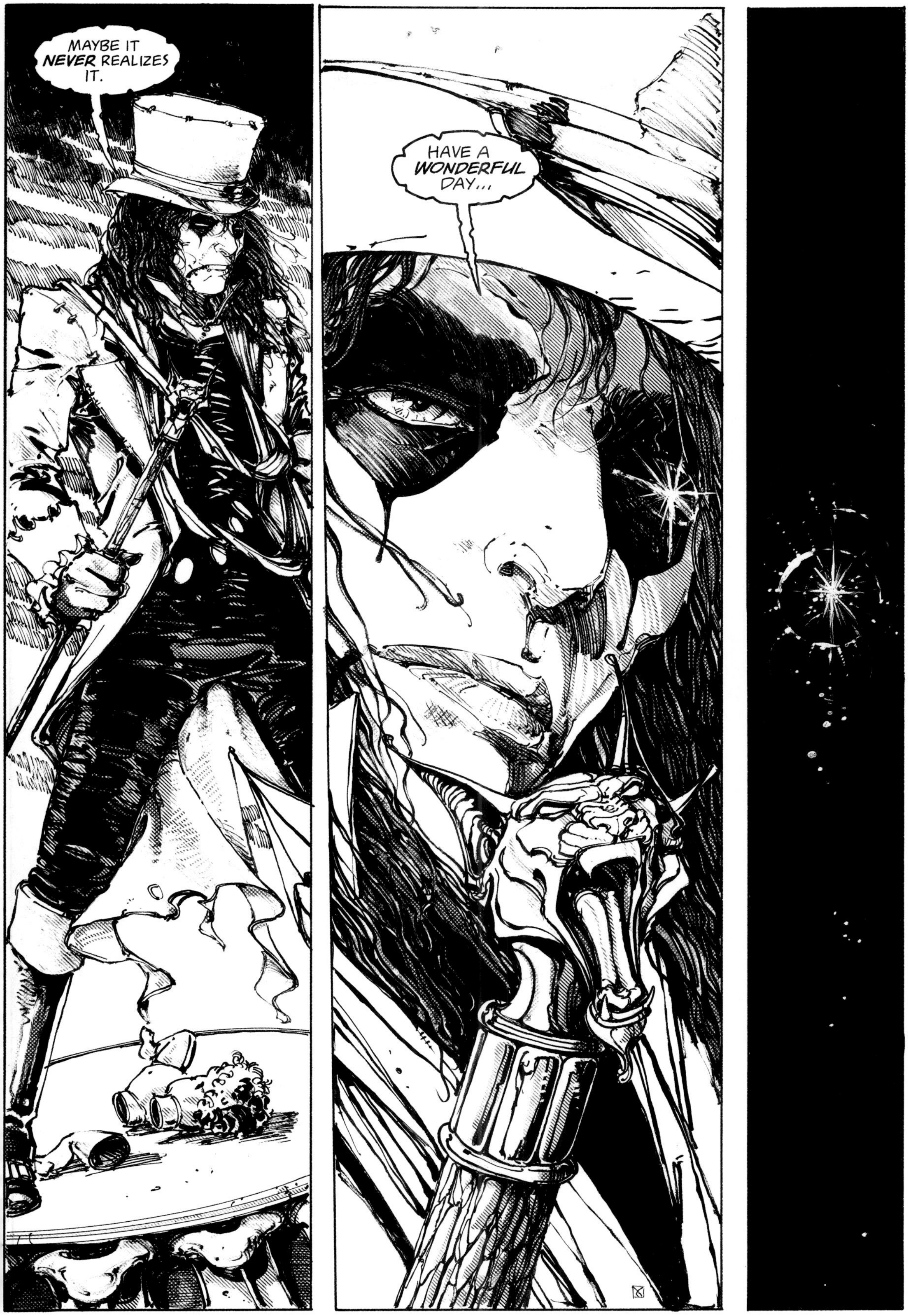
MAYBE IT NEVER REALIZES IT.
HAVE A WONDERFUL DAY...

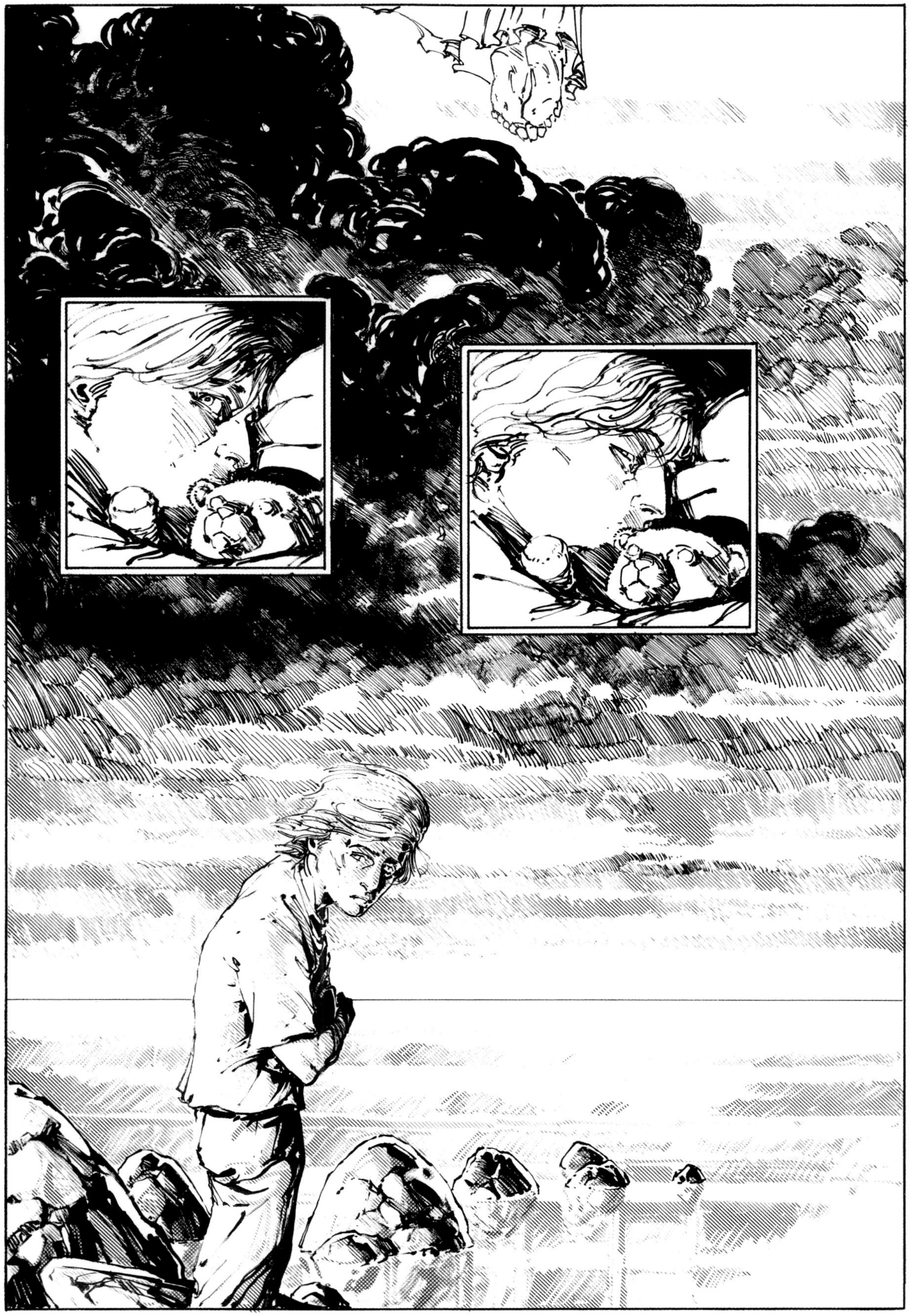

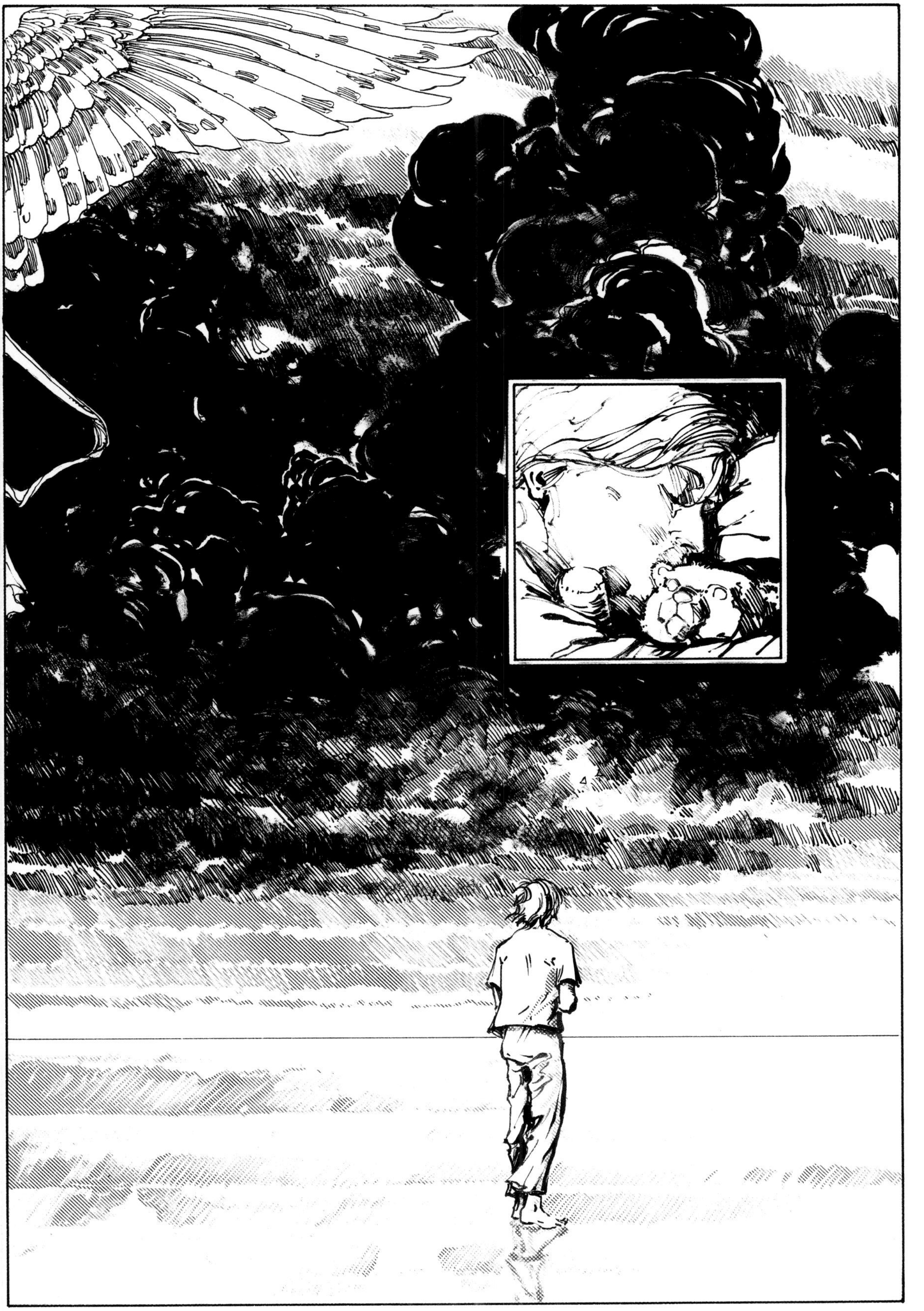

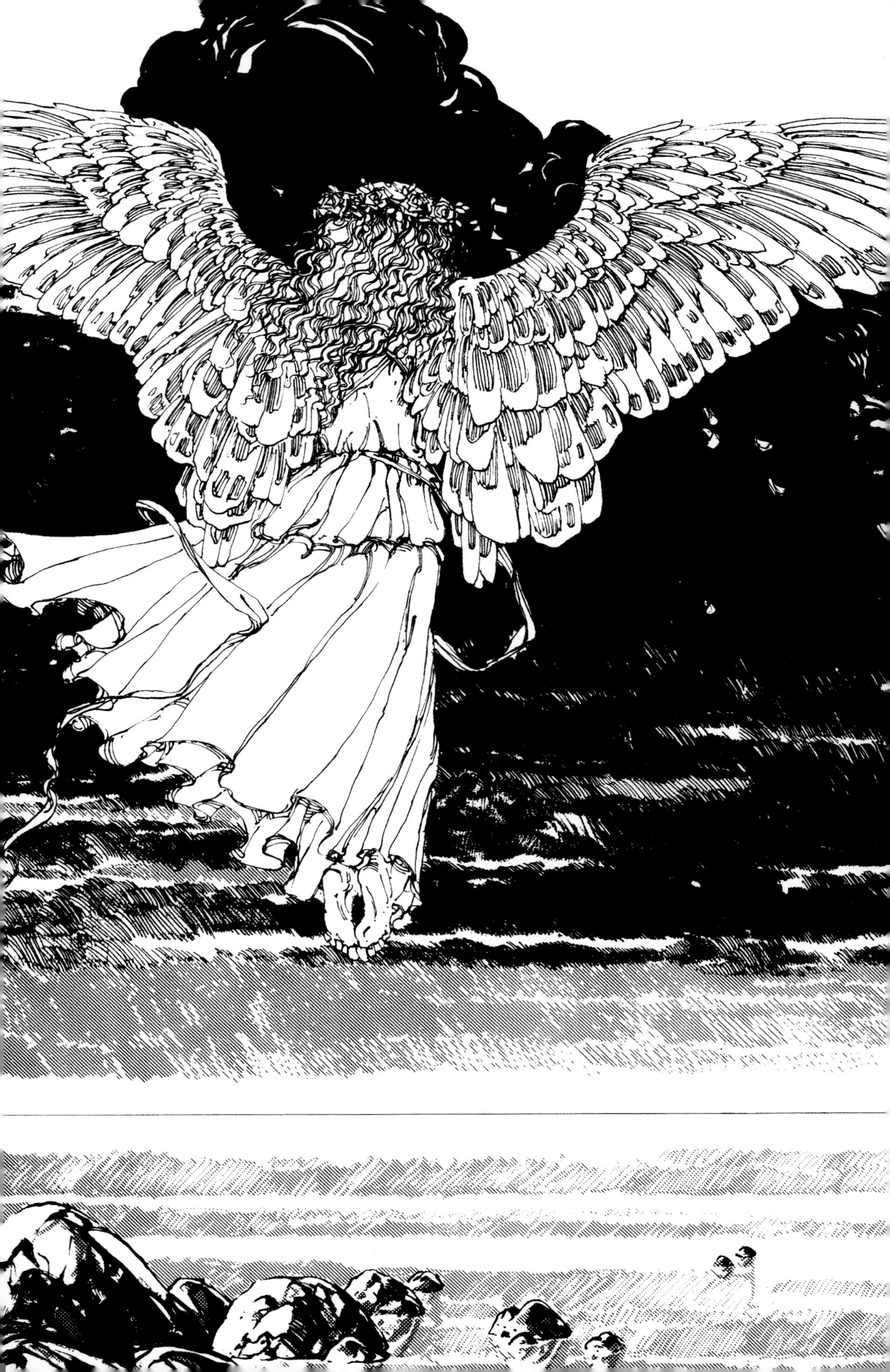

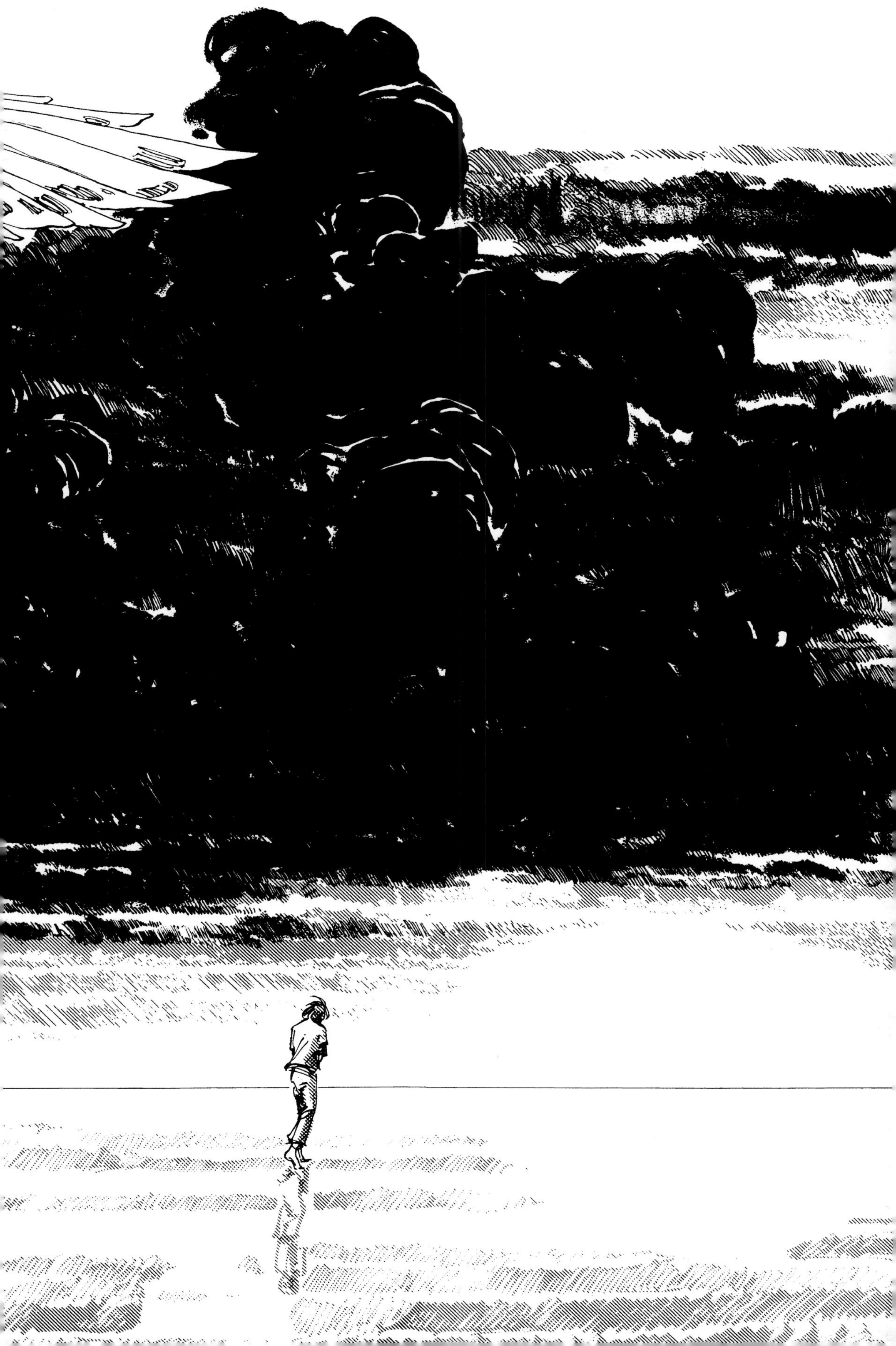

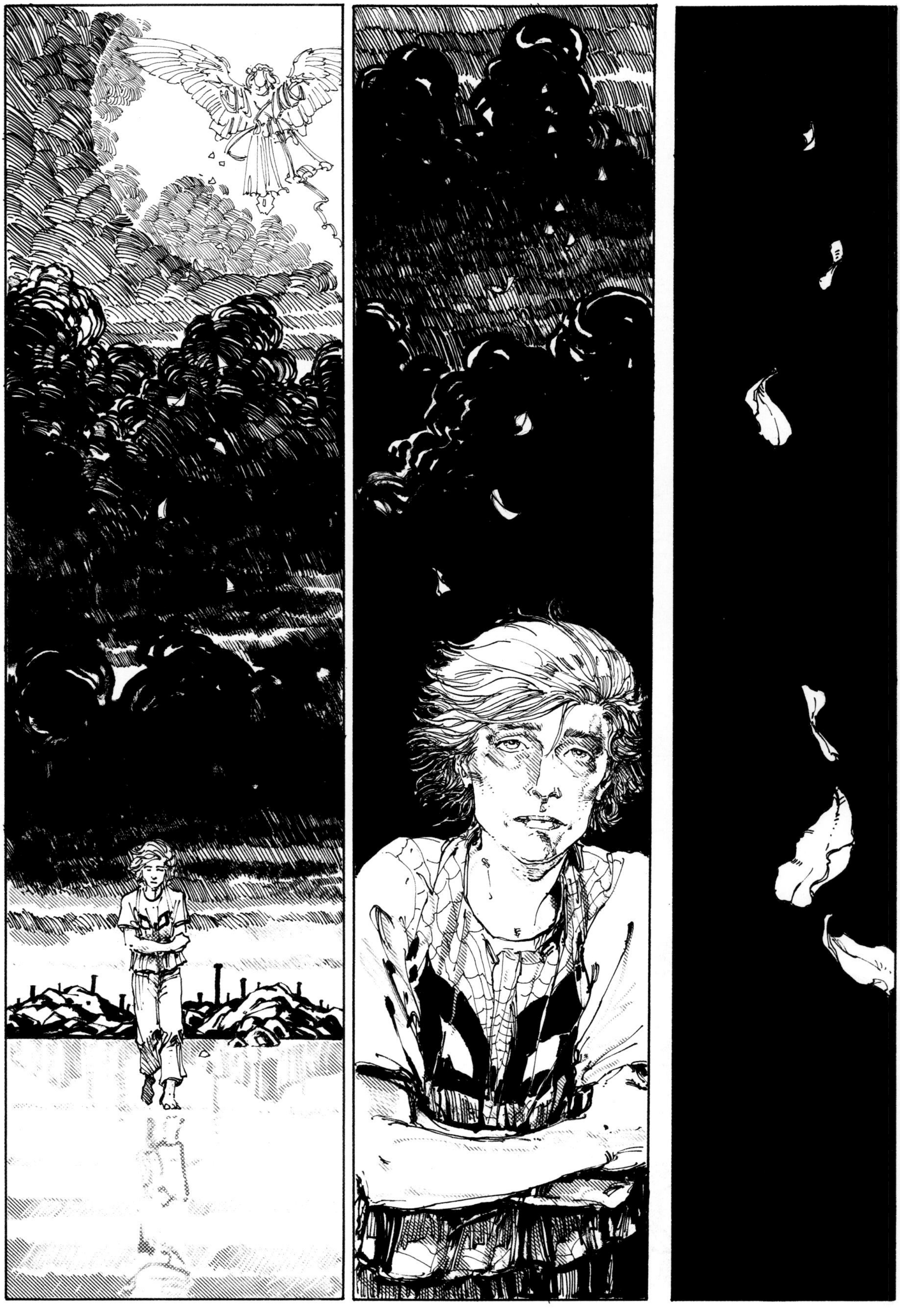

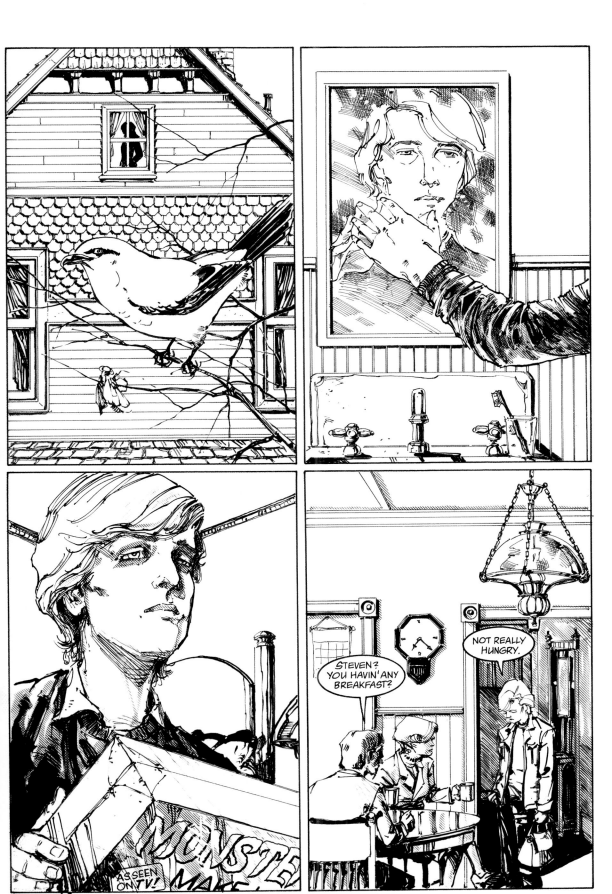

STEVEN? YOU HAVIN' ANY BREAKFAST?

NOT REALLY HUNGRY.

MONSTER MAKE

AS SEEN ON TV!

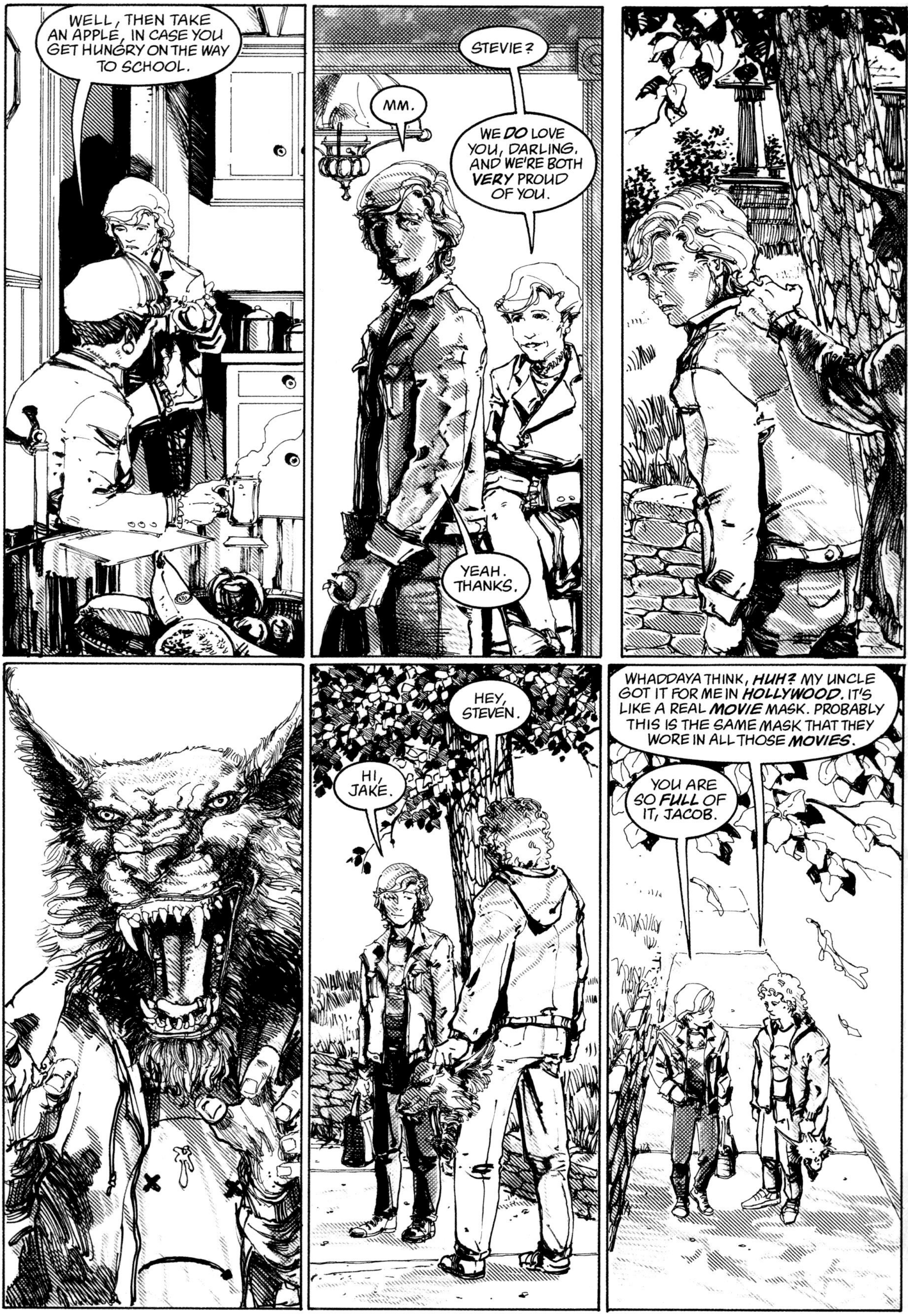
WELL, THEN TAKE AN APPLE, IN CASE YOU GET HUNGRY ON THE WAY TO SCHOOL.
STEVIE?
MM.
WE DO LOVE YOU, DARLING, AND WE'RE BOTH VERY PROUD OF YOU.
YEAH. THANKS.
HEY, STEVEN.
HI, JAKE.
WHADDAYA THINK, HUH? MY UNCLE GOT IT FOR ME IN HOLLYWOOD. IT'S LIKE A REAL MOVIE MASK. PROBABLY THIS IS THE SAME MASK THAT THEY WORE IN ALL THOSE MOVIES.
YOU ARE SO FULL OF IT, JACOB.

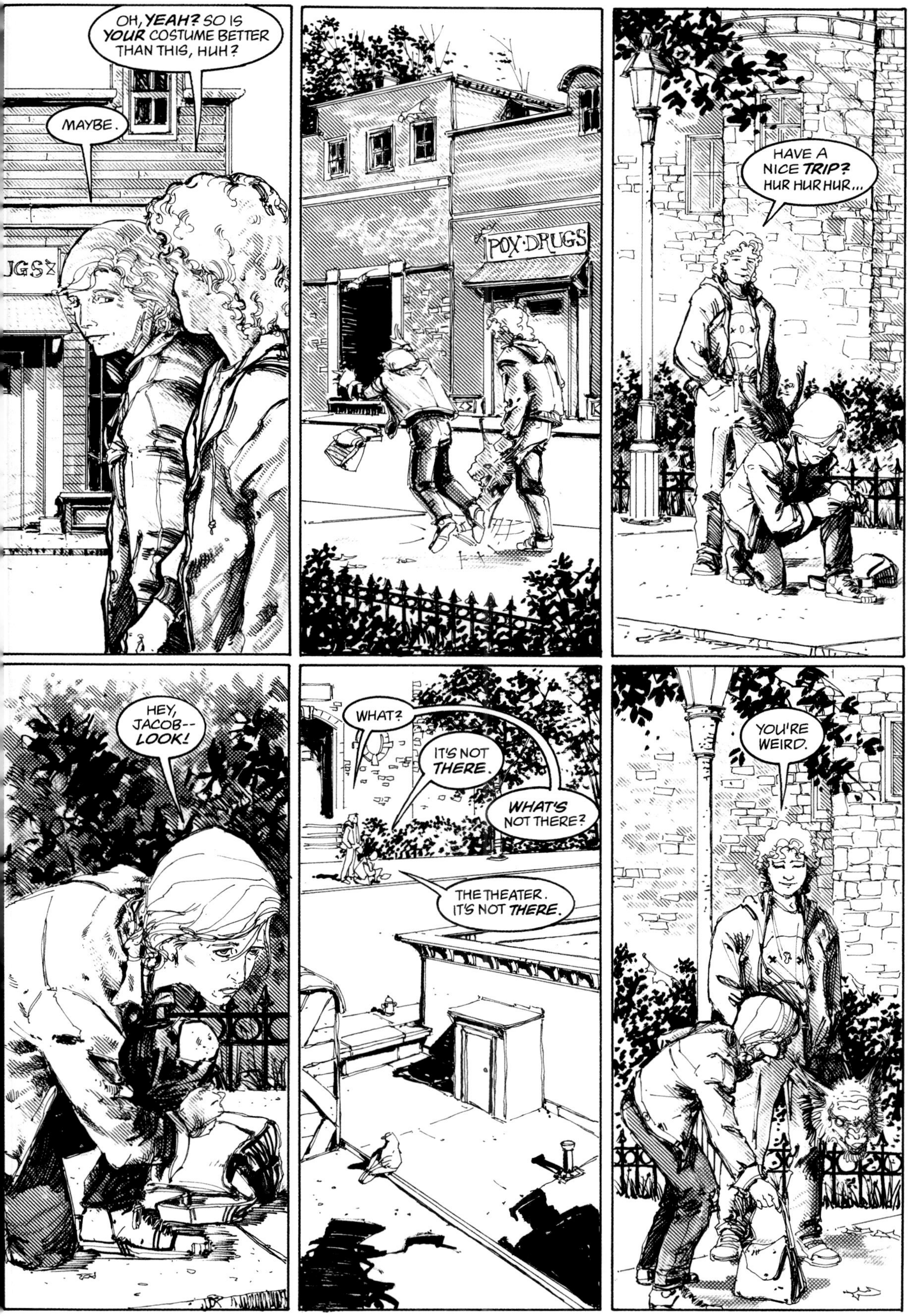

OH, YEAH? SO IS YOUR COSTUME BETTER THAN THIS, HUH?
MAYBE.
UGS
POX·DRUGS
HAVE A NICE TRIP? HUR HUR HUR...
HEY, JACOB-- LOOK!
WHAT?
IT'S NOT THERE.
WHAT'S NOT THERE?
THE THEATER. IT'S NOT THERE.
YOU'RE WEIRD.

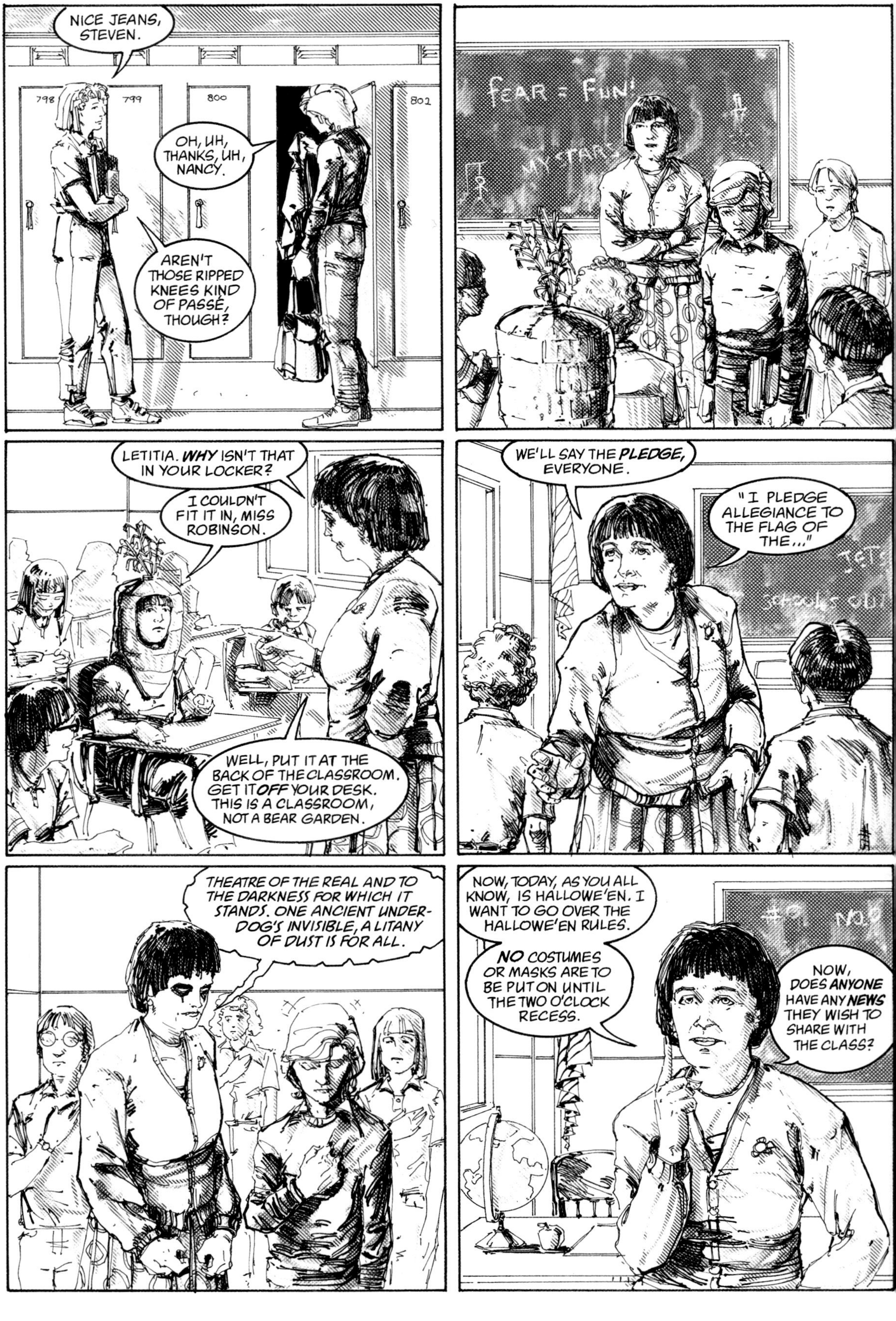
NICE JEANS, STEVEN.
798
799
800
801
OH, UH, THANKS, UH, NANCY.
AREN'T THOSE RIPPED KNEES KIND OF PASSÉ, THOUGH?
LETITIA. WHY ISN'T THAT IN YOUR LOCKER?
I COULDN'T FIT IT IN, MISS ROBINSON.
WELL, PUT IT AT THE BACK OF THE CLASSROOM. GET IT OFF YOUR DESK. THIS IS A CLASSROOM, NOT A BEAR GARDEN.
WE'LL SAY THE PLEDGE, EVERYONE.
"I PLEDGE ALLEGIANCE TO THE FLAG OF THE..."
THEATRE OF THE REAL AND TO THE DARKNESS FOR WHICH IT STANDS. ONE ANCIENT UNDER-DOG'S INVISIBLE, A LITANY OF DUST IS FOR ALL.
NOW, TODAY, AS YOU ALL KNOW, IS HALLOWE'EN. I WANT TO GO OVER THE HALLOWE'EN RULES.
NO COSTUMES OR MASKS ARE TO BE PUT ON UNTIL THE TWO O'CLOCK RECESS.
NOW, DOES ANYONE HAVE ANY NEWS THEY WISH TO SHARE WITH THE CLASS?

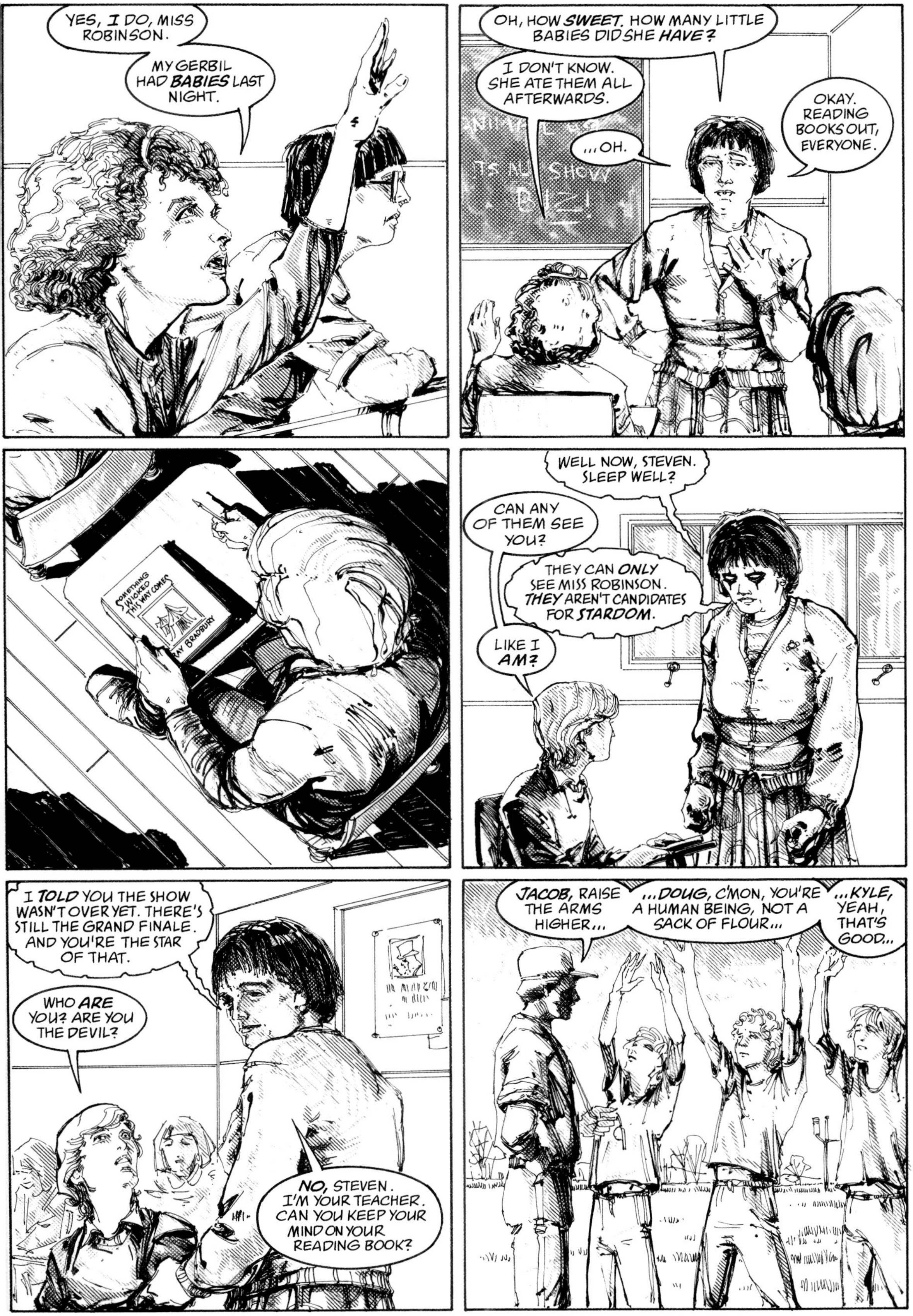
YES, I DO, MISS ROBINSON.
MY GERBIL HAD BABIES LAST NIGHT.
OH, HOW SWEET. HOW MANY LITTLE BABIES DID SHE HAVE?
I DON'T KNOW. SHE ATE THEM ALL AFTERWARDS.
...OH.
OKAY. READING BOOKS OUT, EVERYONE.
SOMETHING WICKED THIS WAY COMES
RAY BRADBURY
WELL NOW, STEVEN. SLEEP WELL?
CAN ANY OF THEM SEE YOU?
THEY CAN ONLY SEE MISS ROBINSON. THEY AREN'T CANDIDATES FOR STARDOM.
LIKE I AM?
I TOLD YOU THE SHOW WASN'T OVER YET. THERE'S STILL THE GRAND FINALE. AND YOU'RE THE STAR OF THAT.
WHO ARE YOU? ARE YOU THE DEVIL?
NO, STEVEN. I'M YOUR TEACHER. CAN YOU KEEP YOUR MIND ON YOUR READING BOOK?
JACOB, RAISE THE ARMS HIGHER...
...DOUG, C'MON, YOU'RE A HUMAN BEING, NOT A SACK OF FLOUR...
...KYLE, YEAH, THAT'S GOOD...

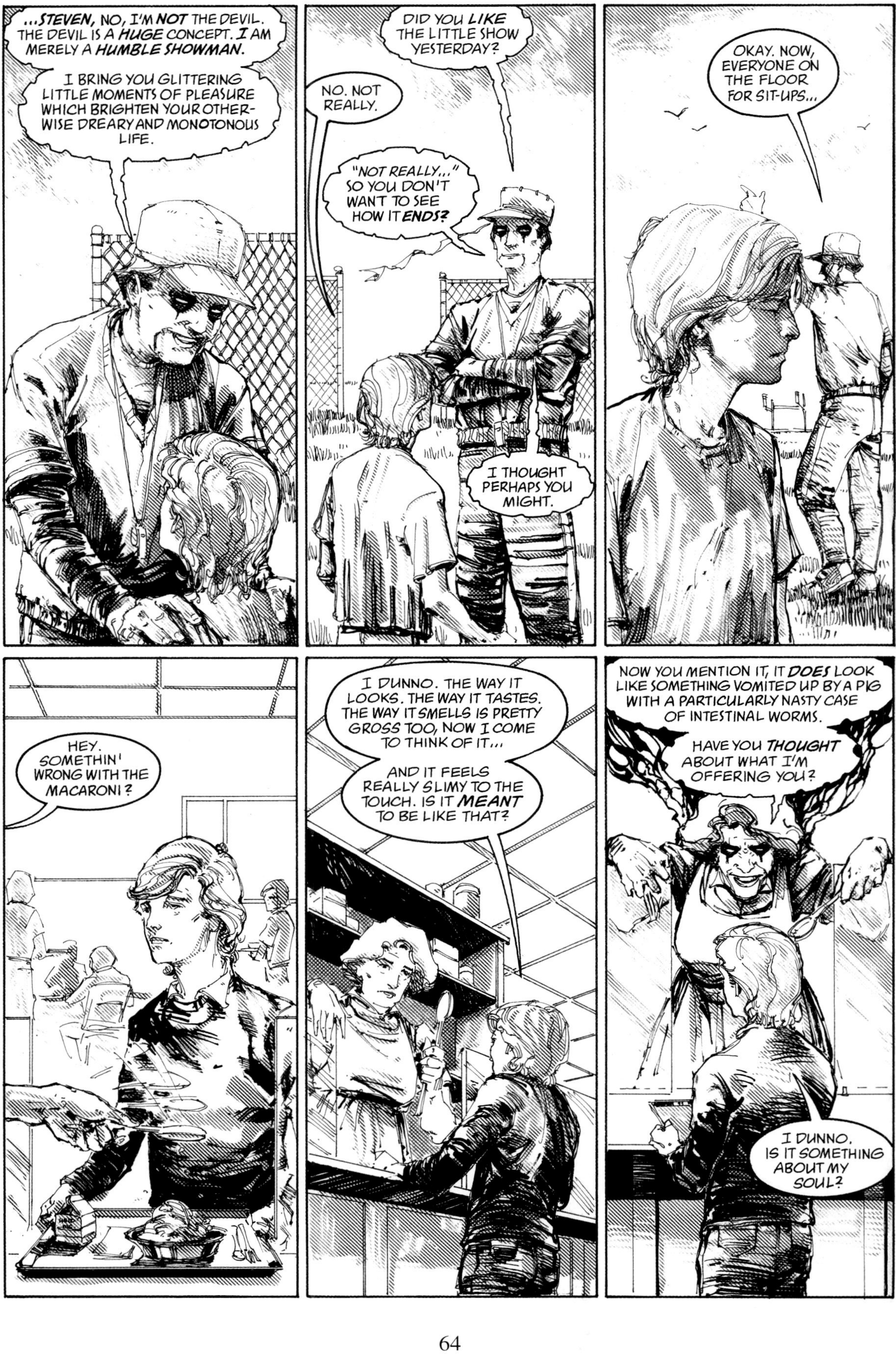
...STEVEN, NO, I'M NOT THE DEVIL. THE DEVIL IS A HUGE CONCEPT. I AM MERELY A HUMBLE SHOWMAN.
I BRING YOU GLITTERING LITTLE MOMENTS OF PLEASURE WHICH BRIGHTEN YOUR OTHER-WISE DREARY AND MONOTONOUS LIFE.
DID YOU LIKE THE LITTLE SHOW YESTERDAY?
NO. NOT REALLY.
"NOT REALLY..." SO YOU DON'T WANT TO SEE HOW IT ENDS?
I THOUGHT PERHAPS YOU MIGHT.
OKAY. NOW, EVERYONE ON THE FLOOR FOR SIT-UPS...
HEY. SOMETHIN' WRONG WITH THE MACARONI?
I DUNNO. THE WAY IT LOOKS. THE WAY IT TASTES. THE WAY IT SMELLS IS PRETTY GROSS TOO, NOW I COME TO THINK OF IT...
AND IT FEELS REALLY SLIMY TO THE TOUCH. IS IT MEANT TO BE LIKE THAT?
NOW YOU MENTION IT, IT DOES LOOK LIKE SOMETHING VOMITED UP BY A PIG WITH A PARTICULARLY NASTY CASE OF INTESTINAL WORMS.
HAVE YOU THOUGHT ABOUT WHAT I'M OFFERING YOU?
I DUNNO. IS IT SOMETHING ABOUT MY SOUL?

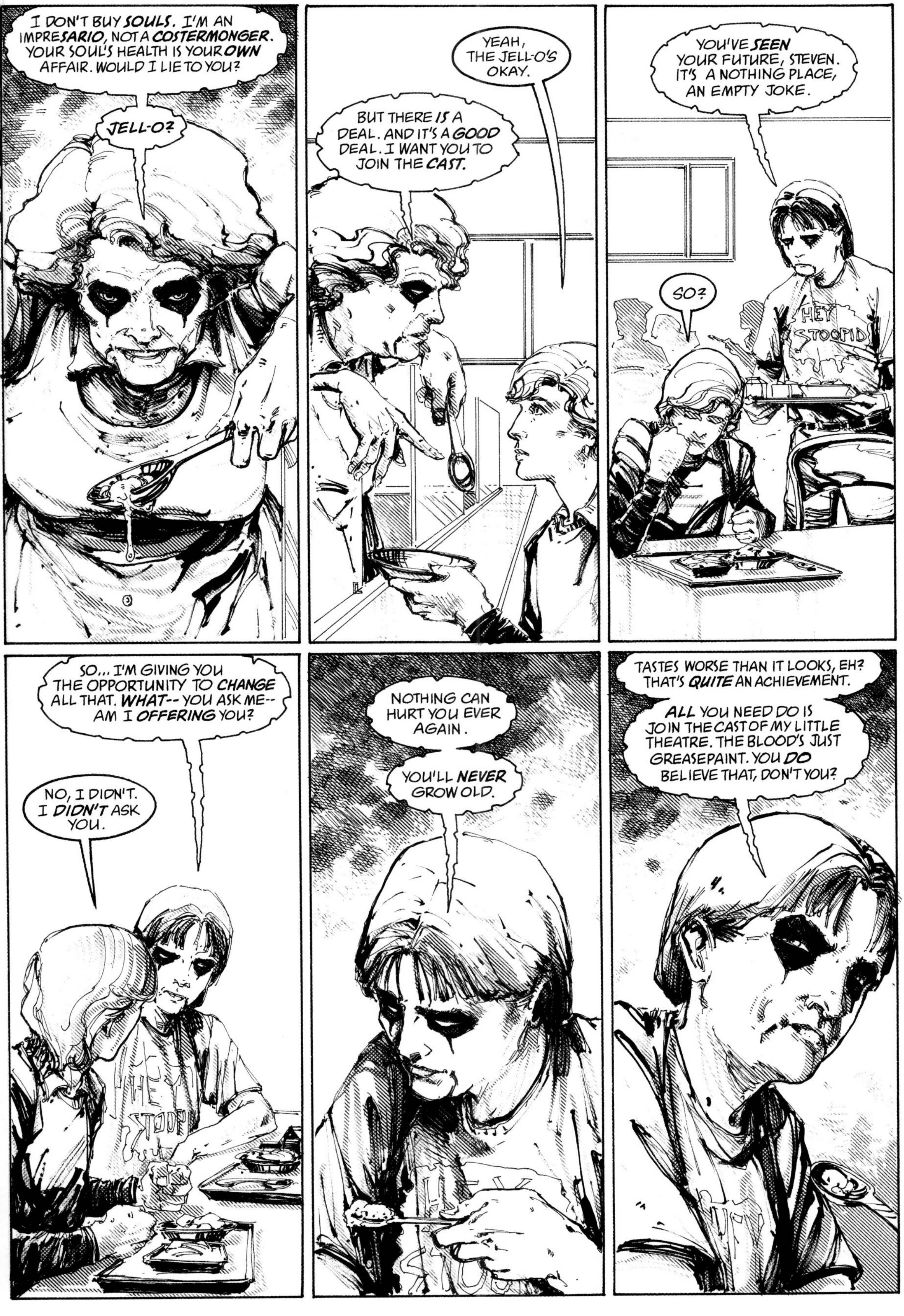
I DON'T BUY SOULS. I'M AN IMPRESARIO, NOT A COSTERMONGER. YOUR SOUL'S HEALTH IS YOUR OWN AFFAIR. WOULD I LIE TO YOU?
JELL-O?
YEAH, THE JELL-O'S OKAY.
BUT THERE IS A DEAL. AND IT'S A GOOD DEAL. I WANT YOU TO JOIN THE CAST.
YOU'VE SEEN YOUR FUTURE, STEVEN. IT'S A NOTHING PLACE, AN EMPTY JOKE.
SO?
HEY STOOPID
SO... I'M GIVING YOU THE OPPORTUNITY TO CHANGE ALL THAT. WHAT-- YOU ASK ME-- AM I OFFERING YOU?
NO, I DIDN'T. I DIDN'T ASK YOU.
NOTHING CAN HURT YOU EVER AGAIN.
YOU'LL NEVER GROW OLD.
TASTES WORSE THAN IT LOOKS, EH? THAT'S QUITE AN ACHIEVEMENT.
ALL YOU NEED DO IS JOIN THE CAST OF MY LITTLE THEATRE. THE BLOOD'S JUST GREASEPAINT. YOU DO BELIEVE THAT, DON'T YOU?

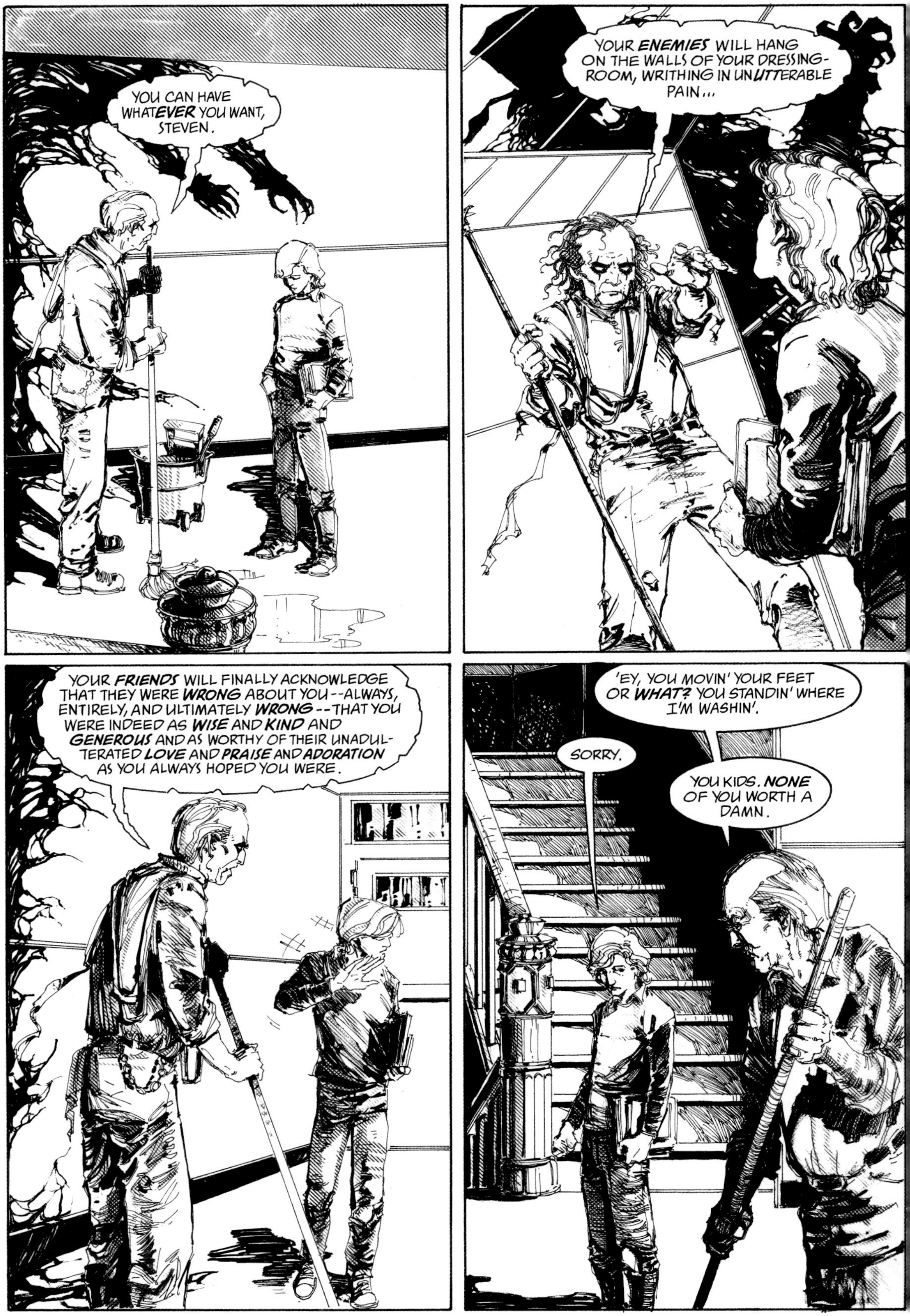
YOU CAN HAVE WHATEVER YOU WANT, STEVEN.
YOUR ENEMIES WILL HANG ON THE WALLS OF YOUR DRESSING-ROOM, WRITHING IN UNUTTERABLE PAIN...
YOUR FRIENDS WILL FINALLY ACKNOWLEDGE THAT THEY WERE WRONG ABOUT YOU--ALWAYS, ENTIRELY, AND ULTIMATELY WRONG--THAT YOU WERE INDEED AS WISE AND KIND AND GENEROUS AND AS WORTHY OF THEIR UNADULTERATED LOVE AND PRAISE AND ADORATION AS YOU ALWAYS HOPED YOU WERE.
'EY, YOU MOVIN' YOUR FEET OR WHAT? YOU STANDIN' WHERE I'M WASHIN'.
SORRY.
YOU KIDS. NONE OF YOU WORTH A DAMN.

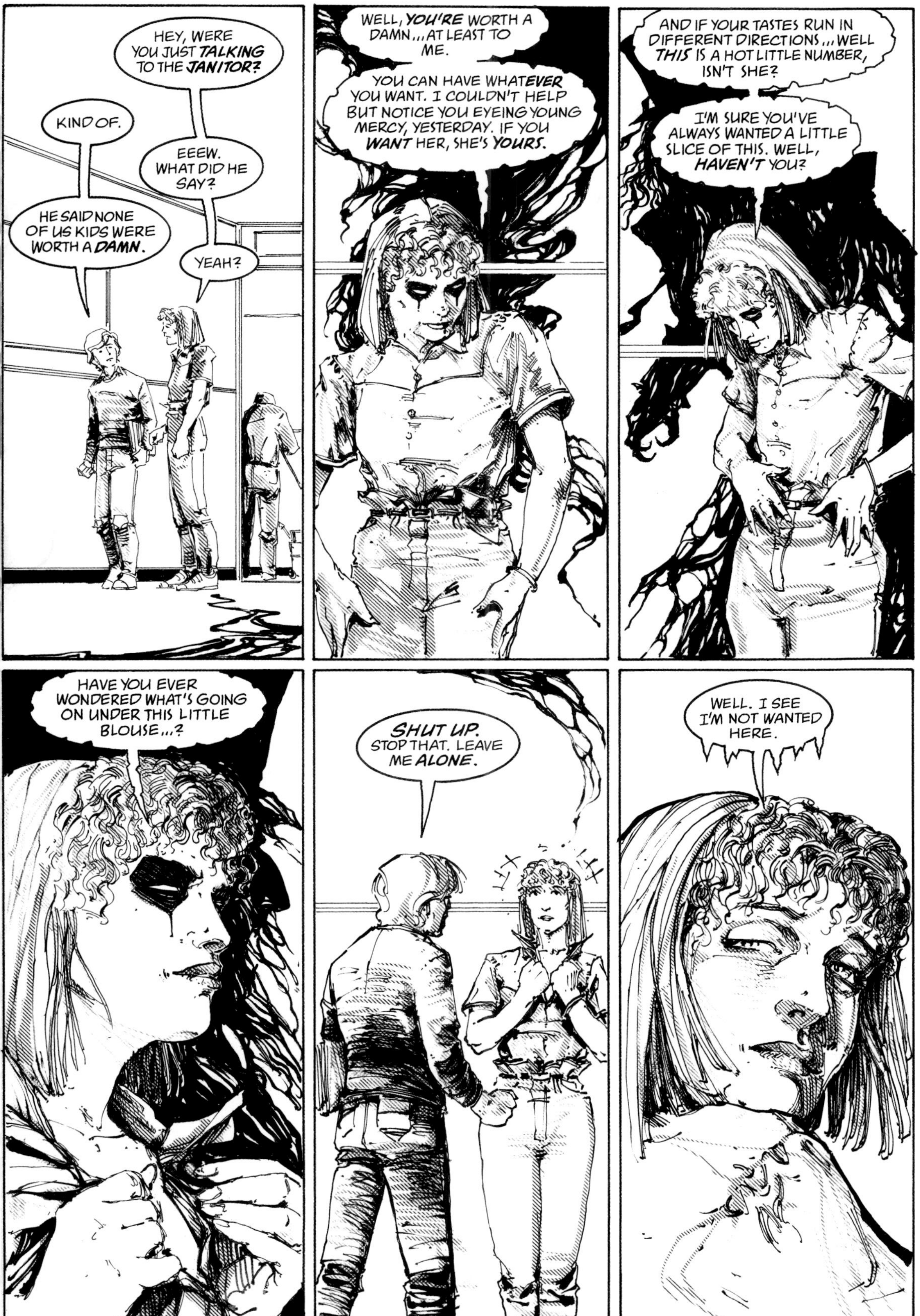
HEY, WERE YOU JUST TALKING TO THE JANITOR?
KIND OF.
EEEW. WHAT DID HE SAY?
HE SAID NONE OF US KIDS WERE WORTH A DAMN.
YEAH?
WELL, YOU'RE WORTH A DAMN... AT LEAST TO ME.
YOU CAN HAVE WHATEVER YOU WANT. I COULDN'T HELP BUT NOTICE YOU EYEING YOUNG MERCY, YESTERDAY. IF YOU WANT HER, SHE'S YOURS.
AND IF YOUR TASTES RUN IN DIFFERENT DIRECTIONS... WELL THIS IS A HOT LITTLE NUMBER, ISN'T SHE?
I'M SURE YOU'VE ALWAYS WANTED A LITTLE SLICE OF THIS. WELL, HAVEN'T YOU?
HAVE YOU EVER WONDERED WHAT'S GOING ON UNDER THIS LITTLE BLOUSE...?
SHUT UP. STOP THAT. LEAVE ME ALONE.
WELL. I SEE I'M NOT WANTED HERE.

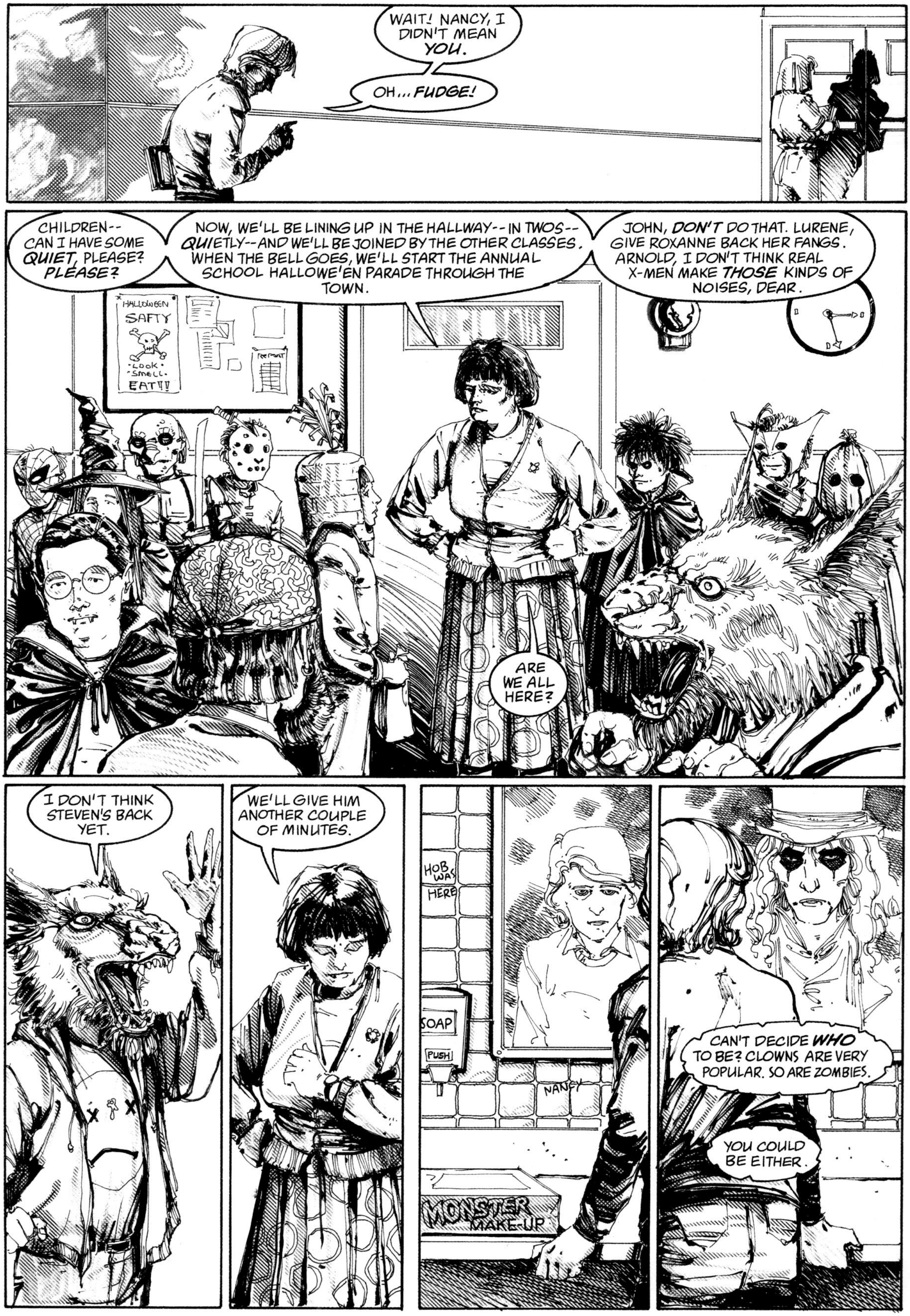
WAIT! NANCY, I DIDN'T MEAN YOU.
OH... FUDGE!
CHILDREN-- CAN I HAVE SOME QUIET, PLEASE? PLEASE?
NOW, WE'LL BE LINING UP IN THE HALLWAY-- IN TWOS-- QUIETLY--AND WE'LL BE JOINED BY THE OTHER CLASSES. WHEN THE BELL GOES, WE'LL START THE ANNUAL SCHOOL HALLOWE'EN PARADE THROUGH THE TOWN.
JOHN, DON'T DO THAT. LURENE, GIVE ROXANNE BACK HER FANGS. ARNOLD, I DON'T THINK REAL X-MEN MAKE THOSE KINDS OF NOISES, DEAR.
HALLOWEEN SAFTY
LOOK SMELL EAT!!!
REPORT
ARE WE ALL HERE?
I DON'T THINK STEVEN'S BACK YET.
WE'LL GIVE HIM ANOTHER COUPLE OF MINUTES.
HOB WAS HERE
SOAP
PUSH
NANCY
MONSTER MAKE-UP
CAN'T DECIDE WHO TO BE? CLOWNS ARE VERY POPULAR. SO ARE ZOMBIES.
YOU COULD BE EITHER.

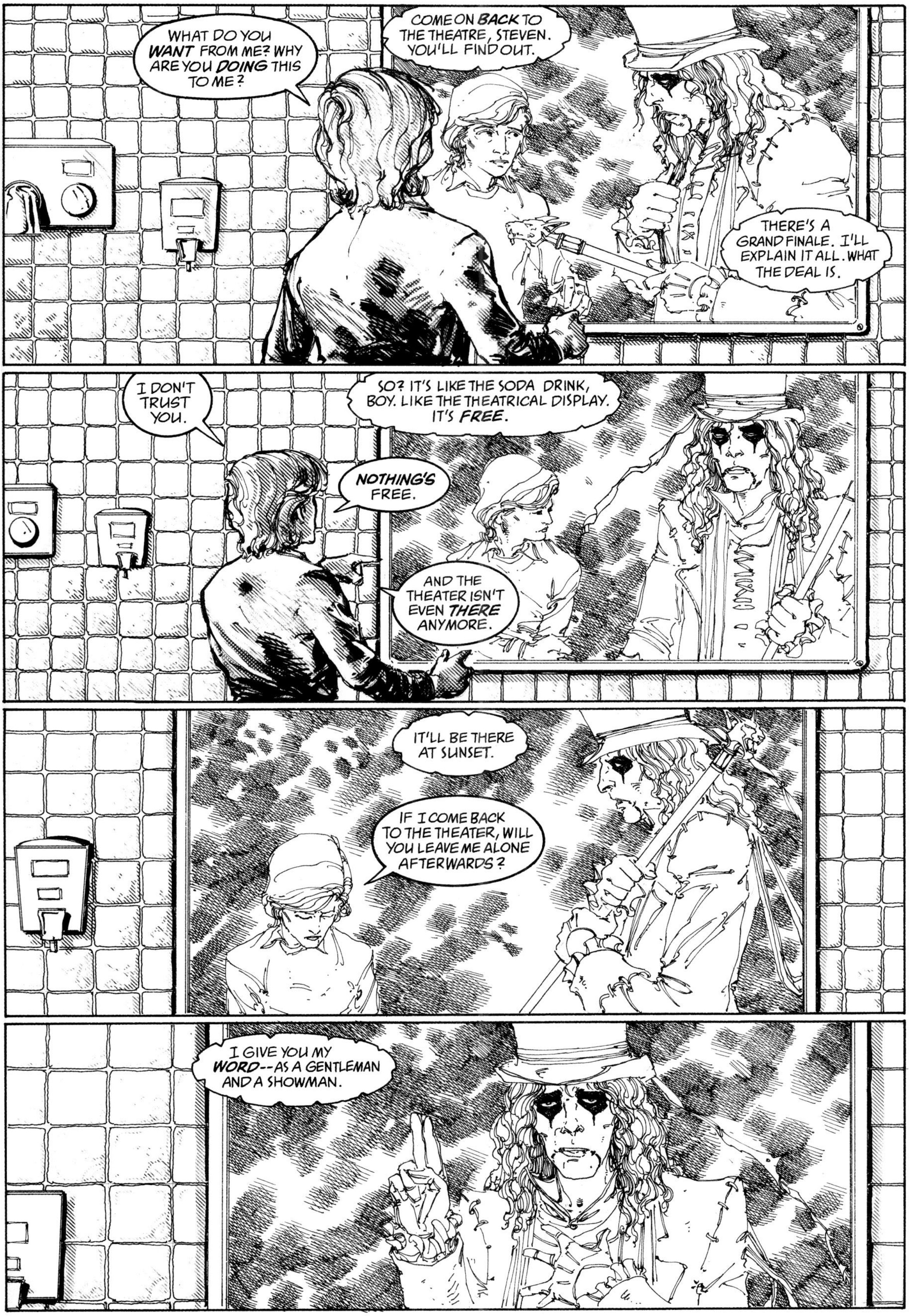
WHAT DO YOU **WANT** FROM ME? WHY ARE YOU **DOING** THIS TO ME?
COME ON **BACK** TO THE THEATRE, STEVEN. YOU'LL FIND OUT.
THERE'S A GRAND FINALE. I'LL EXPLAIN IT ALL. WHAT THE DEAL IS.
I DON'T TRUST YOU.
SO? IT'S LIKE THE SODA DRINK, BOY. LIKE THE THEATRICAL DISPLAY. IT'S **FREE**.
NOTHING'S FREE.
AND THE THEATER ISN'T EVEN **THERE** ANYMORE.
IT'LL BE THERE AT SUNSET.
IF I COME BACK TO THE THEATER, WILL YOU LEAVE ME ALONE AFTERWARDS?
I GIVE YOU MY **WORD**--AS A GENTLEMAN AND A SHOWMAN.

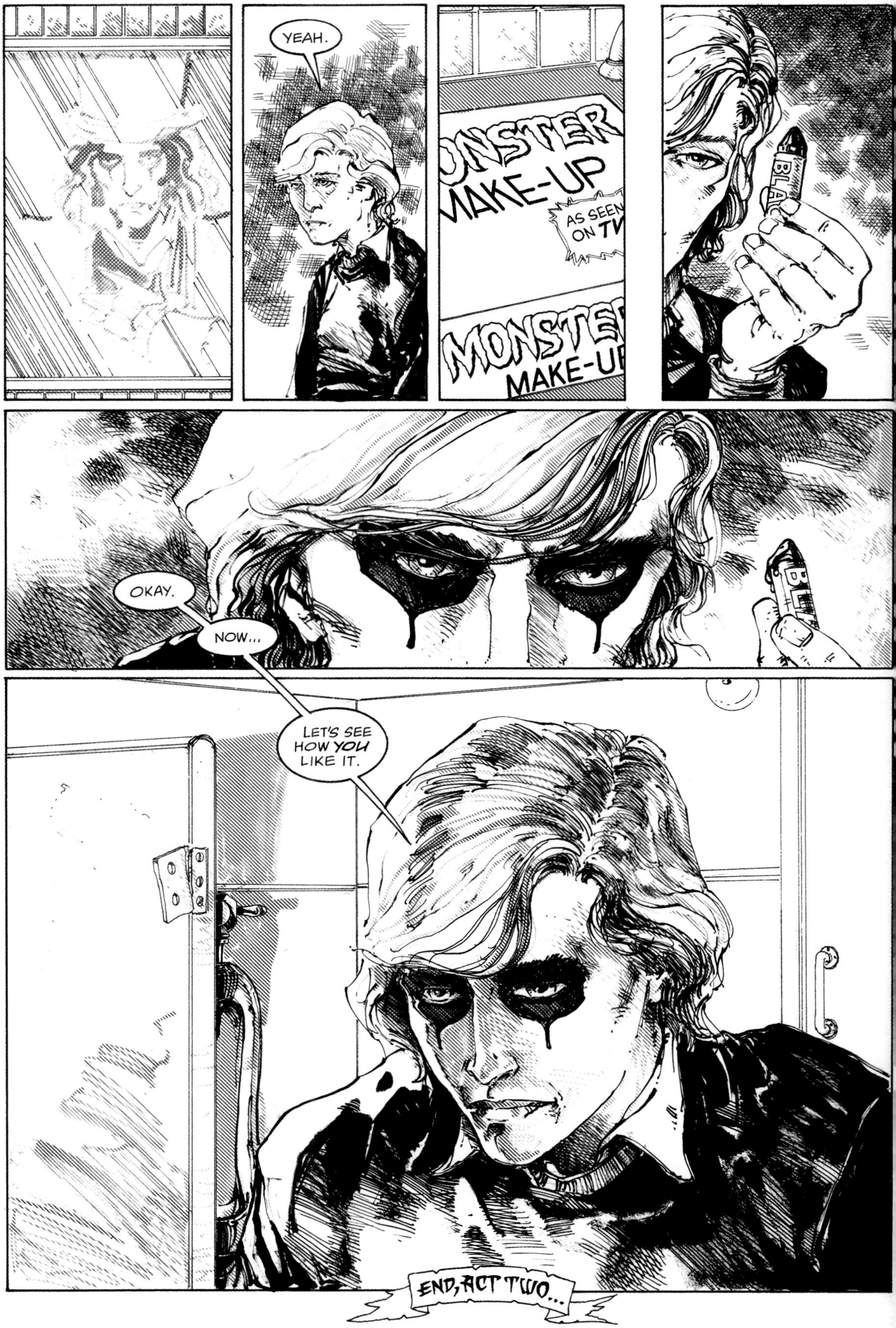
YEAH.
MONSTER MAKE-UP
AS SEEN ON TV
MONSTER MAKE-UP
OKAY.
NOW...
LET'S SEE HOW YOU LIKE IT.
END, ACT TWO...

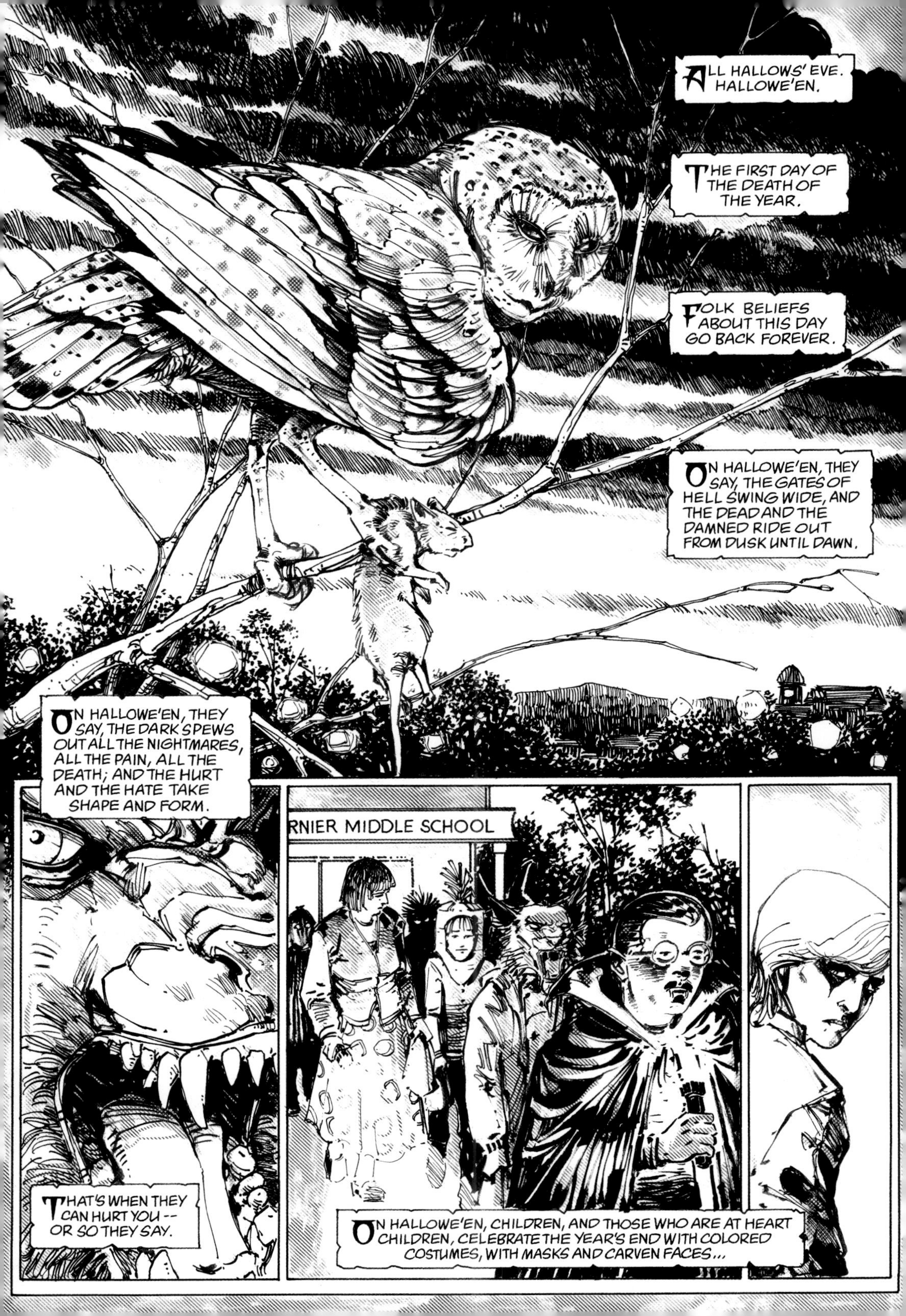
ALL HALLOWS' EVE. HALLOWE'EN.
THE FIRST DAY OF THE DEATH OF THE YEAR.
FOLK BELIEFS ABOUT THIS DAY GO BACK FOREVER.
ON HALLOWE'EN, THEY SAY, THE GATES OF HELL SWING WIDE, AND THE DEAD AND THE DAMNED RIDE OUT FROM DUSK UNTIL DAWN.
ON HALLOWE'EN, THEY SAY, THE DARK SPEWS OUT ALL THE NIGHTMARES, ALL THE PAIN, ALL THE DEATH; AND THE HURT AND THE HATE TAKE SHAPE AND FORM.
THAT'S WHEN THEY CAN HURT YOU -- OR SO THEY SAY.
RNIER MIDDLE SCHOOL
ON HALLOWE'EN, CHILDREN, AND THOSE WHO ARE AT HEART CHILDREN, CELEBRATE THE YEAR'S END WITH COLORED COSTUMES, WITH MASKS AND CARVEN FACES...

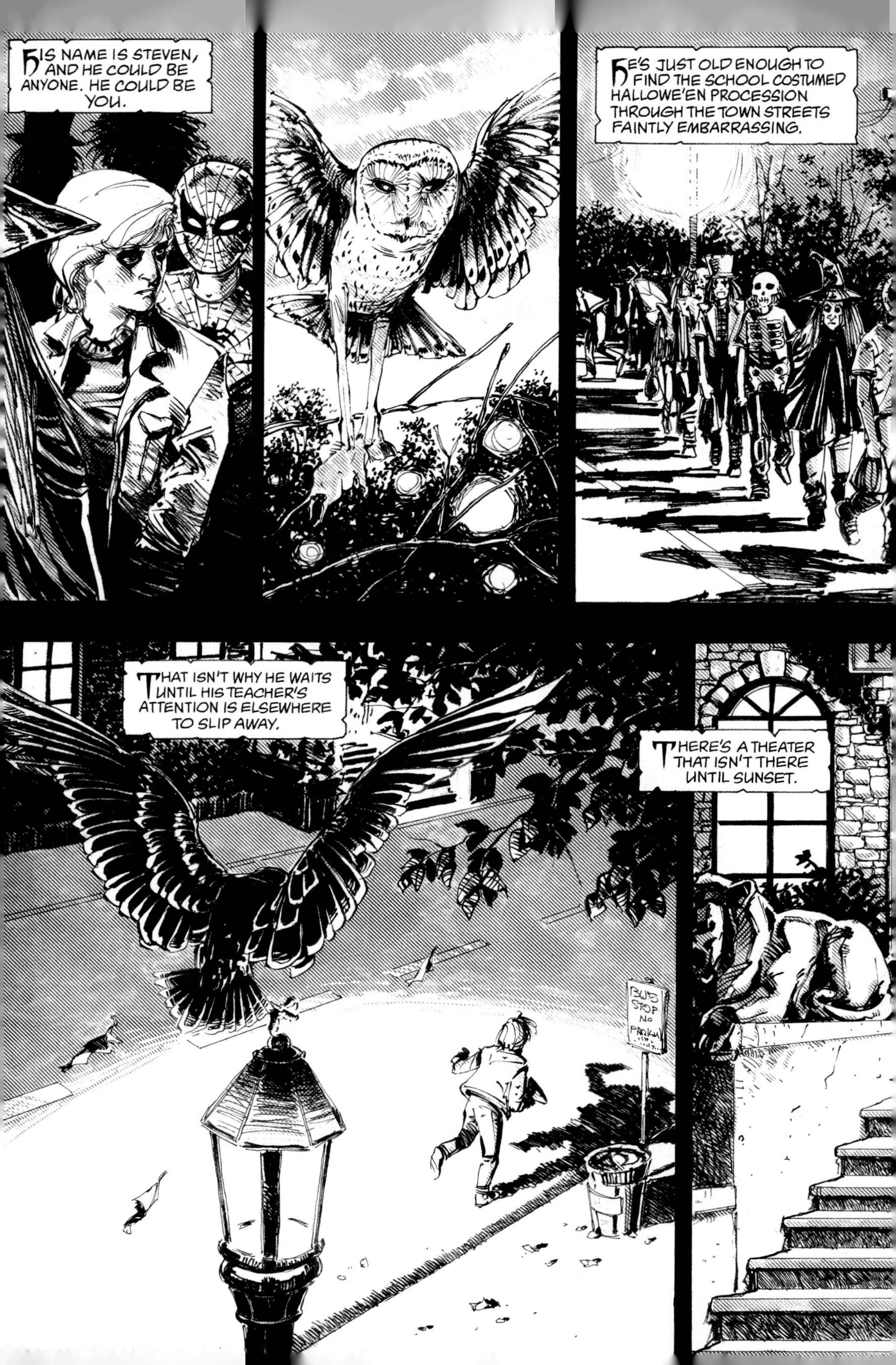
HIS NAME IS STEVEN, AND HE COULD BE ANYONE. HE COULD BE YOU.
HE'S JUST OLD ENOUGH TO FIND THE SCHOOL COSTUMED HALLOWE'EN PROCESSION THROUGH THE TOWN STREETS FAINTLY EMBARRASSING.
THAT ISN'T WHY HE WAITS UNTIL HIS TEACHER'S ATTENTION IS ELSEWHERE TO SLIP AWAY.
BUS STOP NO
THERE'S A THEATER THAT ISN'T THERE UNTIL SUNSET.

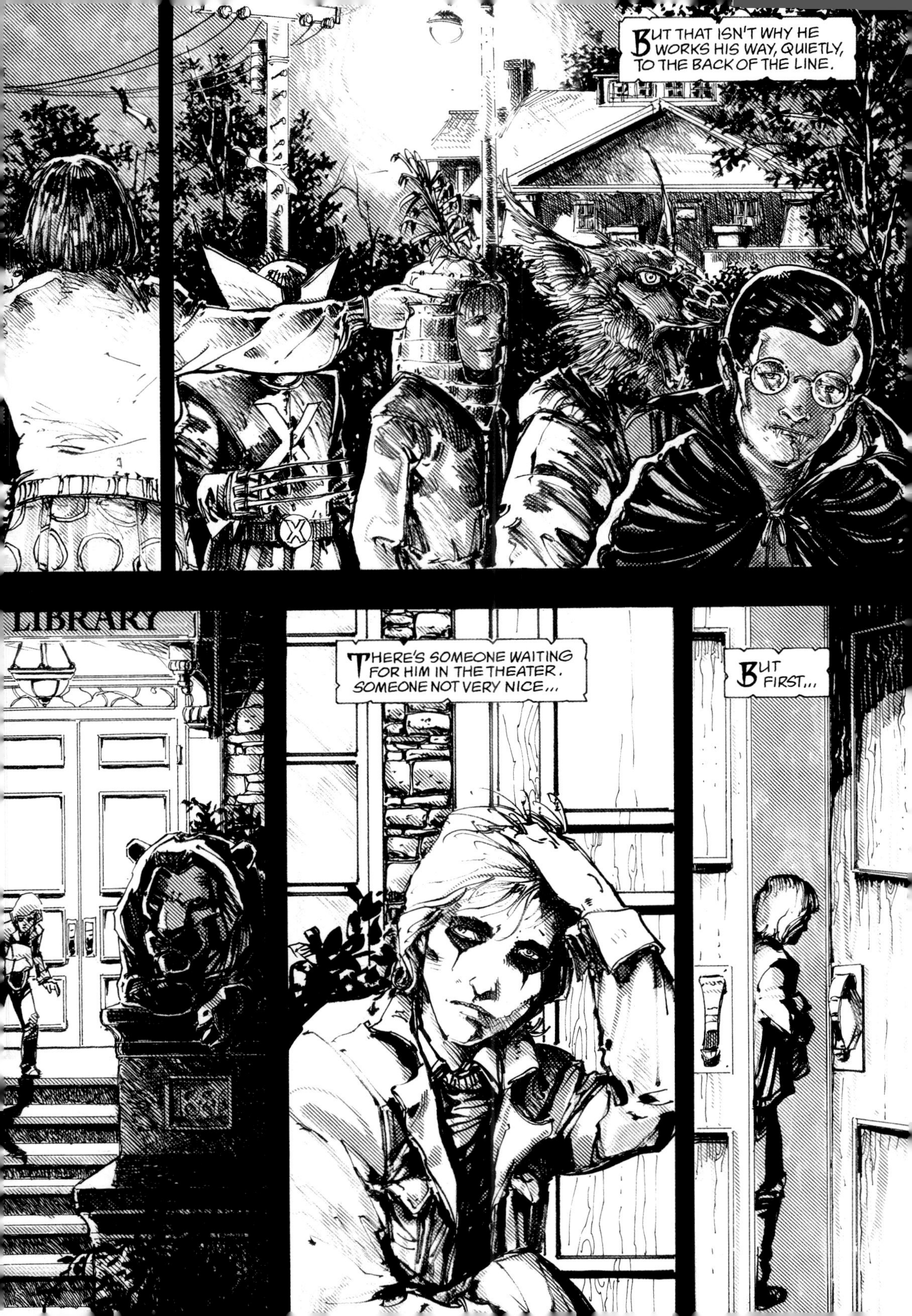
BUT THAT ISN'T WHY HE WORKS HIS WAY, QUIETLY, TO THE BACK OF THE LINE.
LIBRARY
THERE'S SOMEONE WAITING FOR HIM IN THE THEATER. SOMEONE NOT VERY NICE...
BUT FIRST...

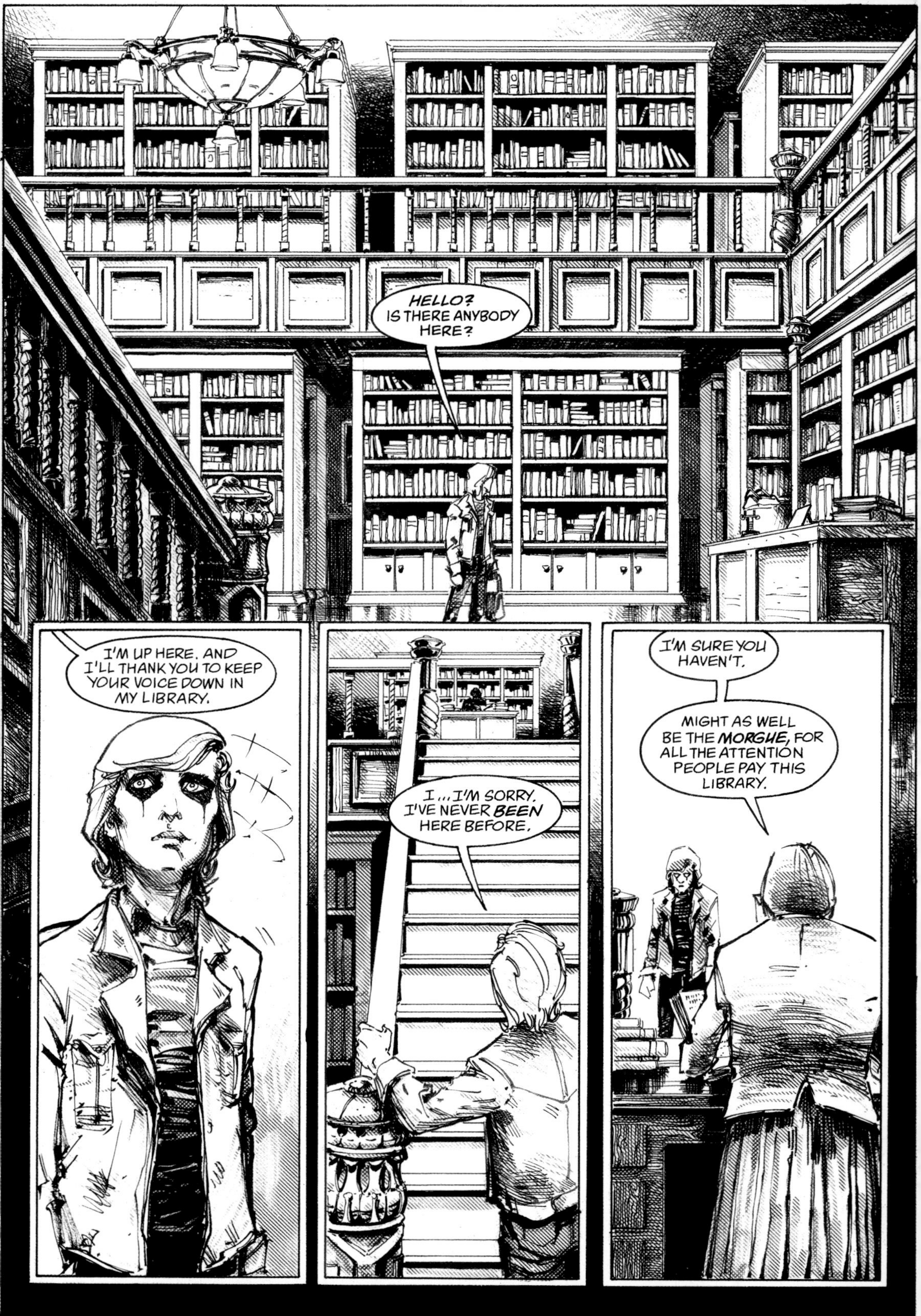
HELLO? IS THERE ANYBODY HERE?
I'M UP HERE. AND I'LL THANK YOU TO KEEP YOUR VOICE DOWN IN MY LIBRARY.
I... I'M SORRY. I'VE NEVER BEEN HERE BEFORE.
I'M SURE YOU HAVEN'T.
MIGHT AS WELL BE THE MORGUE, FOR ALL THE ATTENTION PEOPLE PAY THIS LIBRARY.

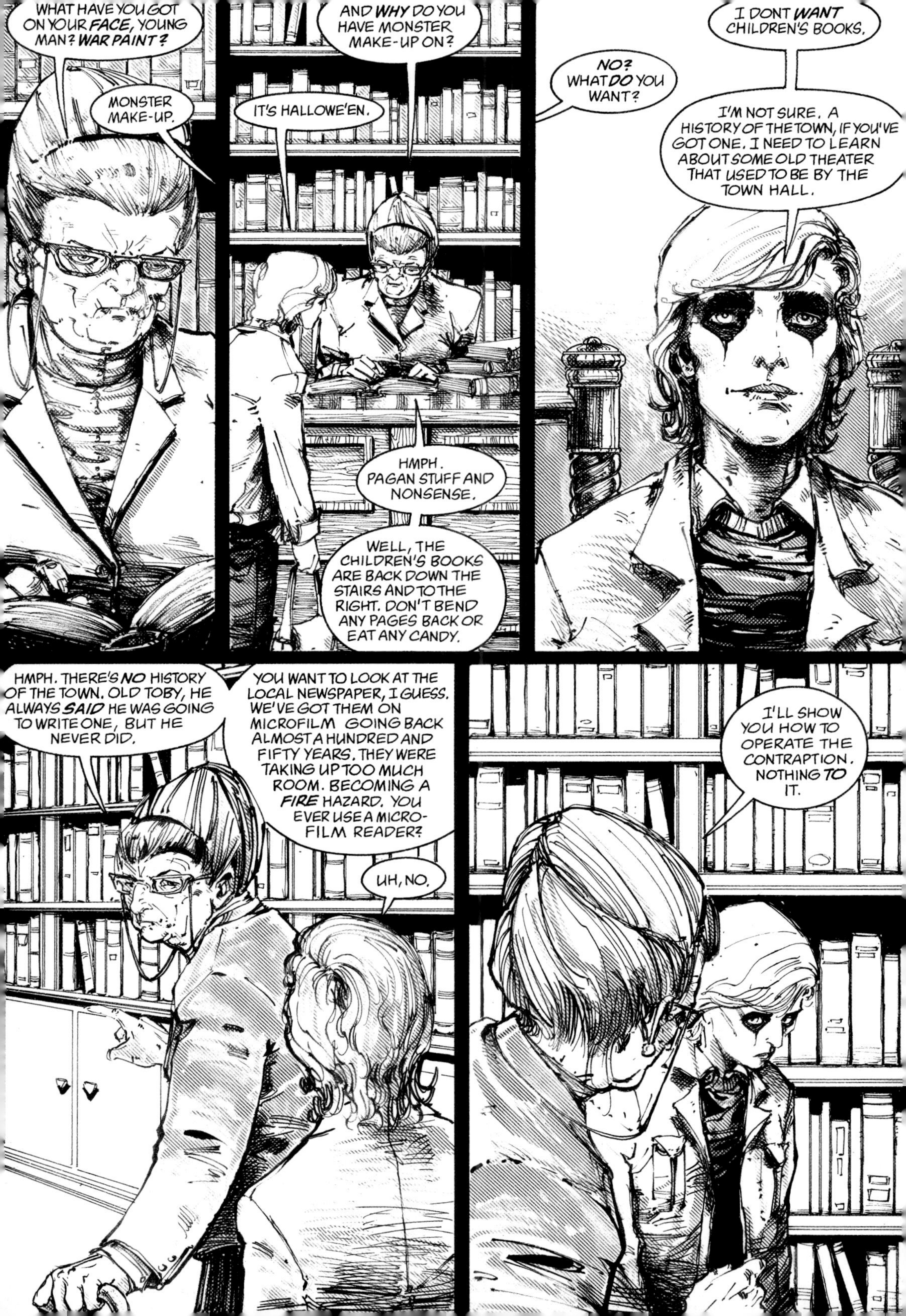
WHAT HAVE YOU GOT ON YOUR FACE, YOUNG MAN? WAR PAINT?
MONSTER MAKE-UP.
AND WHY DO YOU HAVE MONSTER MAKE-UP ON?
IT'S HALLOWE'EN.
HMPH. PAGAN STUFF AND NONSENSE.
WELL, THE CHILDREN'S BOOKS ARE BACK DOWN THE STAIRS AND TO THE RIGHT. DON'T BEND ANY PAGES BACK OR EAT ANY CANDY.
I DONT WANT CHILDREN'S BOOKS.
NO? WHAT DO YOU WANT?
I'M NOT SURE. A HISTORY OF THE TOWN, IF YOU'VE GOT ONE. I NEED TO LEARN ABOUT SOME OLD THEATER THAT USED TO BE BY THE TOWN HALL.
HMPH. THERE'S NO HISTORY OF THE TOWN. OLD TOBY, HE ALWAYS SAID HE WAS GOING TO WRITE ONE, BUT HE NEVER DID.
YOU WANT TO LOOK AT THE LOCAL NEWSPAPER, I GUESS. WE'VE GOT THEM ON MICROFILM GOING BACK ALMOST A HUNDRED AND FIFTY YEARS. THEY WERE TAKING UP TOO MUCH ROOM. BECOMING A FIRE HAZARD. YOU EVER USE A MICRO-FILM READER?
UH, NO.
I'LL SHOW YOU HOW TO OPERATE THE CONTRAPTION. NOTHING TO IT.

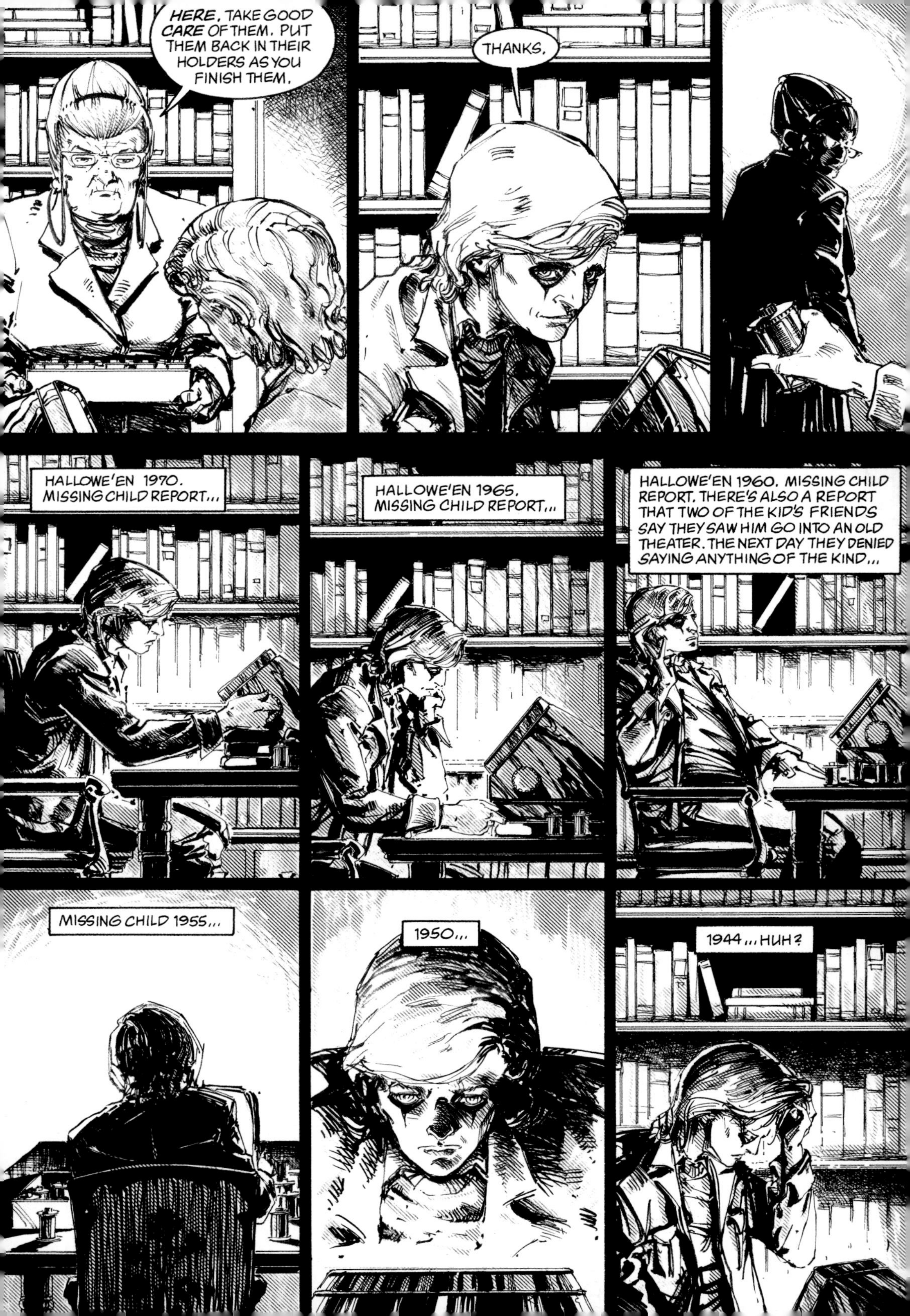
HERE. TAKE GOOD CARE OF THEM. PUT THEM BACK IN THEIR HOLDERS AS YOU FINISH THEM.
THANKS.
HALLOWE'EN 1970. MISSING CHILD REPORT...
HALLOWE'EN 1965. MISSING CHILD REPORT...
HALLOWE'EN 1960. MISSING CHILD REPORT. THERE'S ALSO A REPORT THAT TWO OF THE KID'S FRIENDS SAY THEY SAW HIM GO INTO AN OLD THEATER. THE NEXT DAY THEY DENIED SAYING ANYTHING OF THE KIND...
MISSING CHILD 1955...
1950...
1944... HUH?

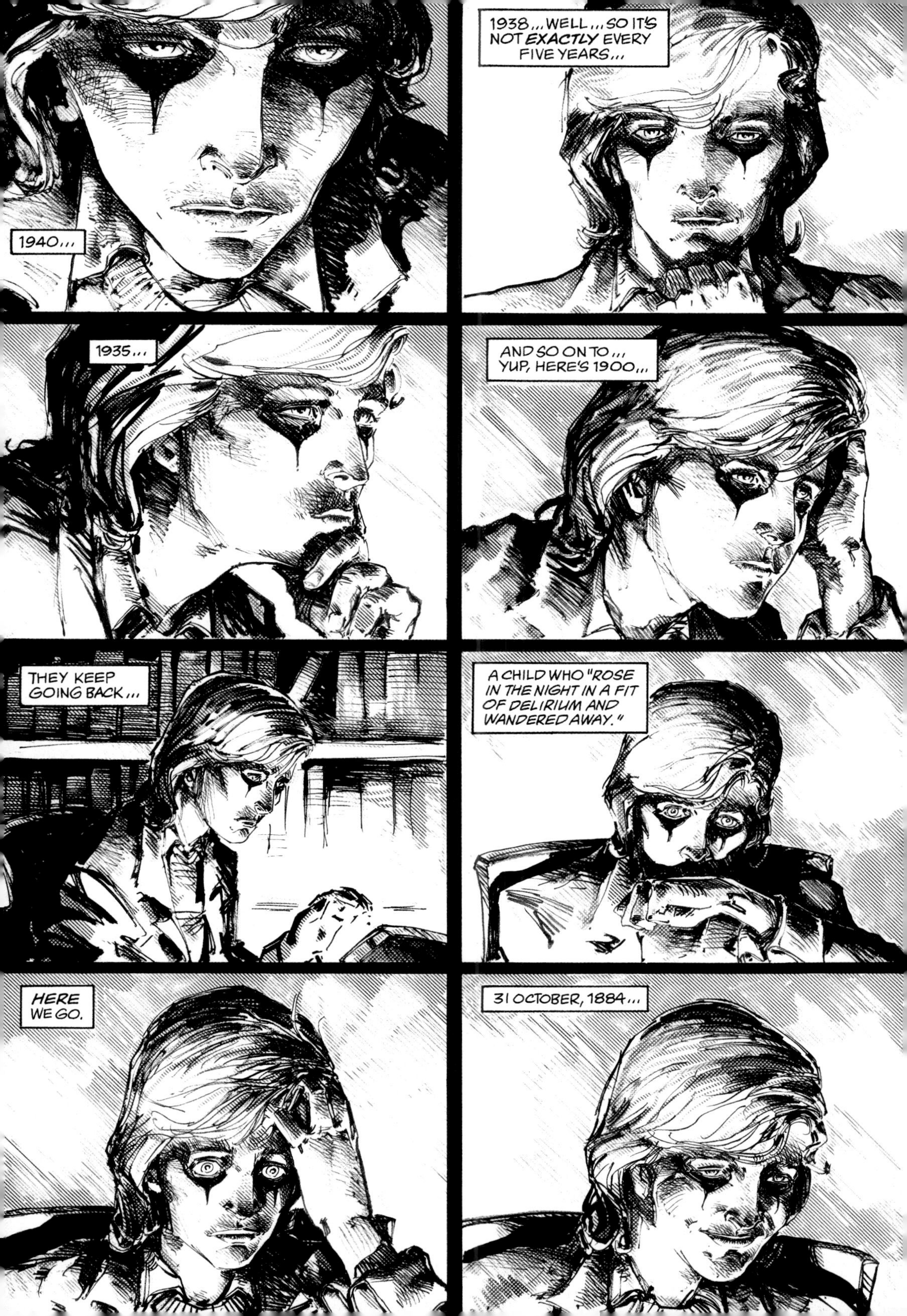
1940...
1938... WELL... SO IT'S NOT EXACTLY EVERY FIVE YEARS...
1935...
AND SO ON TO... YUP, HERE'S 1900...
THEY KEEP GOING BACK...
A CHILD WHO "ROSE IN THE NIGHT IN A FIT OF DELIRIUM AND WANDERED AWAY."
HERE WE GO.
31 OCTOBER, 1884...

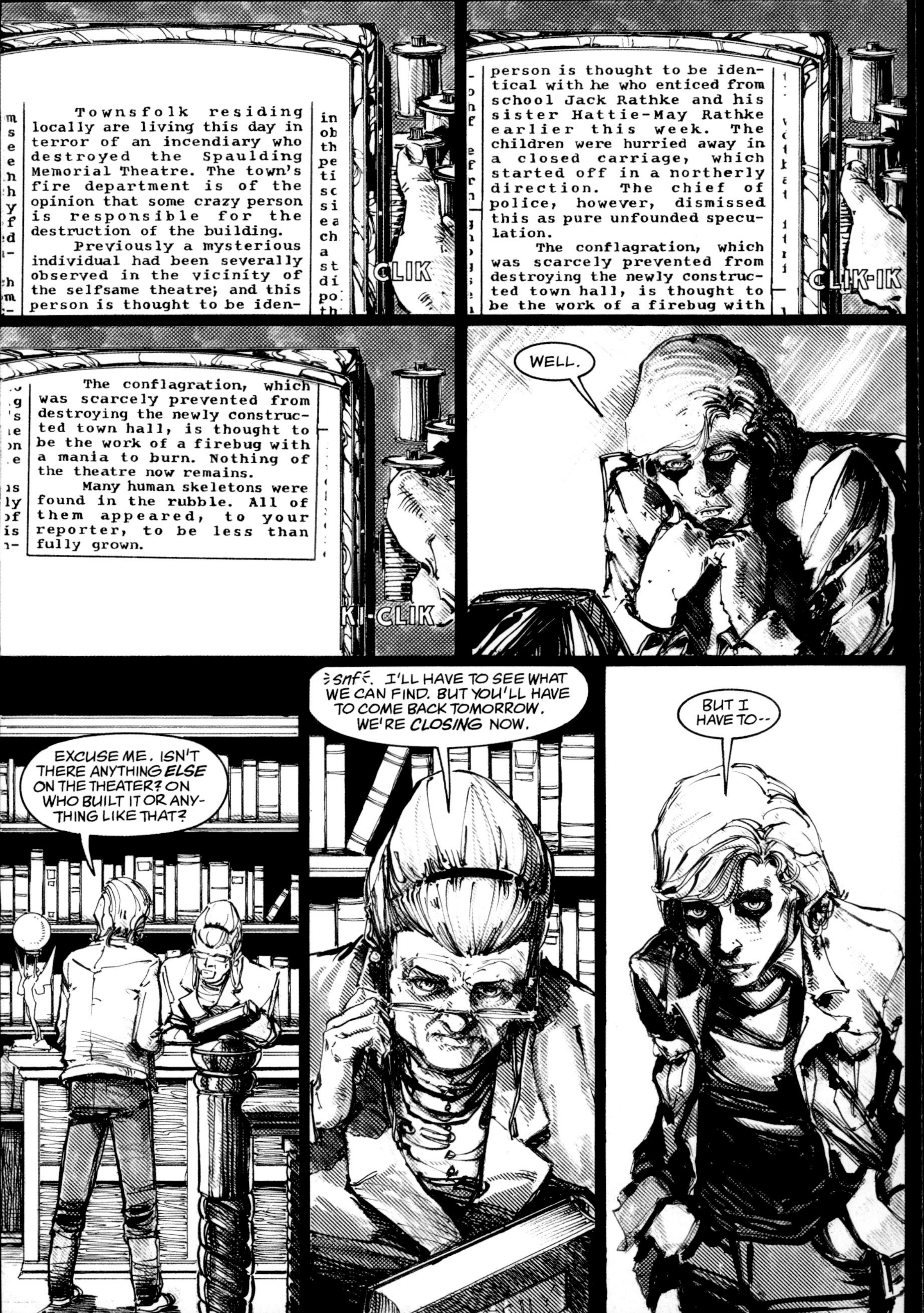
Townsfolk residing locally are living this day in terror of an incendiary who destroyed the Spaulding Memorial Theatre. The town's fire department is of the opinion that some crazy person is responsible for the destruction of the building.
Previously a mysterious individual had been severally observed in the vicinity of the selfsame theatre; and this person is thought to be iden-
CLIK
person is thought to be identical with he who enticed from school Jack Rathke and his sister Hattie-May Rathke earlier this week. The children were hurried away in a closed carriage, which started off in a northerly direction. The chief of police, however, dismissed this as pure unfounded speculation.
The conflagration, which was scarcely prevented from destroying the newly constructed town hall, is thought to be the work of a firebug with
CLIK-IK
The conflagration, which was scarcely prevented from destroying the newly constructed town hall, is thought to be the work of a firebug with a mania to burn. Nothing of the theatre now remains.
Many human skeletons were found in the rubble. All of them appeared, to your reporter, to be less than fully grown.
KI-CLIK
WELL.
EXCUSE ME. ISN'T THERE ANYTHING ELSE ON THE THEATER? ON WHO BUILT IT OR ANYTHING LIKE THAT?
SNF. I'LL HAVE TO SEE WHAT WE CAN FIND. BUT YOU'LL HAVE TO COME BACK TOMORROW. WE'RE CLOSING NOW.
BUT I HAVE TO--

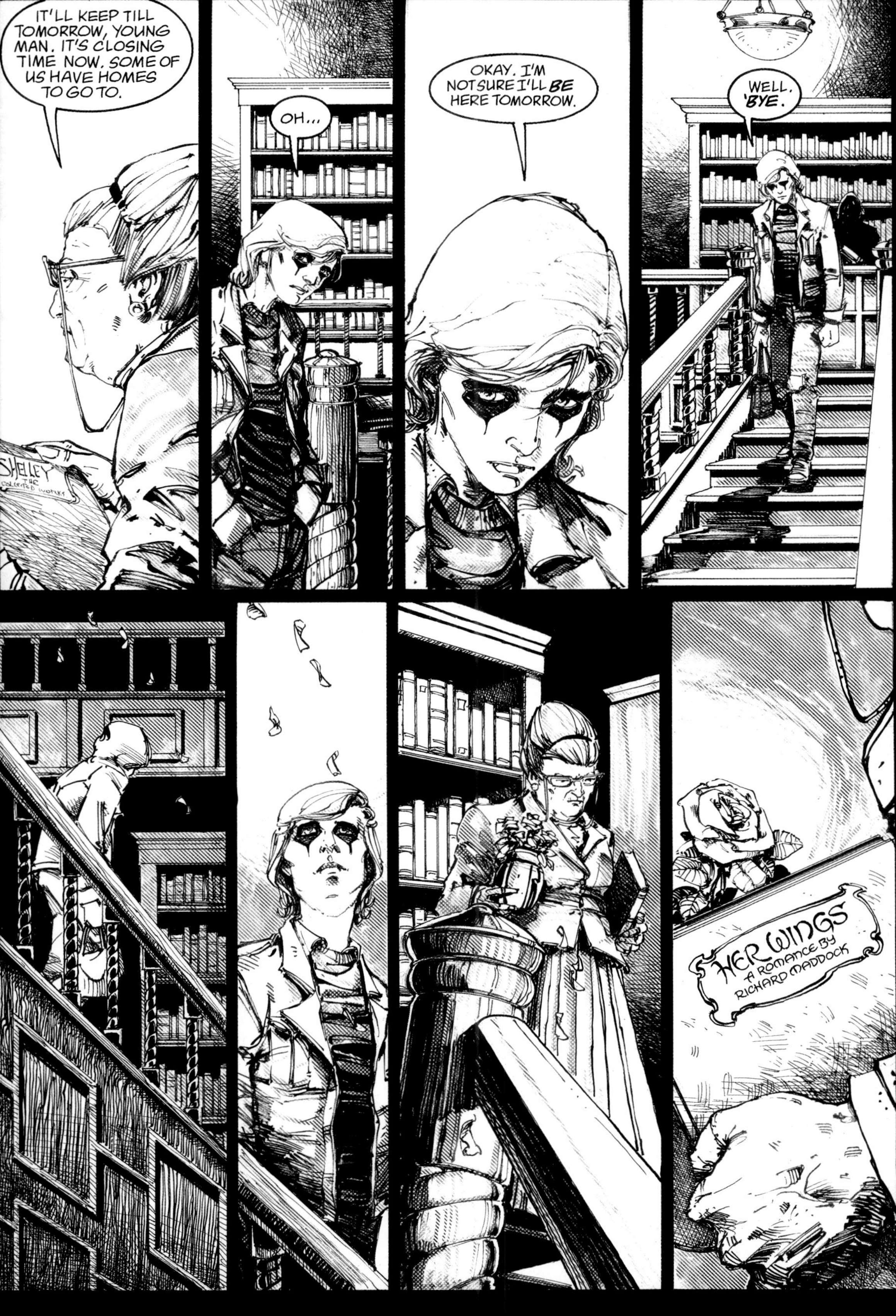

IT'LL KEEP TILL TOMORROW, YOUNG MAN. IT'S CLOSING TIME NOW. SOME OF US HAVE HOMES TO GO TO.
SHELLEY THE COLLECTED WORKS
OH...
OKAY. I'M NOT SURE I'LL BE HERE TOMORROW.
WELL. 'BYE.
HER WINGS A ROMANCE BY RICHARD MADDOCK

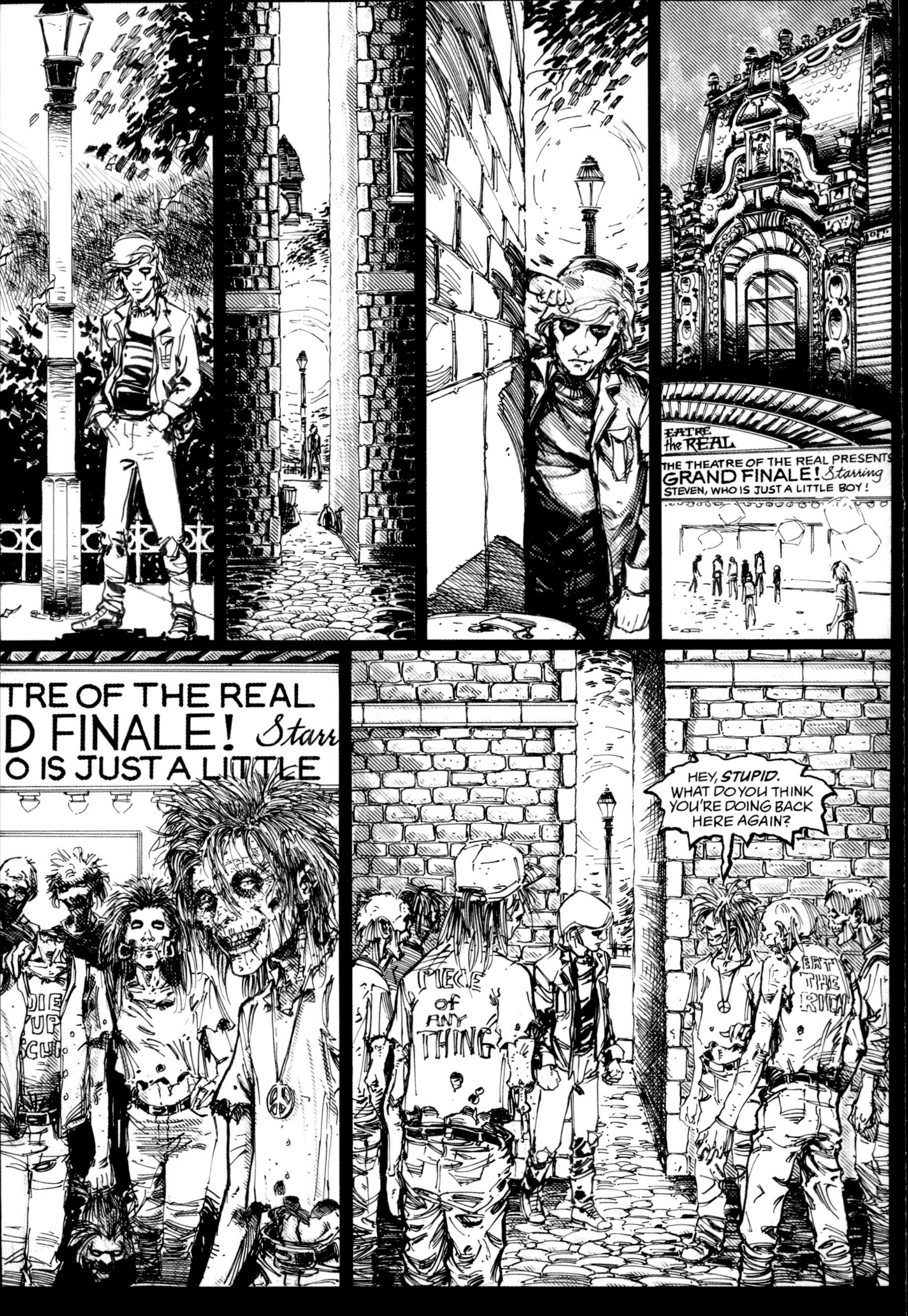
EATRE the REAL
THE THEATRE OF THE REAL PRESENTS
GRAND FINALE! Starring
STEVEN, WHO IS JUST A LITTLE BOY!
TRE OF THE REAL
D FINALE! Starr
O IS JUST A LITTLE
PIECE of ANY THING
EAT THE RICH
HEY, STUPID. WHAT DO YOU THINK YOU'RE DOING BACK HERE AGAIN?

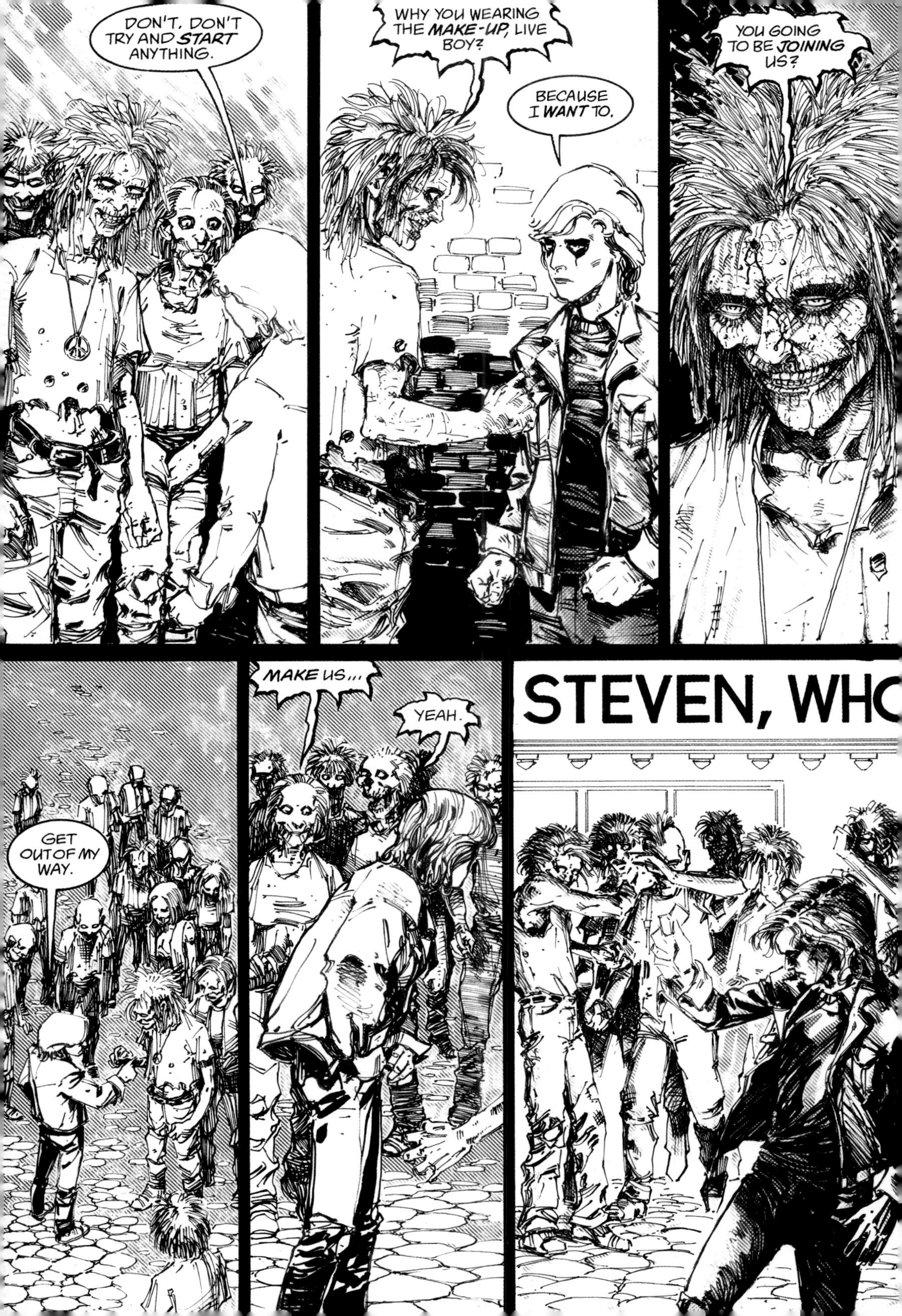
DON'T. DON'T TRY AND START ANYTHING.
WHY YOU WEARING THE MAKE-UP, LIVE BOY?
BECAUSE I WANT TO.
YOU GOING TO BE JOINING US?
GET OUT OF MY WAY.
MAKE US...
YEAH.
STEVEN, WHO

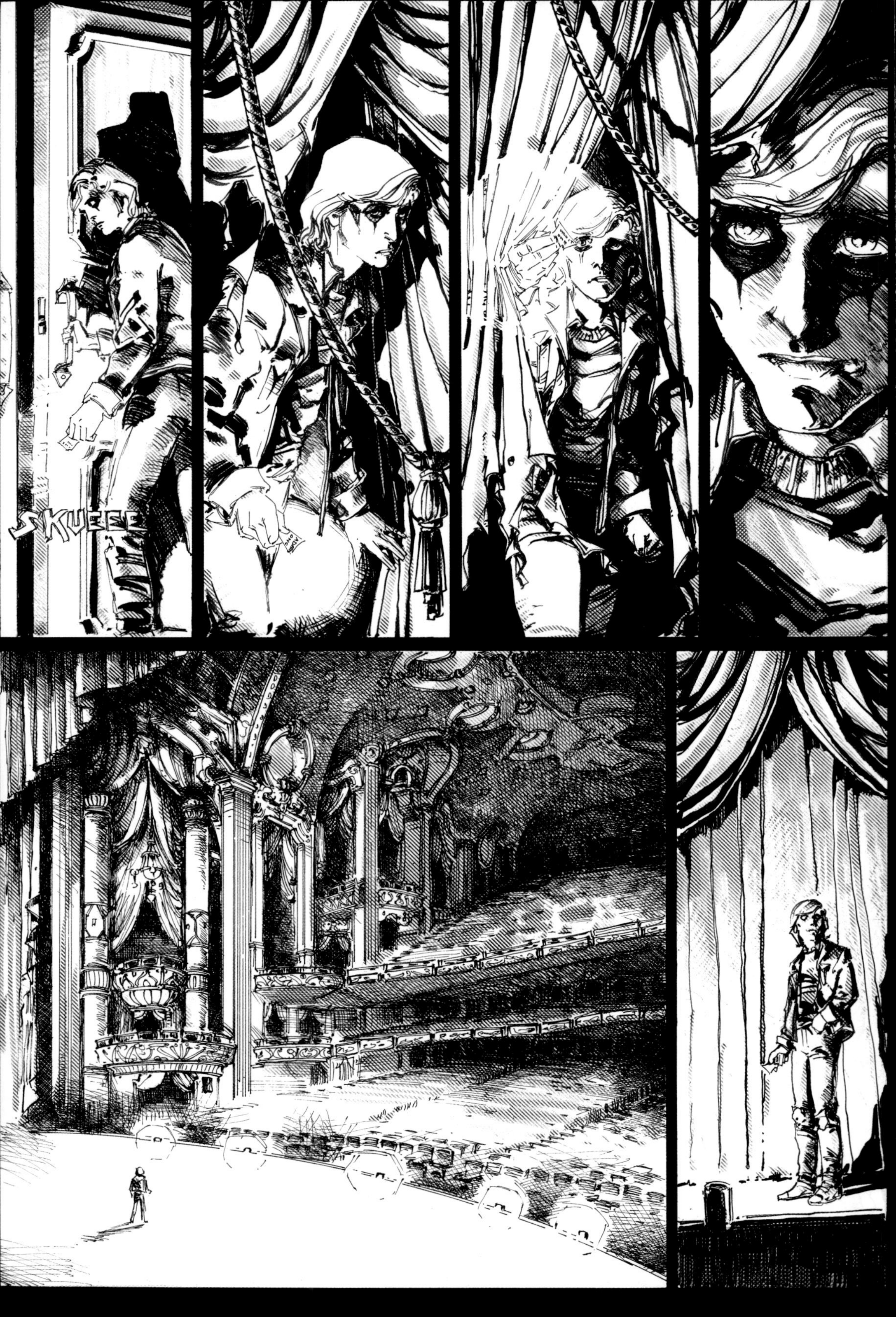
SKUEEE

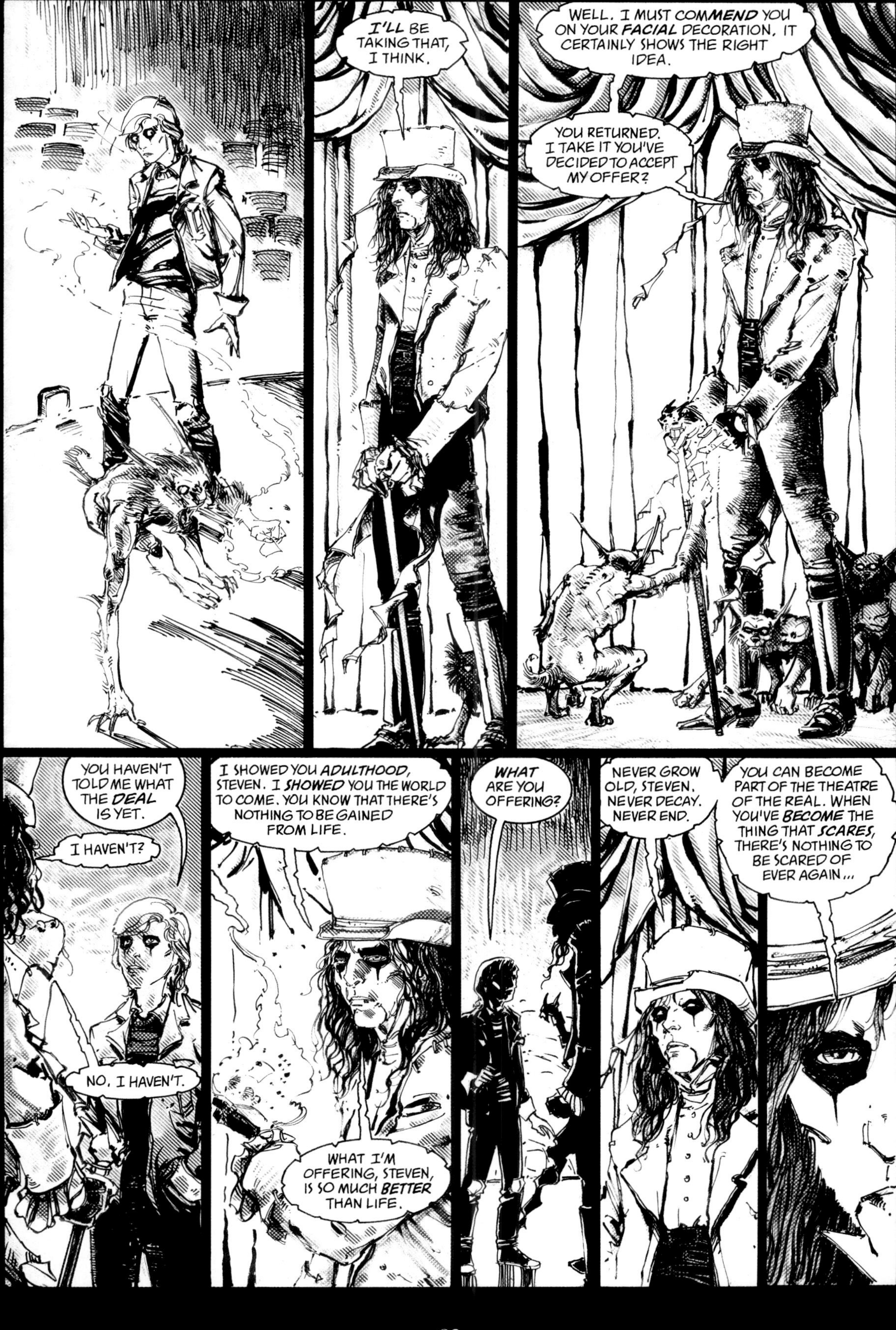

I'LL BE TAKING THAT, I THINK.
WELL, I MUST COMMEND YOU ON YOUR FACIAL DECORATION. IT CERTAINLY SHOWS THE RIGHT IDEA.
YOU RETURNED. I TAKE IT YOU'VE DECIDED TO ACCEPT MY OFFER?
YOU HAVEN'T TOLD ME WHAT THE DEAL IS YET.
I HAVEN'T?
NO, I HAVEN'T.
I SHOWED YOU ADULTHOOD, STEVEN. I SHOWED YOU THE WORLD TO COME. YOU KNOW THAT THERE'S NOTHING TO BE GAINED FROM LIFE.
WHAT I'M OFFERING, STEVEN, IS SO MUCH BETTER THAN LIFE.
WHAT ARE YOU OFFERING?
NEVER GROW OLD, STEVEN. NEVER DECAY. NEVER END.
YOU CAN BECOME PART OF THE THEATRE OF THE REAL. WHEN YOU'VE BECOME THE THING THAT SCARES, THERE'S NOTHING TO BE SCARED OF EVER AGAIN...

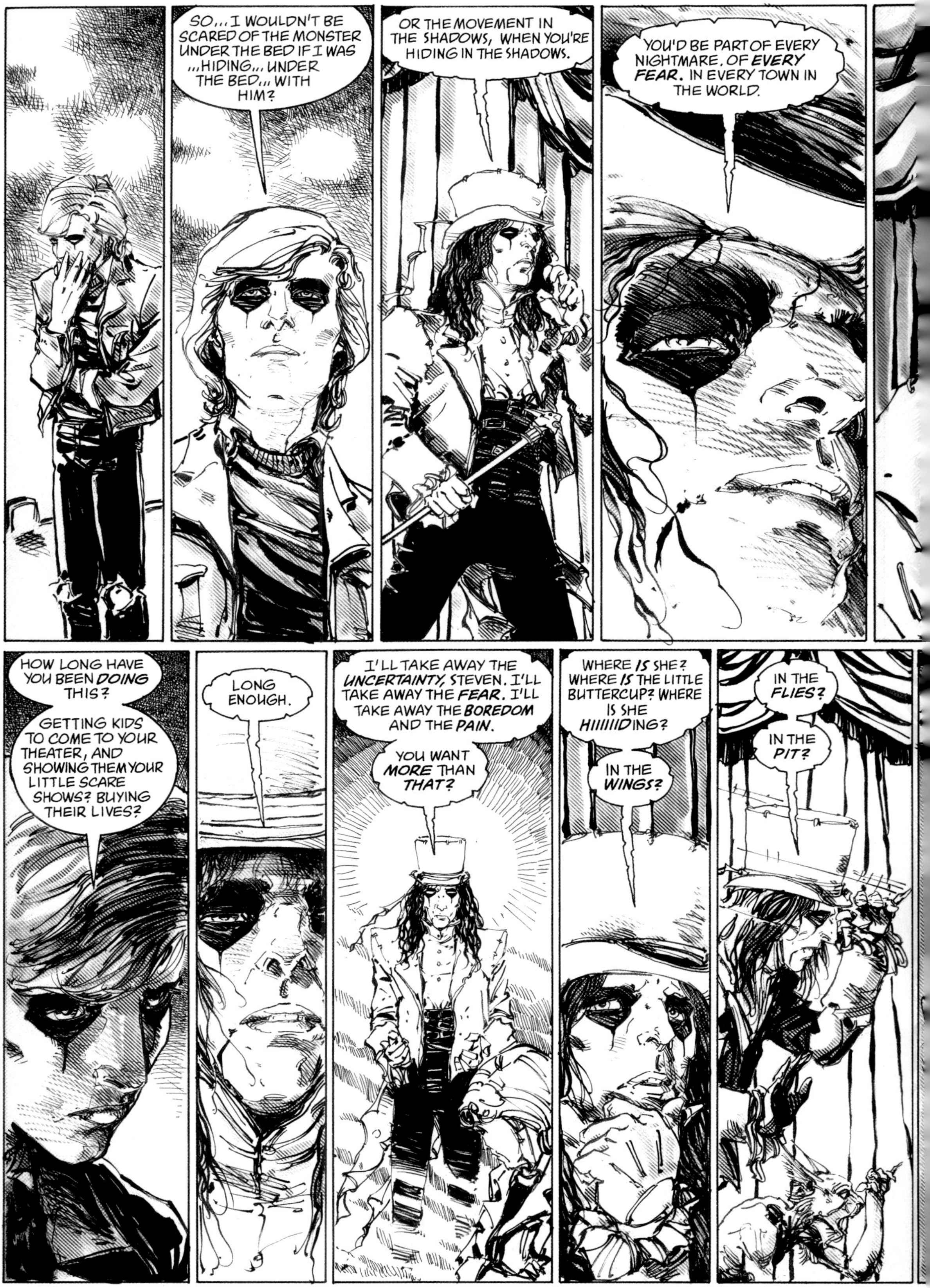
SO,.. I WOULDN'T BE SCARED OF THE MONSTER UNDER THE BED IF I WAS ..HIDING... UNDER THE BED... WITH HIM?
OR THE MOVEMENT IN THE SHADOWS, WHEN YOU'RE HIDING IN THE SHADOWS.
YOU'D BE PART OF EVERY NIGHTMARE. OF EVERY FEAR. IN EVERY TOWN IN THE WORLD.
HOW LONG HAVE YOU BEEN DOING THIS?
GETTING KIDS TO COME TO YOUR THEATER, AND SHOWING THEM YOUR LITTLE SCARE SHOWS? BUYING THEIR LIVES?
LONG ENOUGH.
I'LL TAKE AWAY THE UNCERTAINTY, STEVEN. I'LL TAKE AWAY THE FEAR. I'LL TAKE AWAY THE BOREDOM AND THE PAIN.
YOU WANT MORE THAN THAT?
WHERE IS SHE? WHERE IS THE LITTLE BUTTERCUP? WHERE IS SHE HIIIIIIDING?
IN THE WINGS?
IN THE FLIES?
IN THE PIT?

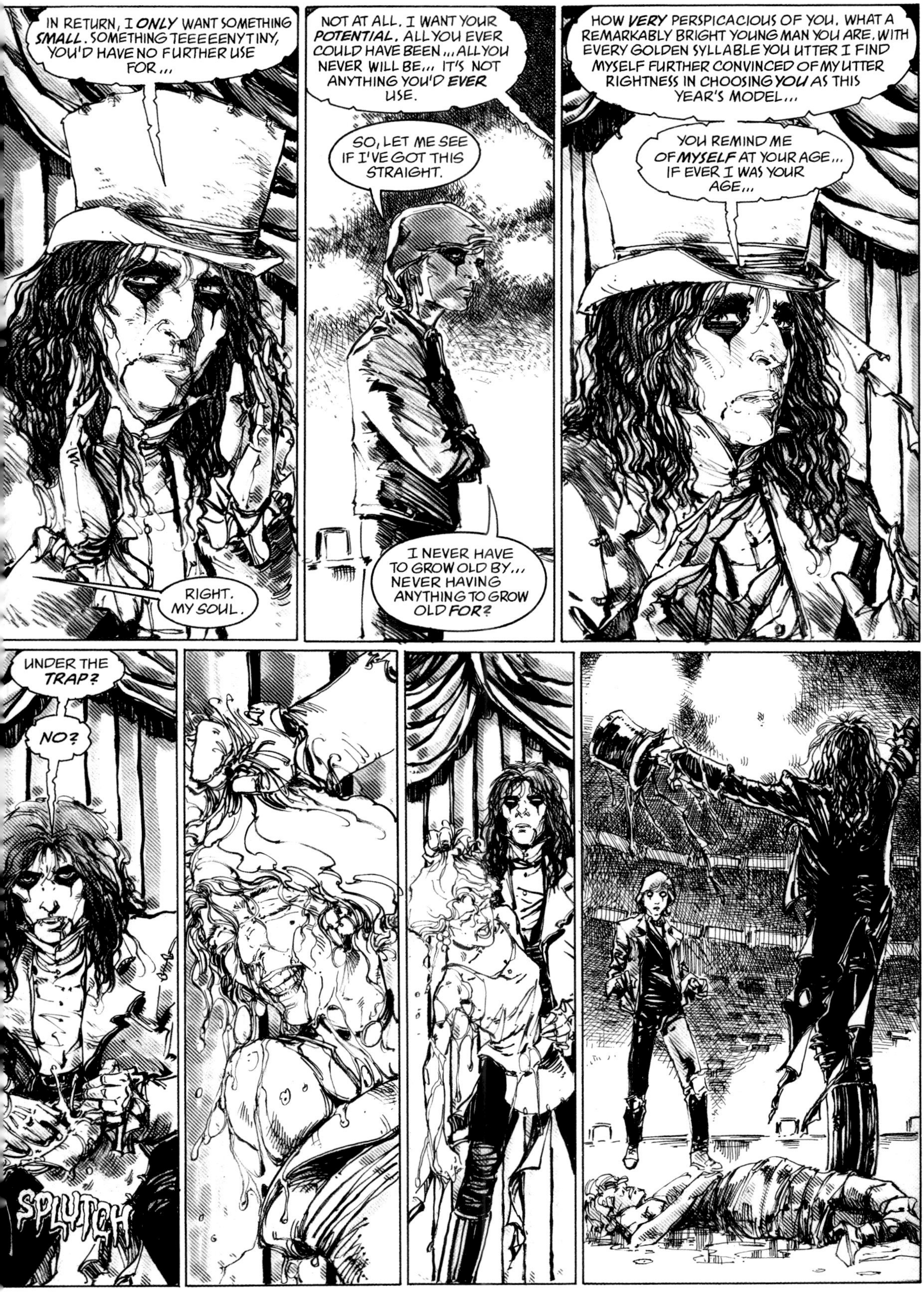
IN RETURN, I ONLY WANT SOMETHING SMALL. SOMETHING TEEEEENYTINY, YOU'D HAVE NO FURTHER USE FOR...
RIGHT. MY SOUL.
NOT AT ALL. I WANT YOUR POTENTIAL. ALL YOU EVER COULD HAVE BEEN... ALL YOU NEVER WILL BE... IT'S NOT ANYTHING YOU'D EVER USE.
SO, LET ME SEE IF I'VE GOT THIS STRAIGHT.
I NEVER HAVE TO GROW OLD BY... NEVER HAVING ANYTHING TO GROW OLD FOR?
HOW VERY PERSPICACIOUS OF YOU. WHAT A REMARKABLY BRIGHT YOUNG MAN YOU ARE. WITH EVERY GOLDEN SYLLABLE YOU UTTER I FIND MYSELF FURTHER CONVINCED OF MY UTTER RIGHTNESS IN CHOOSING YOU AS THIS YEAR'S MODEL...
YOU REMIND ME OF MYSELF AT YOUR AGE... IF EVER I WAS YOUR AGE...
UNDER THE TRAP?
NO?
SPLUTCH

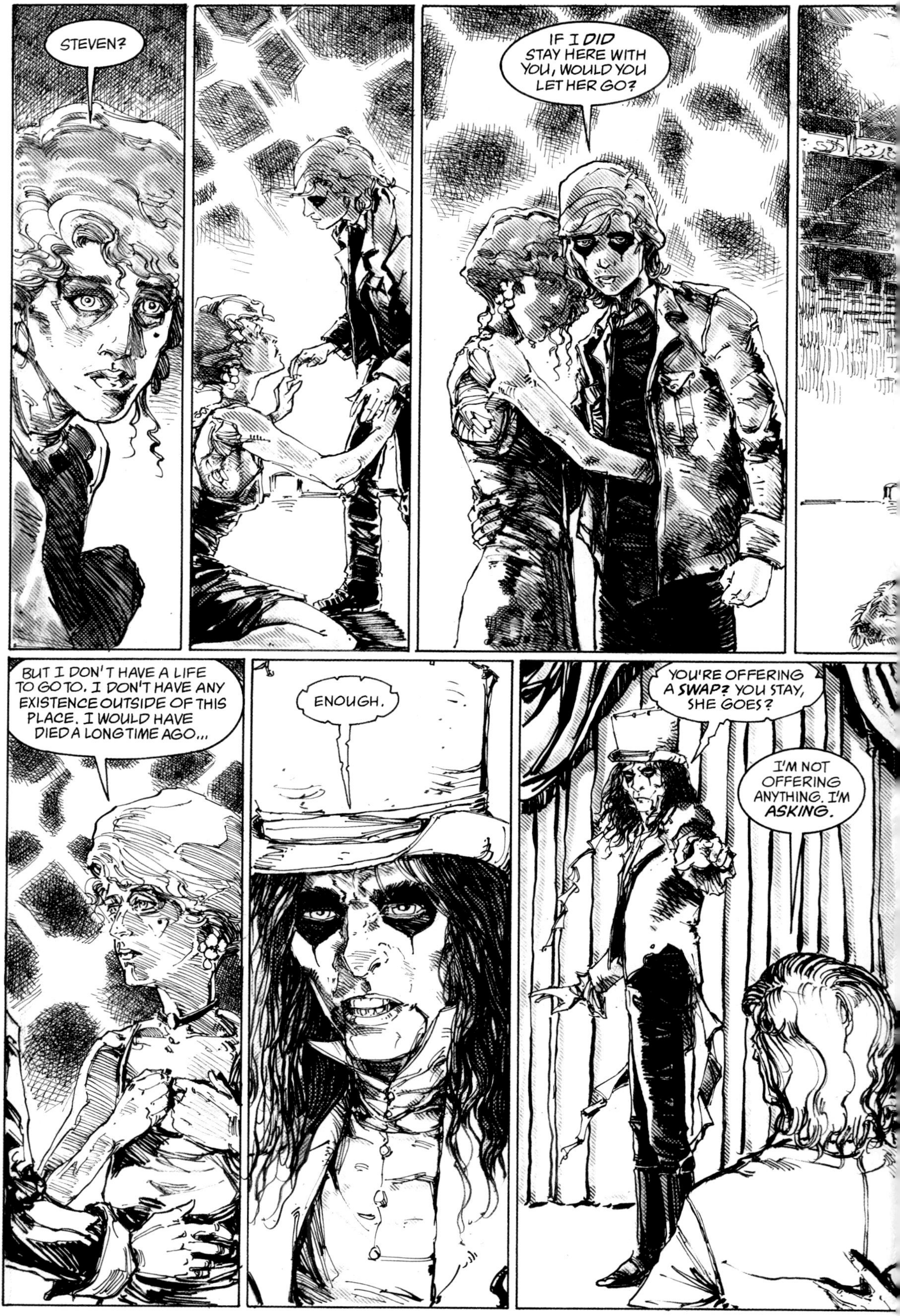
STEVEN?
IF I DID STAY HERE WITH YOU, WOULD YOU LET HER GO?
BUT I DON'T HAVE A LIFE TO GO TO. I DON'T HAVE ANY EXISTENCE OUTSIDE OF THIS PLACE. I WOULD HAVE DIED A LONG TIME AGO...
ENOUGH.
YOU'RE OFFERING A SWAP? YOU STAY, SHE GOES?
I'M NOT OFFERING ANYTHING. I'M ASKING.

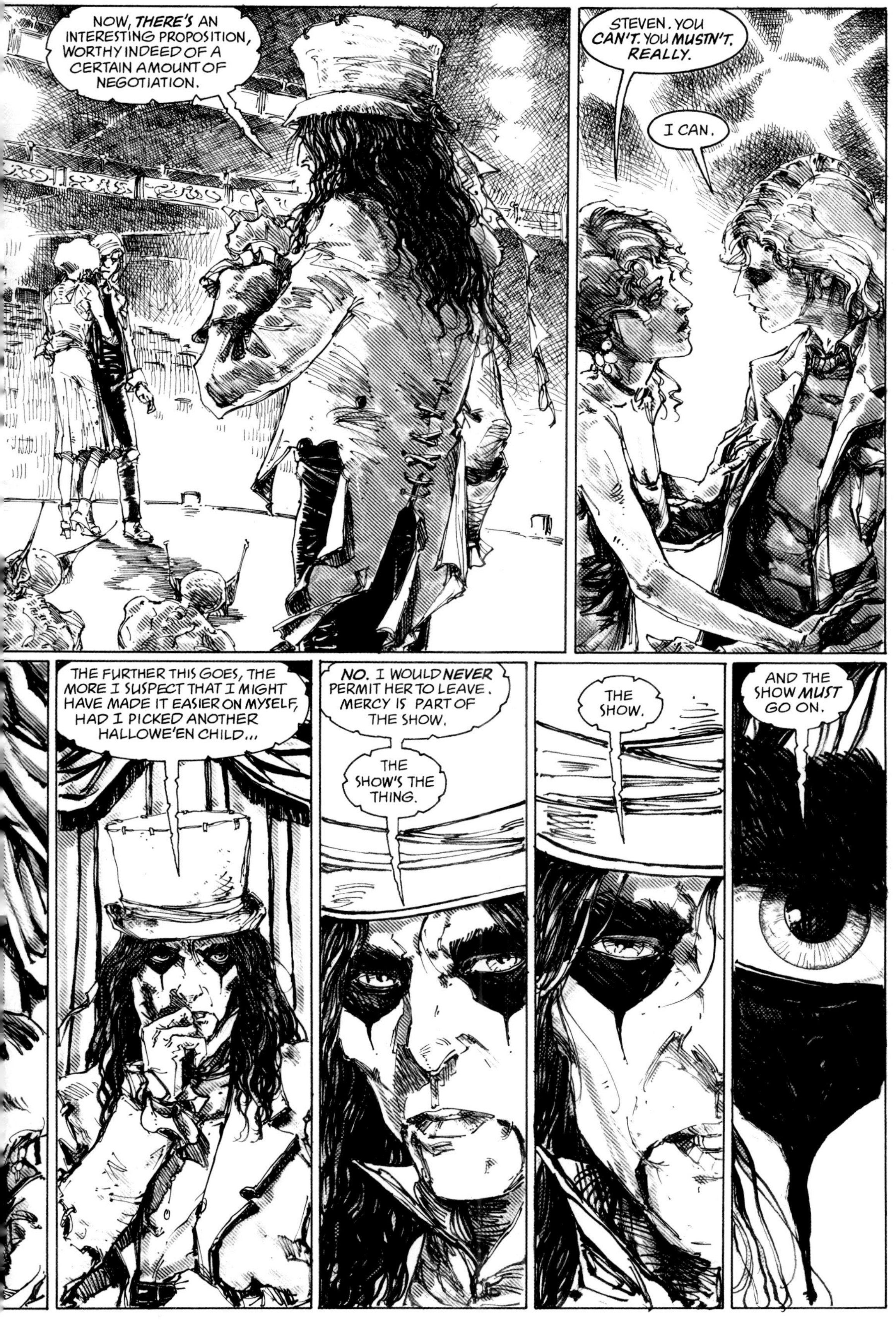
NOW, THERE'S AN INTERESTING PROPOSITION, WORTHY INDEED OF A CERTAIN AMOUNT OF NEGOTIATION.
STEVEN. YOU CAN'T. YOU MUSTN'T. REALLY.
I CAN.
THE FURTHER THIS GOES, THE MORE I SUSPECT THAT I MIGHT HAVE MADE IT EASIER ON MYSELF, HAD I PICKED ANOTHER HALLOWE'EN CHILD...
NO. I WOULD NEVER PERMIT HER TO LEAVE. MERCY IS PART OF THE SHOW.
THE SHOW'S THE THING.
THE SHOW.
AND THE SHOW MUST GO ON.

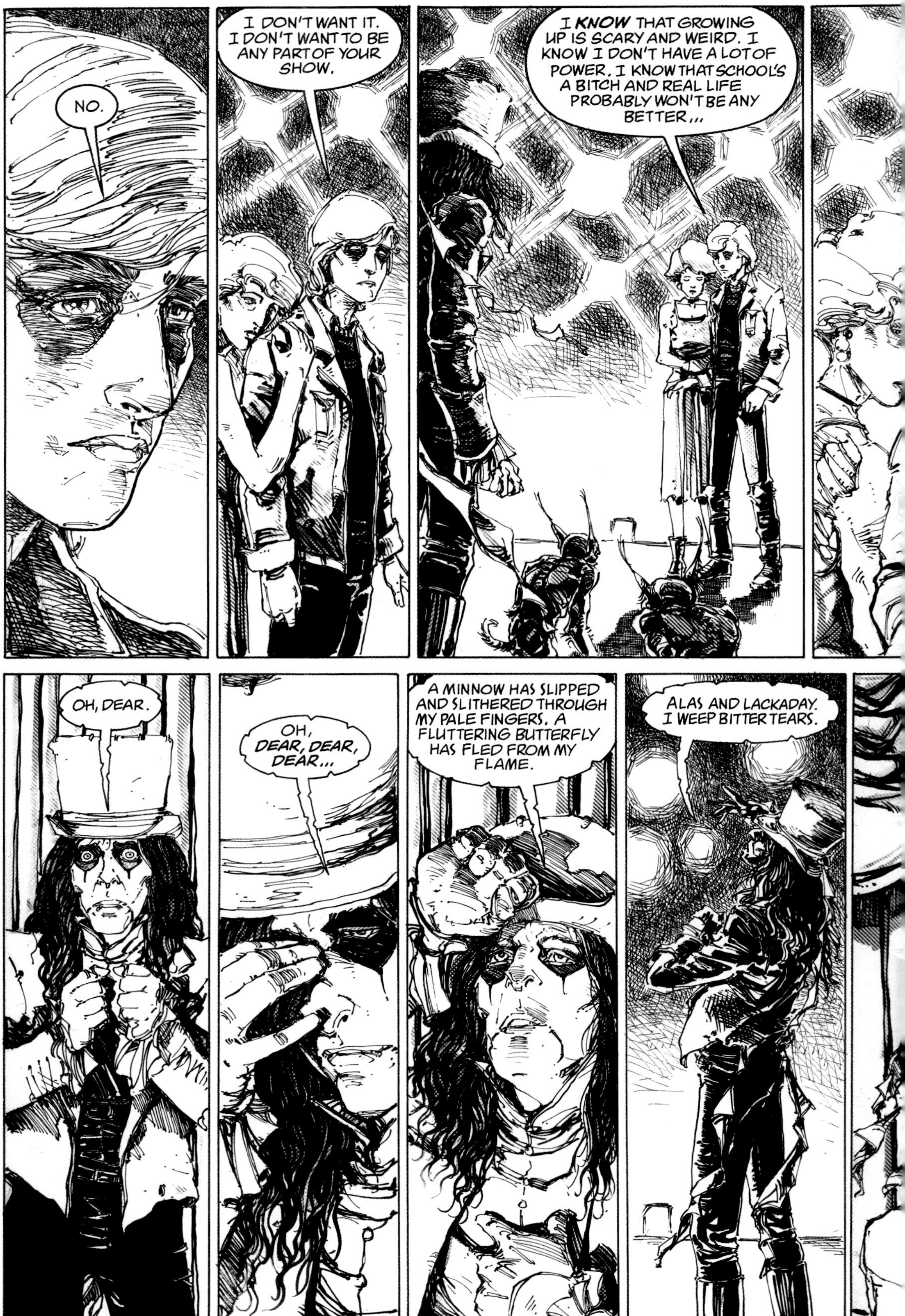
NO.
I DON'T WANT IT. I DON'T WANT TO BE ANY PART OF YOUR SHOW.
I **KNOW** THAT GROWING UP IS SCARY AND WEIRD. I KNOW I DON'T HAVE A LOT OF POWER. I KNOW THAT SCHOOL'S A BITCH AND REAL LIFE PROBABLY WON'T BE ANY BETTER...
OH, DEAR.
OH, ***DEAR, DEAR, DEAR***...
A MINNOW HAS SLIPPED AND SLITHERED THROUGH MY PALE FINGERS. A FLUTTERING BUTTERFLY HAS FLED FROM MY FLAME.
ALAS AND LACKADAY. I WEEP BITTER TEARS.

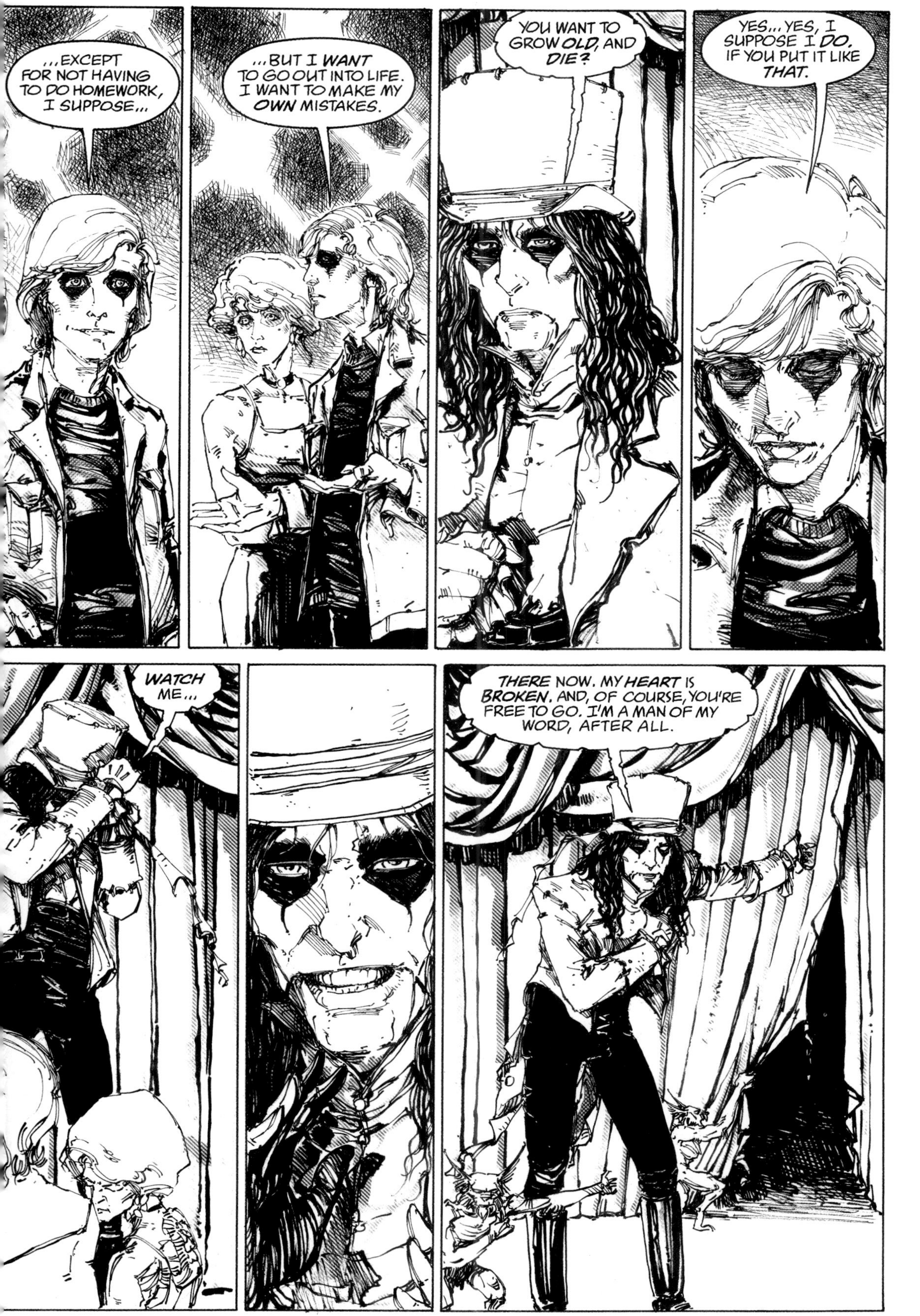
...EXCEPT FOR NOT HAVING TO DO HOMEWORK, I SUPPOSE...
...BUT I WANT TO GO OUT INTO LIFE. I WANT TO MAKE MY OWN MISTAKES.
YOU WANT TO GROW OLD, AND DIE?
YES... YES, I SUPPOSE I DO, IF YOU PUT IT LIKE THAT.
WATCH ME...
THERE NOW. MY HEART IS BROKEN. AND, OF COURSE, YOU'RE FREE TO GO. I'M A MAN OF MY WORD, AFTER ALL.

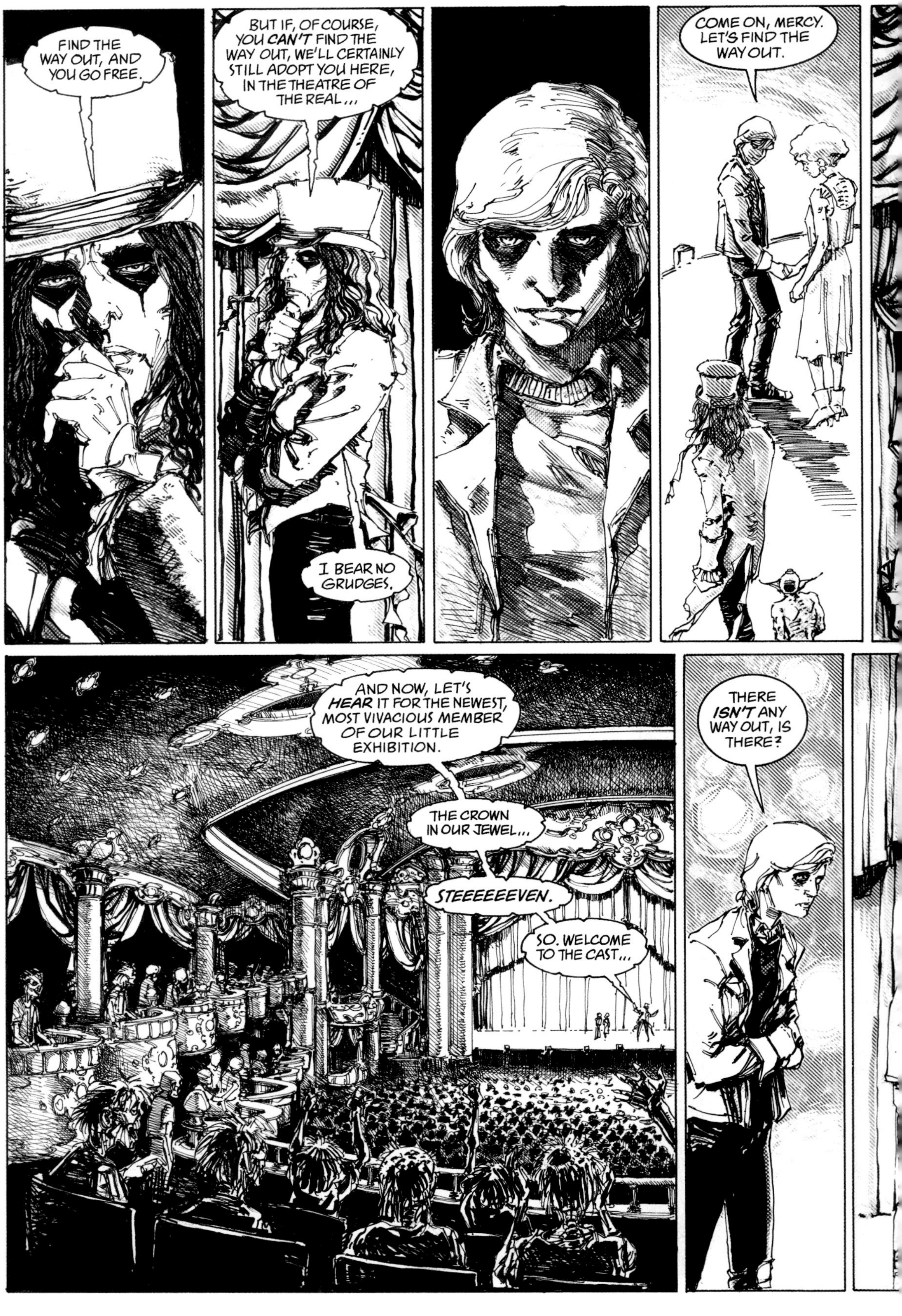
FIND THE WAY OUT, AND YOU GO FREE.
BUT IF, OF COURSE, YOU CAN'T FIND THE WAY OUT, WE'LL CERTAINLY STILL ADOPT YOU HERE, IN THE THEATRE OF THE REAL...
I BEAR NO GRUDGES.
COME ON, MERCY. LET'S FIND THE WAY OUT.
AND NOW, LET'S HEAR IT FOR THE NEWEST, MOST VIVACIOUS MEMBER OF OUR LITTLE EXHIBITION.
THE CROWN IN OUR JEWEL...
STEEEEEEVEN.
SO. WELCOME TO THE CAST...
THERE ISN'T ANY WAY OUT, IS THERE?

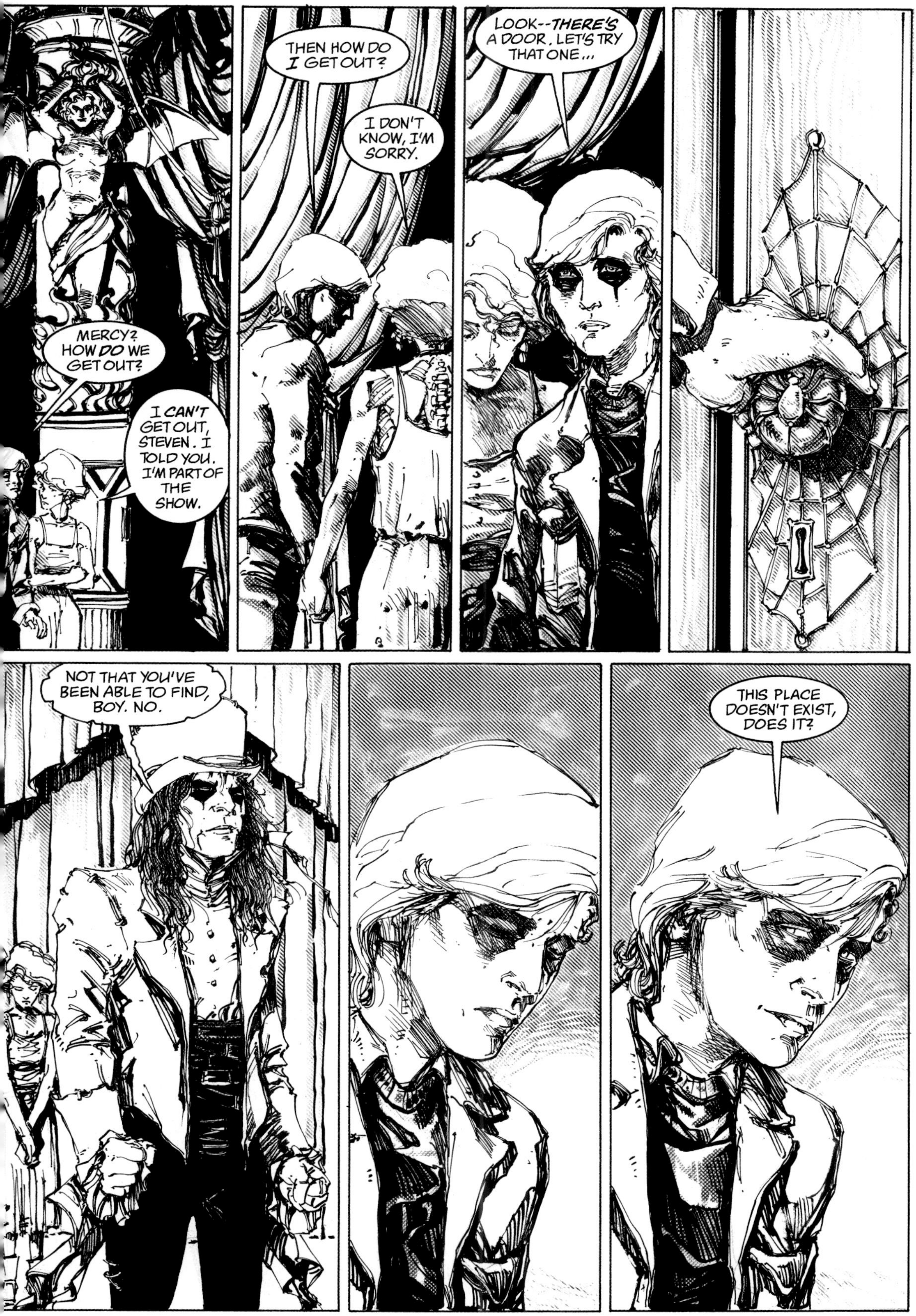
MERCY? HOW DO WE GET OUT?
I CAN'T GET OUT, STEVEN. I TOLD YOU. I'M PART OF THE SHOW.
THEN HOW DO I GET OUT?
I DON'T KNOW, I'M SORRY.
LOOK--THERE'S A DOOR. LET'S TRY THAT ONE...
NOT THAT YOU'VE BEEN ABLE TO FIND, BOY. NO.
THIS PLACE DOESN'T EXIST, DOES IT?

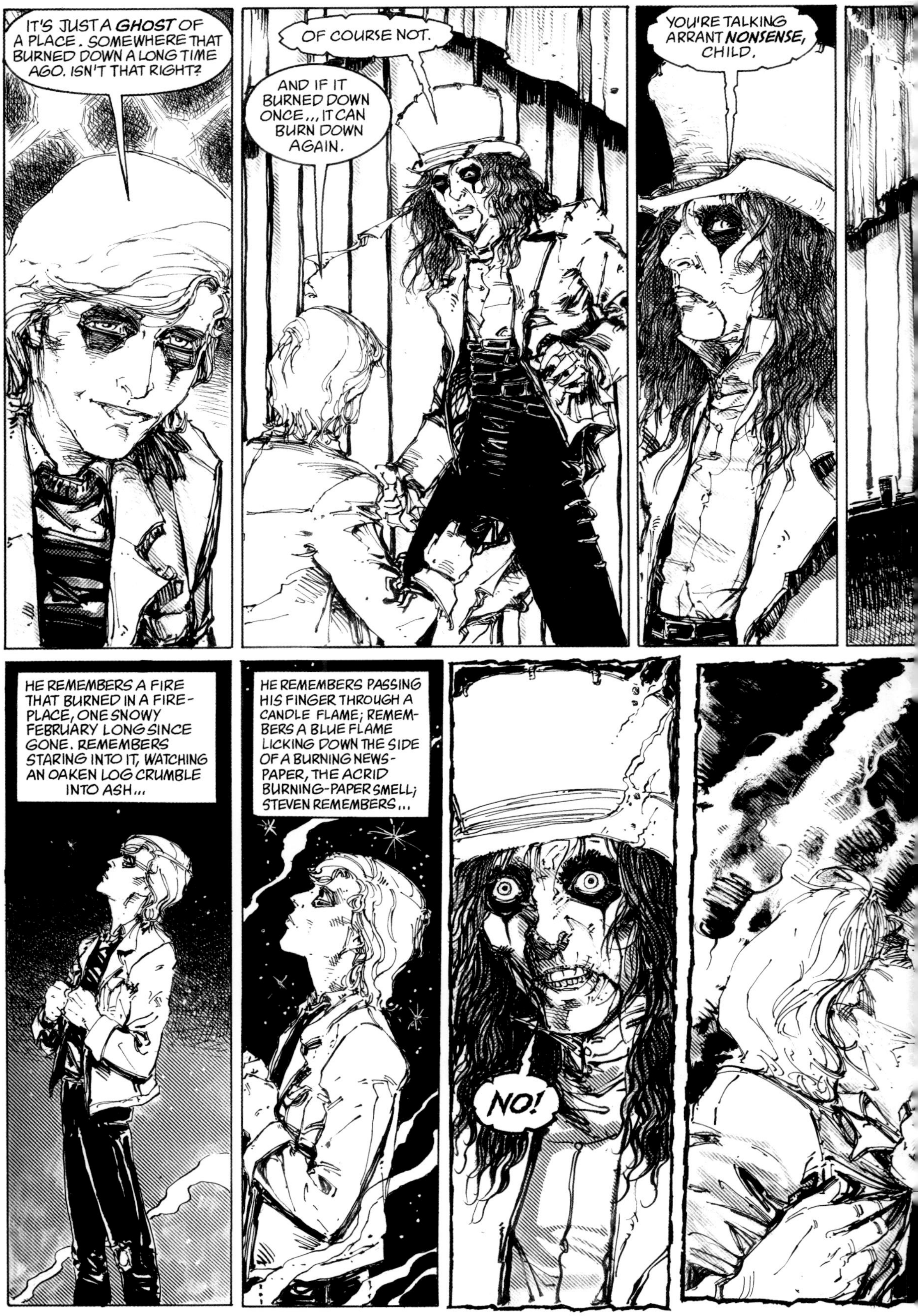
IT'S JUST A GHOST OF A PLACE. SOMEWHERE THAT BURNED DOWN A LONG TIME AGO. ISN'T THAT RIGHT?
OF COURSE NOT.
AND IF IT BURNED DOWN ONCE,,, IT CAN BURN DOWN AGAIN.
YOU'RE TALKING ARRANT NONSENSE, CHILD.
HE REMEMBERS A FIRE THAT BURNED IN A FIRE-PLACE, ONE SNOWY FEBRUARY LONG SINCE GONE. REMEMBERS STARING INTO IT, WATCHING AN OAKEN LOG CRUMBLE INTO ASH...
HE REMEMBERS PASSING HIS FINGER THROUGH A CANDLE FLAME; REMEM-BERS A BLUE FLAME LICKING DOWN THE SIDE OF A BURNING NEWS-PAPER, THE ACRID BURNING-PAPER SMELL; STEVEN REMEMBERS...
NO!

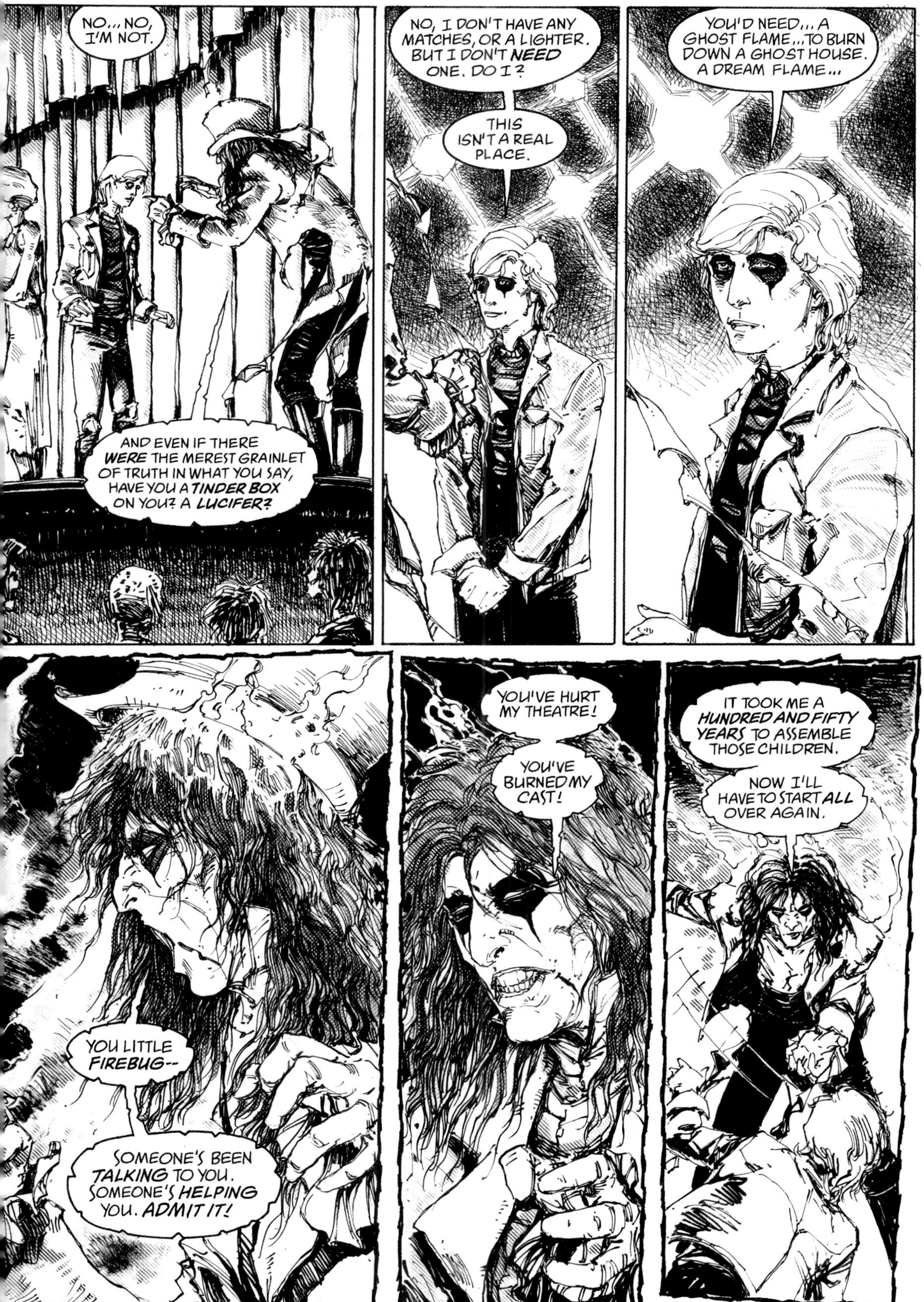
NO... NO, I'M NOT.
AND EVEN IF THERE WERE THE MEREST GRAINLET OF TRUTH IN WHAT YOU SAY, HAVE YOU A TINDER BOX ON YOU? A LUCIFER?
NO, I DON'T HAVE ANY MATCHES, OR A LIGHTER. BUT I DON'T NEED ONE. DO I?
THIS ISN'T A REAL PLACE.
YOU'D NEED... A GHOST FLAME... TO BURN DOWN A GHOST HOUSE. A DREAM FLAME...
YOU LITTLE FIREBUG--
SOMEONE'S BEEN TALKING TO YOU. SOMEONE'S HELPING YOU. ADMIT IT!
YOU'VE HURT MY THEATRE!
YOU'VE BURNED MY CAST!
IT TOOK ME A HUNDRED AND FIFTY YEARS TO ASSEMBLE THOSE CHILDREN.
NOW I'LL HAVE TO START ALL OVER AGAIN.

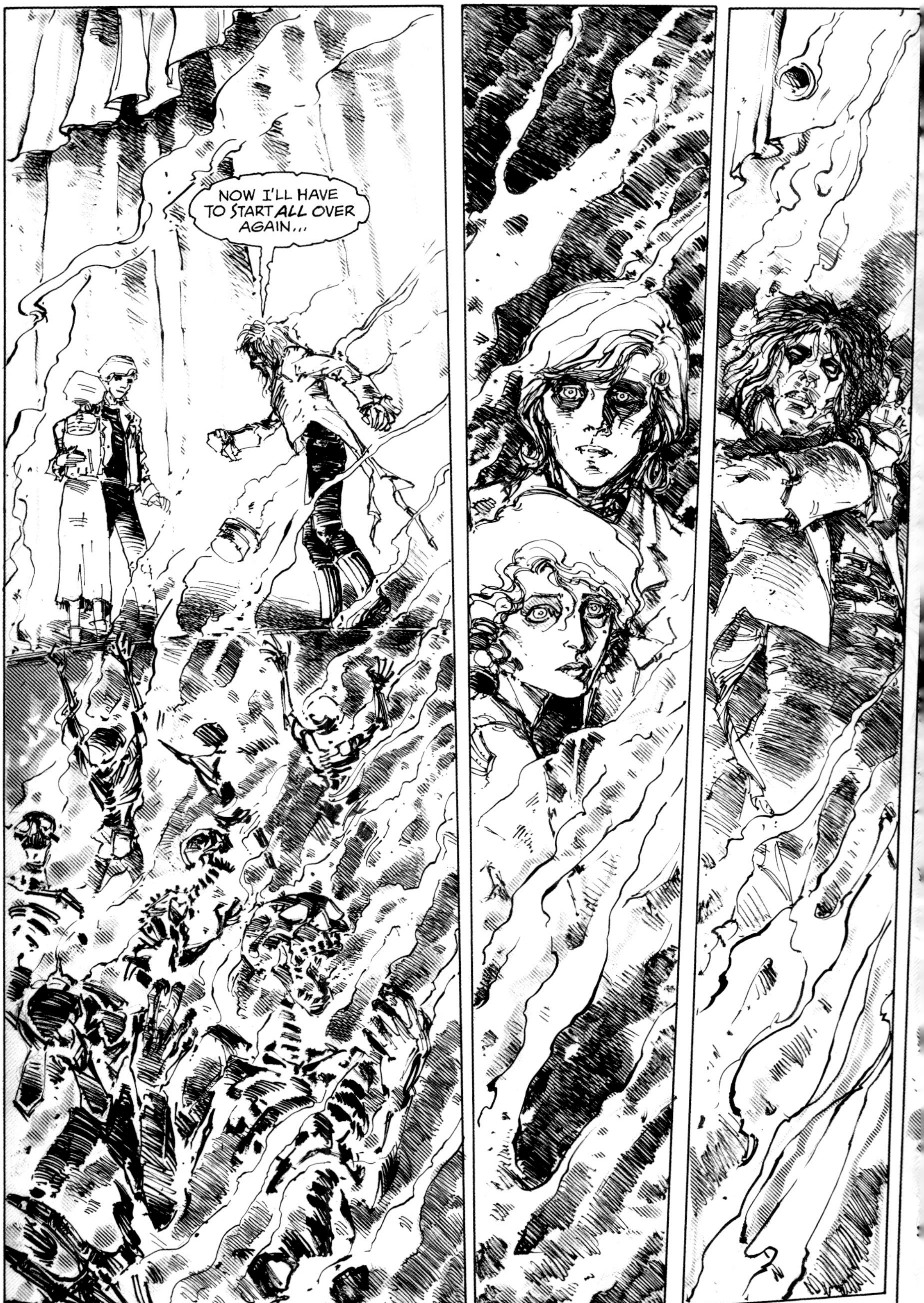
NOW I'LL HAVE TO START ALL OVER AGAIN...

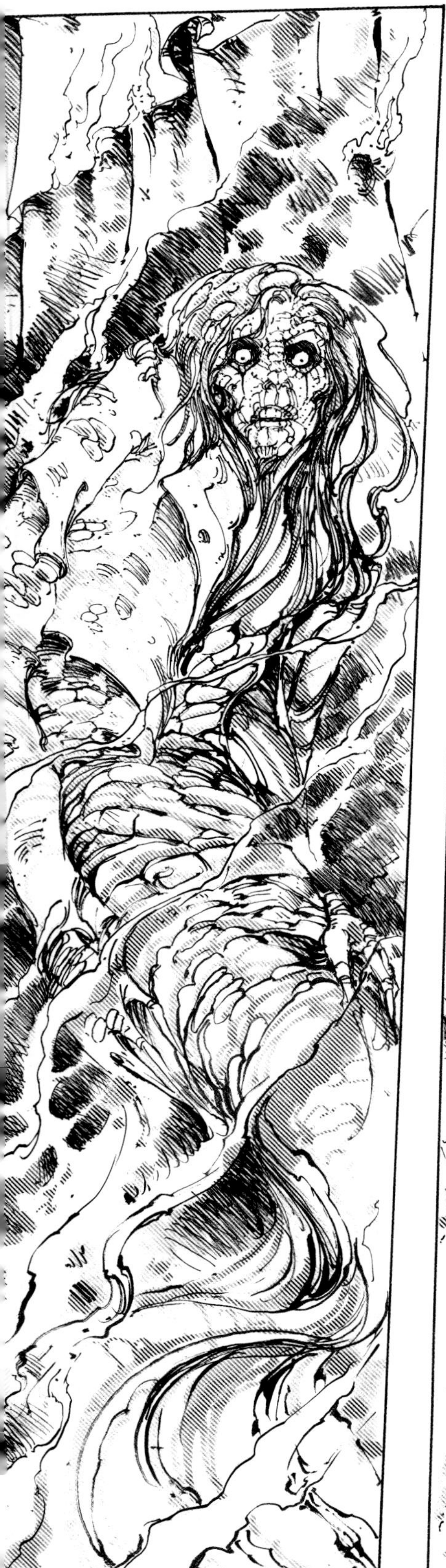

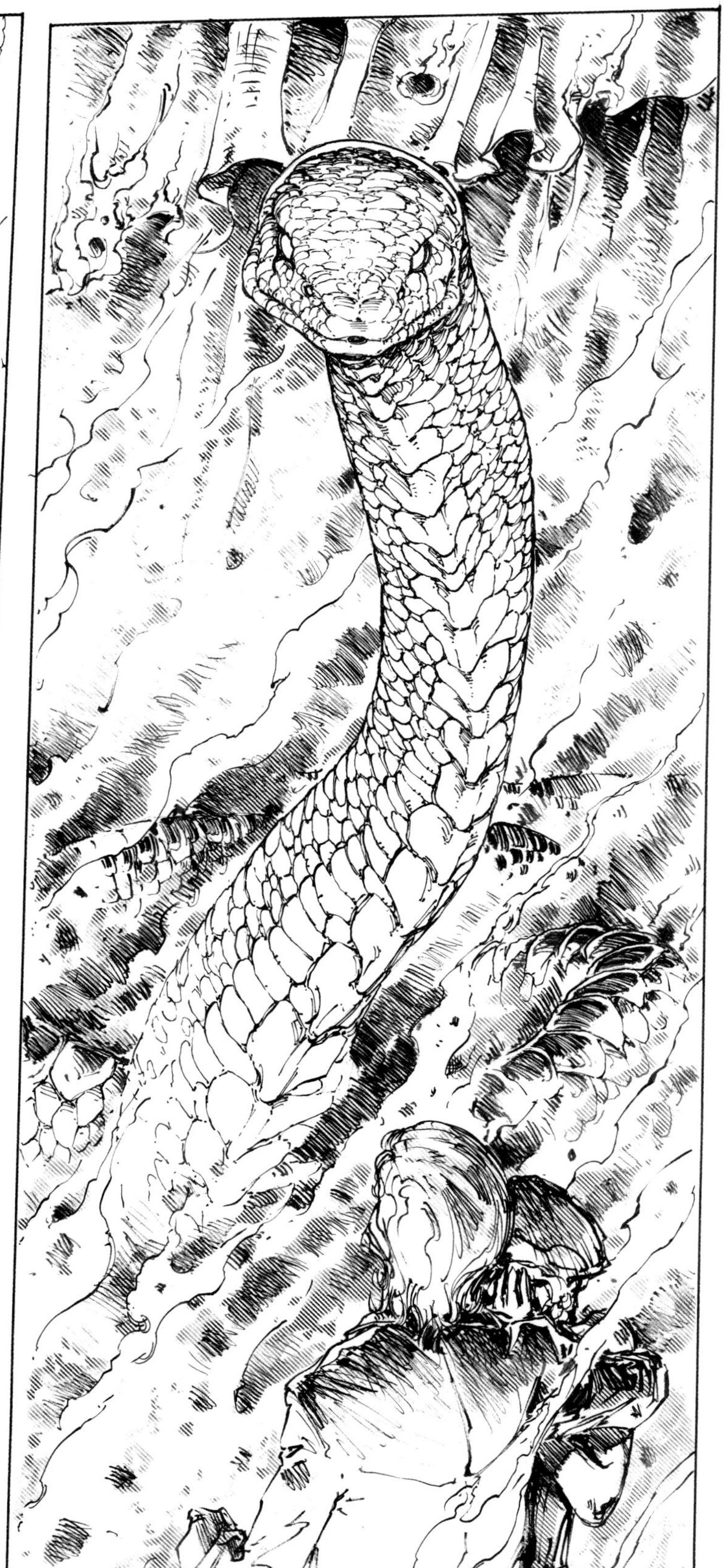

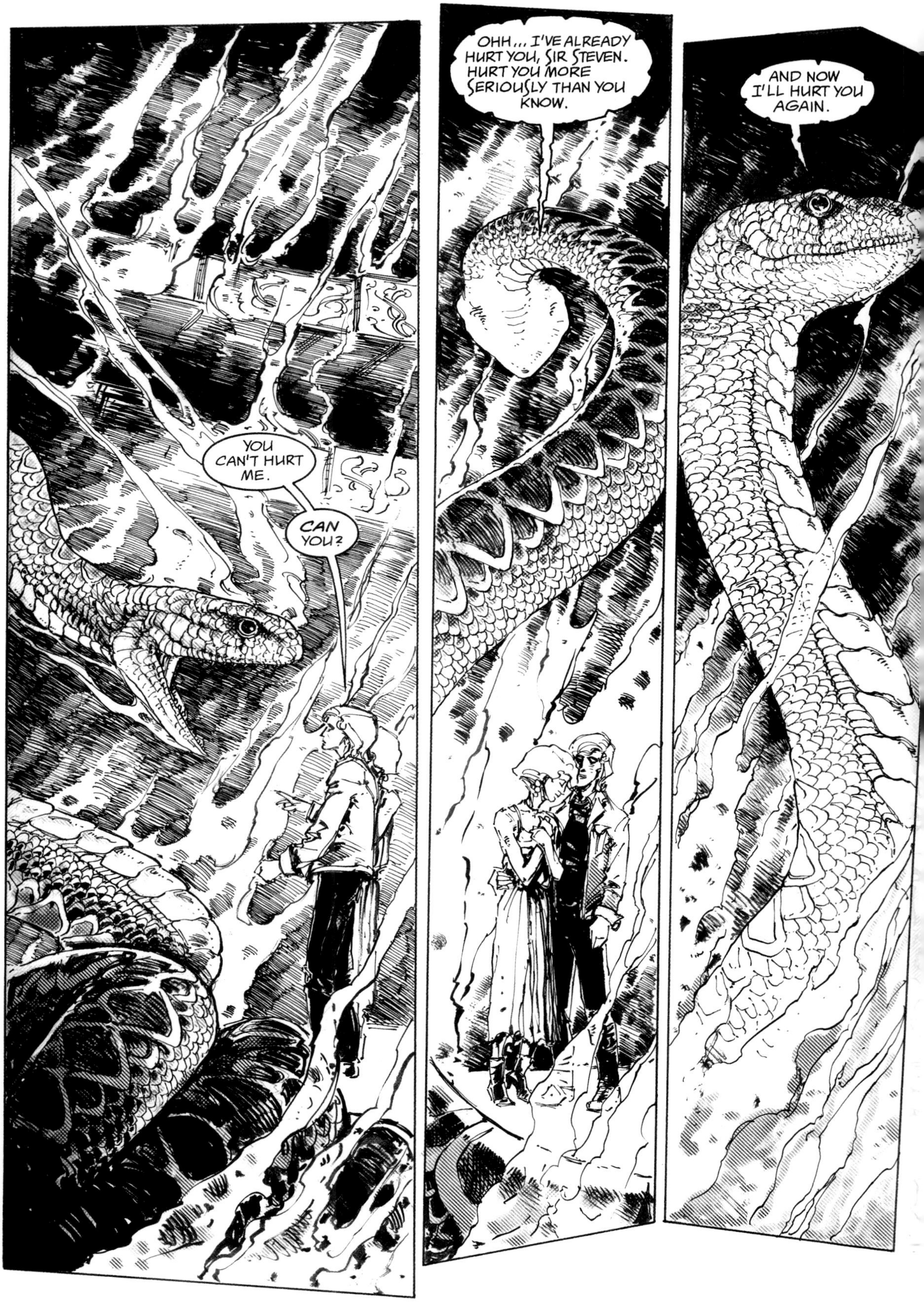
YOU CAN'T HURT ME.
CAN YOU?
OHH... I'VE ALREADY HURT YOU, SIR STEVEN. HURT YOU MORE SERIOUSLY THAN YOU KNOW.
AND NOW I'LL HURT YOU AGAIN.

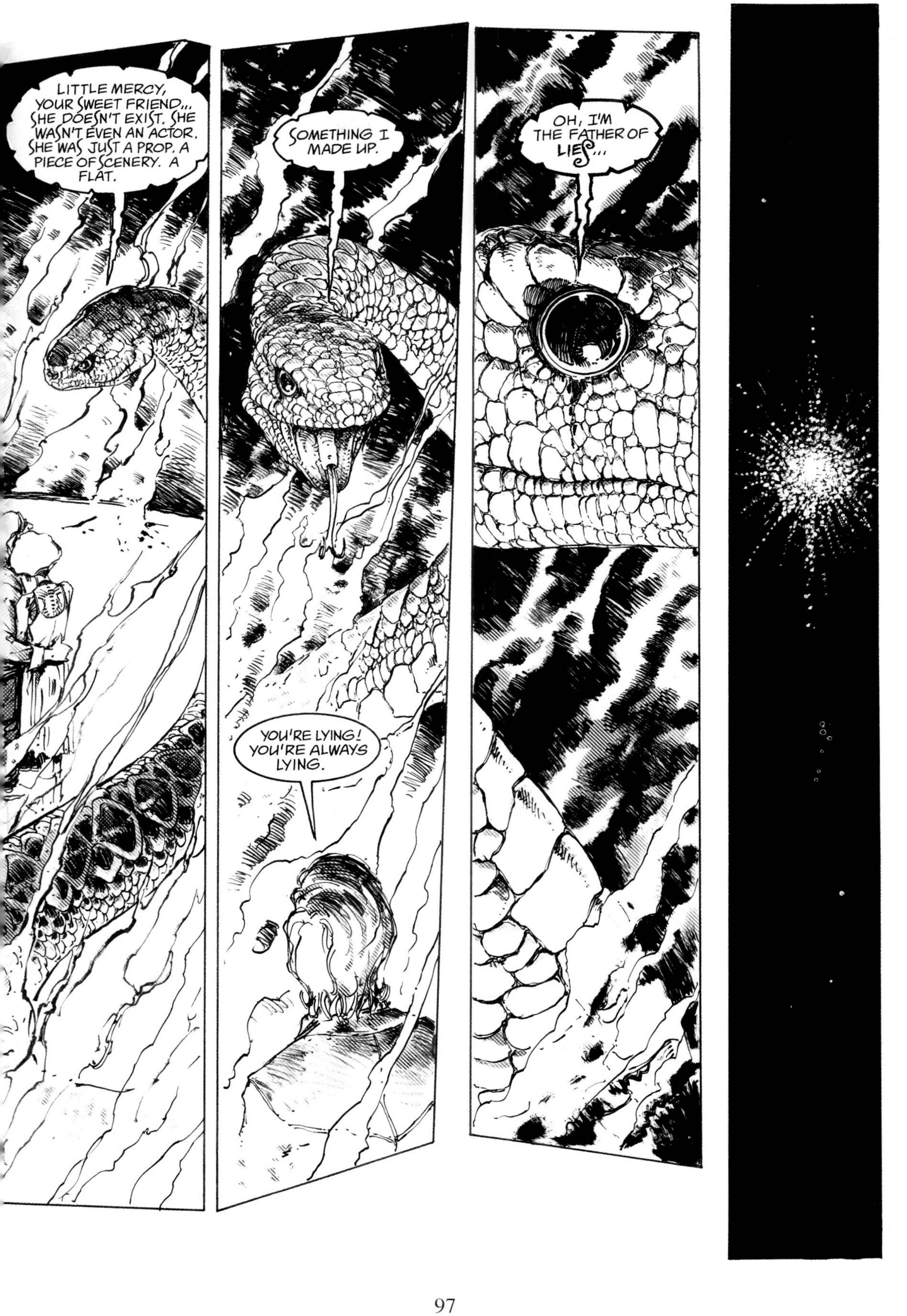
LITTLE MERCY, YOUR SWEET FRIEND... SHE DOESN'T EXIST. SHE WASN'T EVEN AN ACTOR. SHE WAS JUST A PROP. A PIECE OF SCENERY. A FLAT.
SOMETHING I MADE UP.
YOU'RE LYING! YOU'RE ALWAYS LYING.
OH, I'M THE FATHER OF LIES...

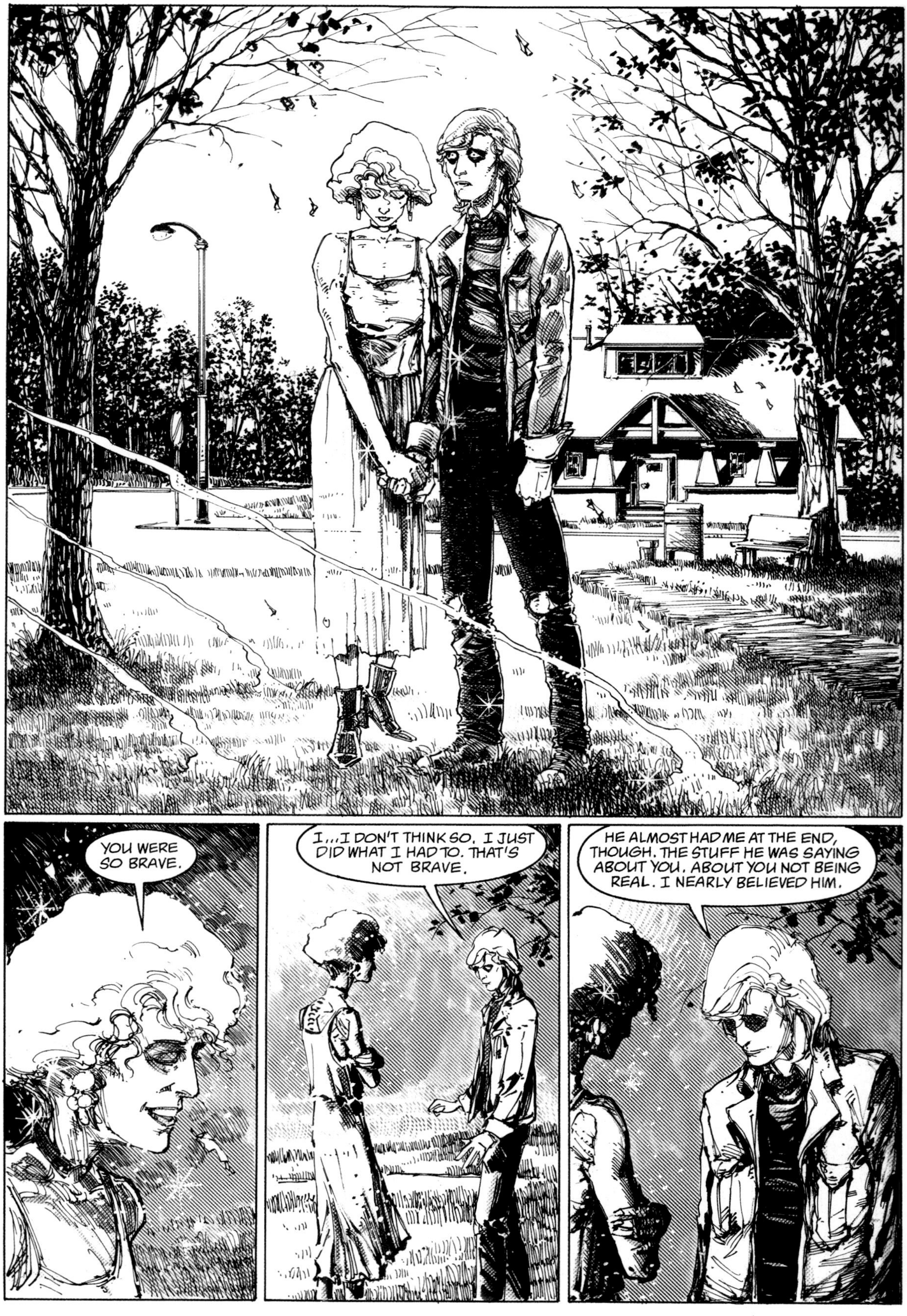
YOU WERE SO BRAVE.
I...I DON'T THINK SO. I JUST DID WHAT I HAD TO. THAT'S NOT BRAVE.
HE ALMOST HAD ME AT THE END, THOUGH. THE STUFF HE WAS SAYING ABOUT YOU. ABOUT YOU NOT BEING REAL. I NEARLY BELIEVED HIM.

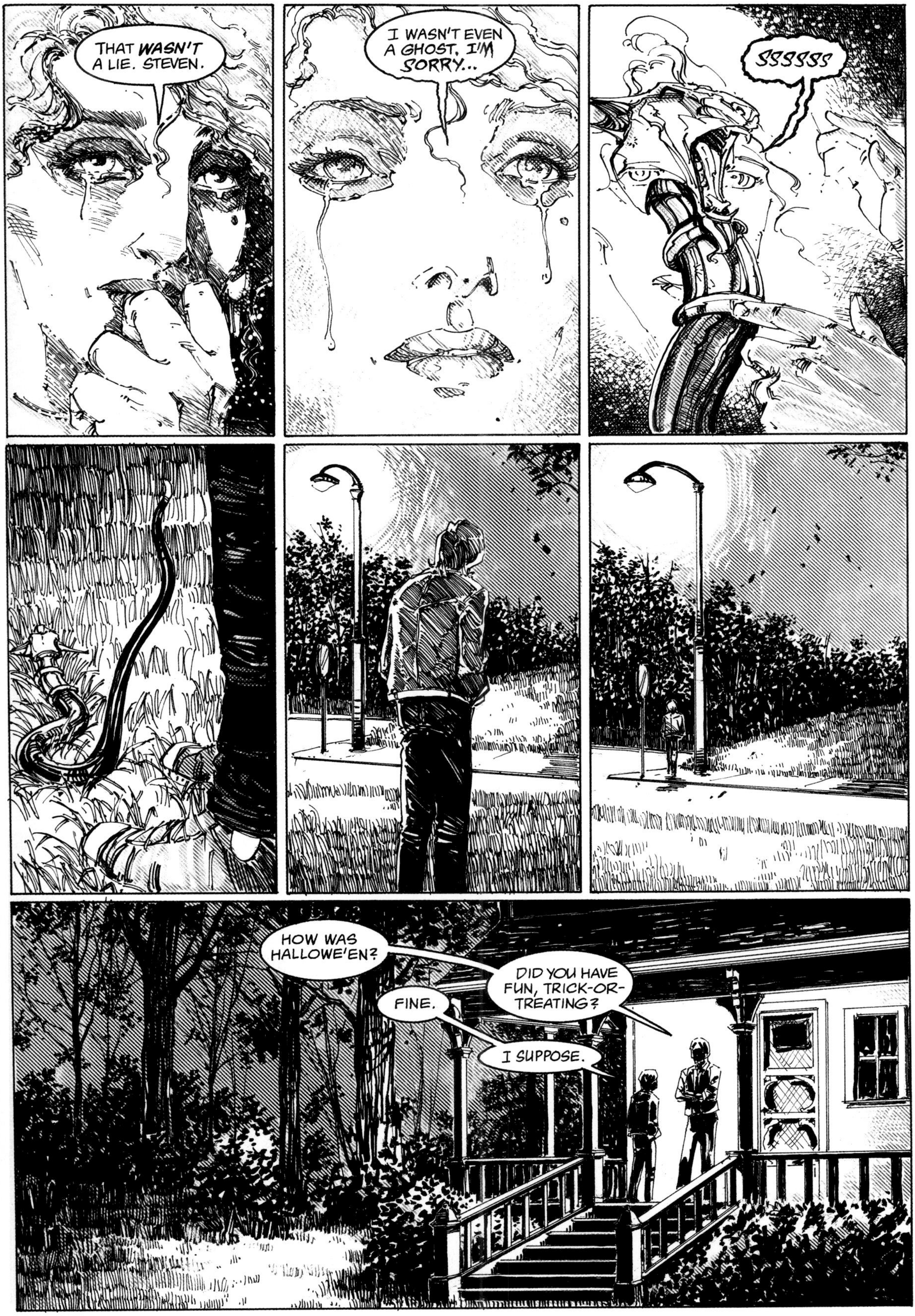
THAT WASN'T A LIE. STEVEN.
I WASN'T EVEN A GHOST, I'M SORRY...
SSSSSS
HOW WAS HALLOWE'EN?
DID YOU HAVE FUN, TRICK-OR-TREATING?
FINE.
I SUPPOSE.

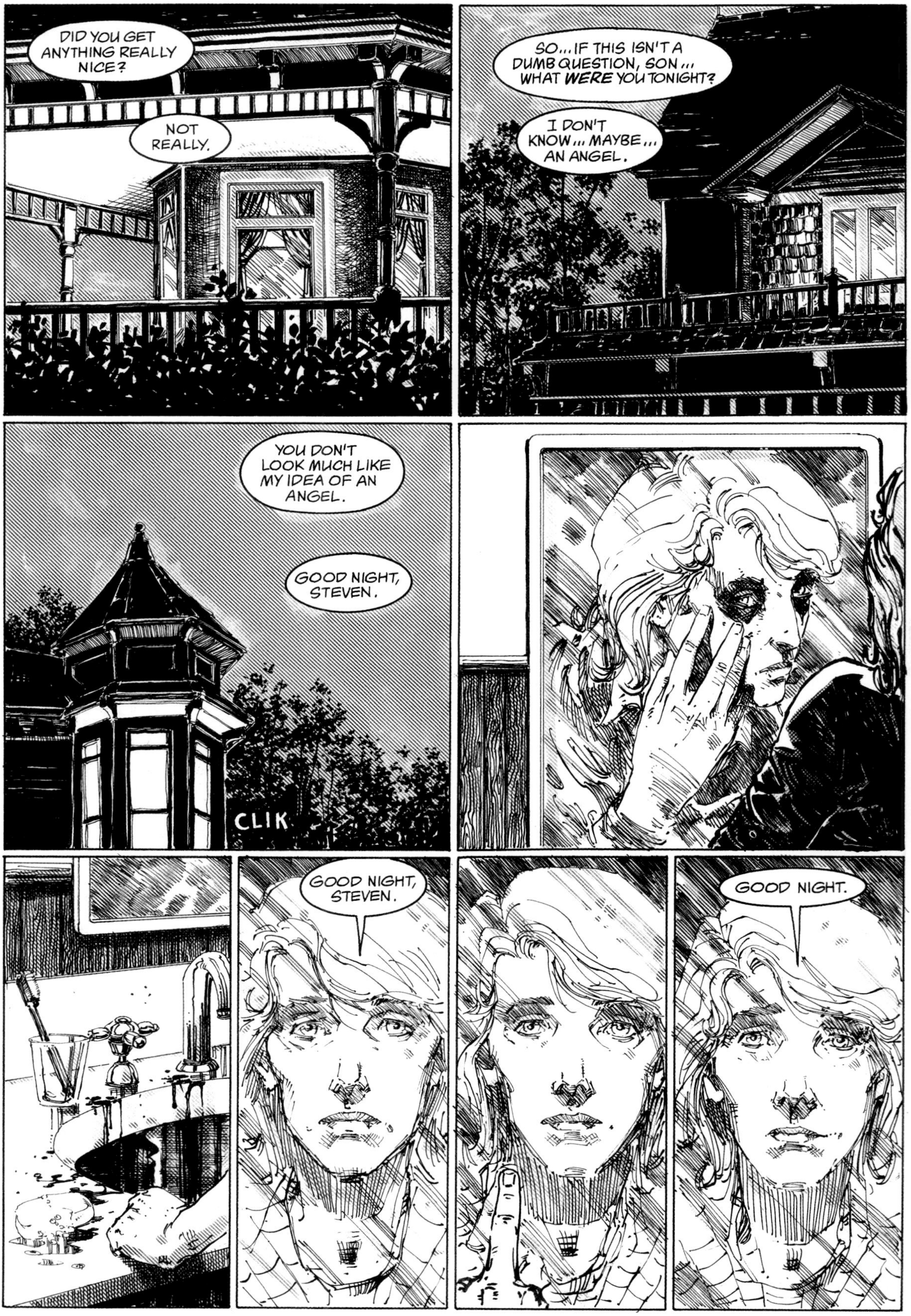
DID YOU GET ANYTHING REALLY NICE?
NOT REALLY.
SO... IF THIS ISN'T A DUMB QUESTION, SON... WHAT WERE YOU TONIGHT?
I DON'T KNOW... MAYBE... AN ANGEL.
YOU DON'T LOOK MUCH LIKE MY IDEA OF AN ANGEL.
GOOD NIGHT, STEVEN.
CLIK
GOOD NIGHT, STEVEN.
GOOD NIGHT.

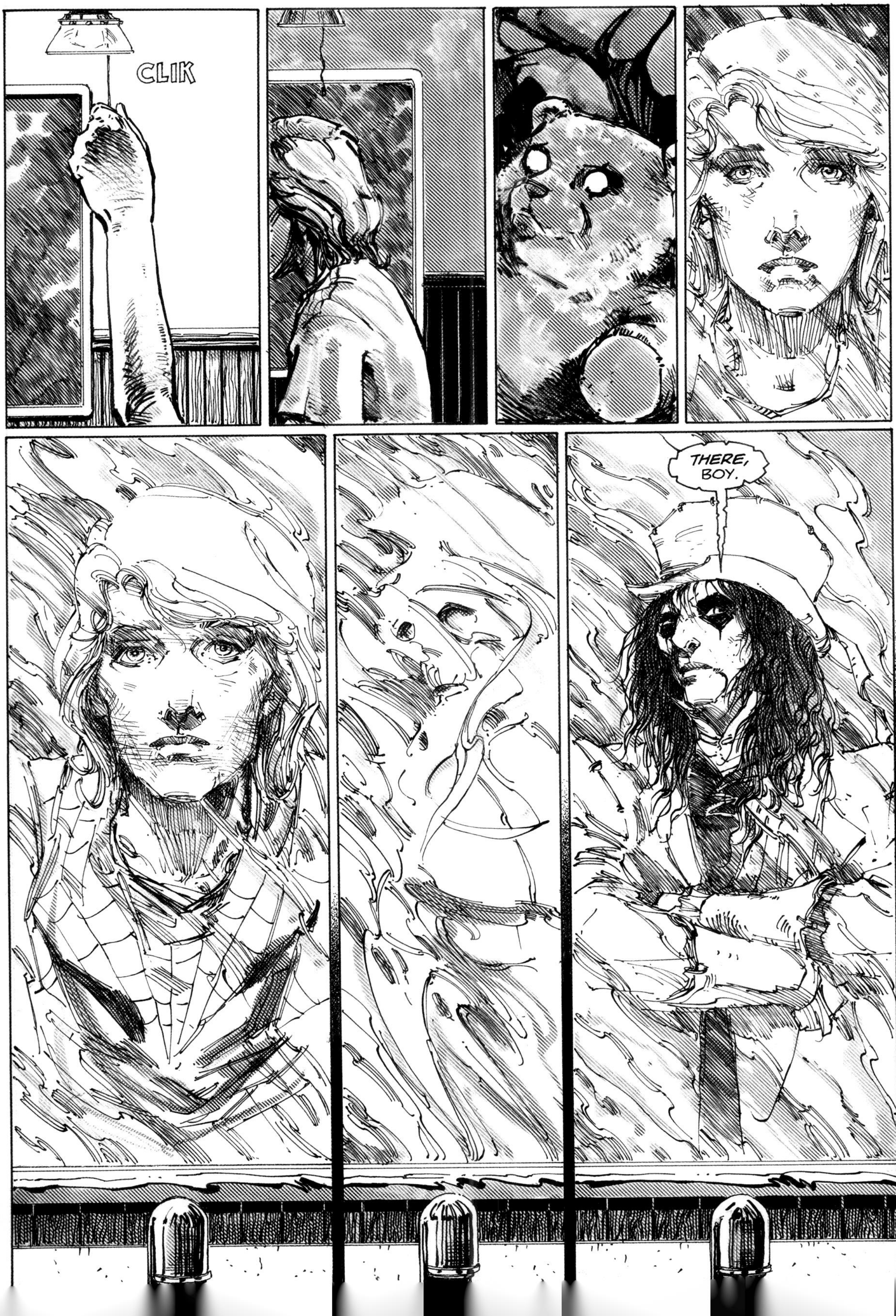
CLIK
THERE, BOY.

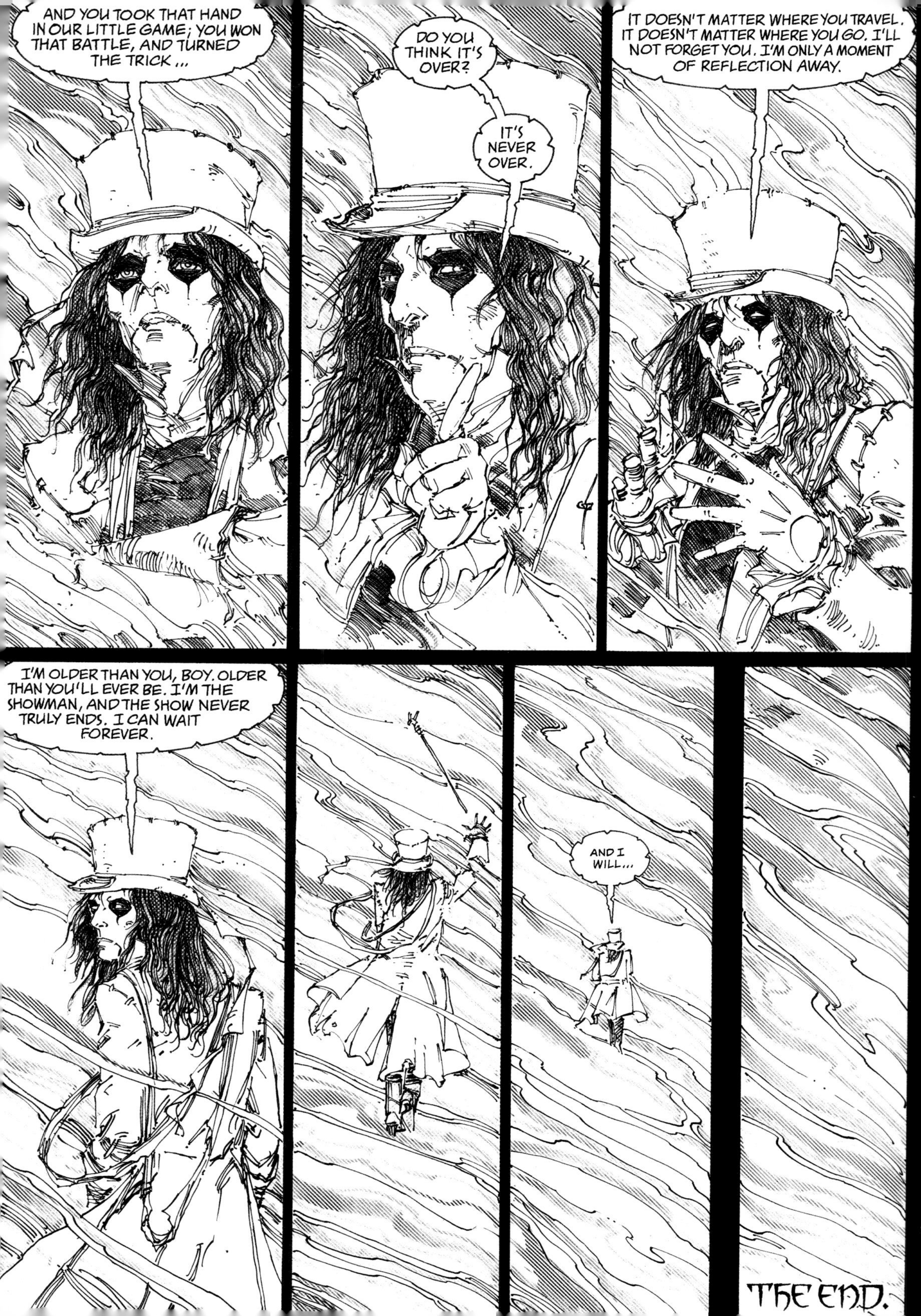
AND YOU TOOK THAT HAND IN OUR LITTLE GAME; YOU WON THAT BATTLE, AND TURNED THE TRICK...
DO YOU THINK IT'S OVER?
IT'S NEVER OVER.
IT DOESN'T MATTER WHERE YOU TRAVEL. IT DOESN'T MATTER WHERE YOU GO. I'LL NOT FORGET YOU. I'M ONLY A MOMENT OF REFLECTION AWAY.
I'M OLDER THAN YOU, BOY. OLDER THAN YOU'LL EVER BE. I'M THE SHOWMAN, AND THE SHOW NEVER TRULY ENDS. I CAN WAIT FOREVER.
AND I WILL...
THE END.

editor
DIANA SCHUTZ

digital production
JASON HVAM & CHRIS HORN

book design
CARY GRAZZINI

publisher
MIKE RICHARDSON

This book collects issues 1 through 3 of
The Last Temptation, originally edited by Mort Todd and published
by Marvel Music, an imprint of Marvel Comics.

Dark Horse Books™

Published by
Dark Horse Books
A division of Dark Horse Comics, Inc.
10956 SE Main Street
Milwaukie, Oregon 97222

First hardcover edition: September 2005
ISBN-10: 1-59307-414-X
ISBN-13: 978-1-59307-414-2

3 5 7 9 10 8 6 4
Printed in China

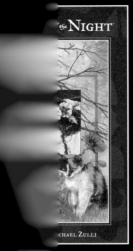

E NIGHT HC
el Zulli
71-936-5
5971-936-7

HARLEQUIN VALENTINE HC
with John Bolton
ISBN-10: 1-56971-620-X
ISBN-13: 978-1-56971-620-5
$10.95

MURDER MYSTERIES HC
with P. Craig Russell
ISBN-10: 1-56971-634-X
ISBN-13: 978-1-56971-634-2
$13.95

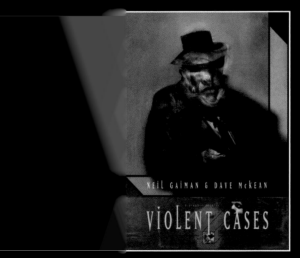

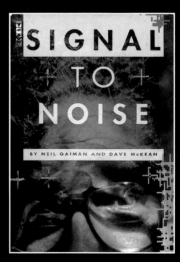

VIOLENT CASES GN
with Dave McKean
ISBN-10: 1-56971-606-4
ISBN-13: 978-1-56971-606-9
$14.95

SIGNAL TO NOISE HC
with Dave McKean
ISBN-10: 1-59307-752-1
ISBN-13: 978-1-59307-752-5
$24.95